S. D. Ford.
1974.

The Trout and the Stream

BOOKS BY CHARLES E. BROOKS
Larger Trout for the Western Fly Fisherman
The Trout and the Stream

Assam Dragon

Riffle Devil larva

Yellow Stone Nymph

White-wing Midge,
Invisible

Little Green Caddis
(larva and pupa)

Little Gray Caddis—larva,
pupa, dry

Cream Wiggler, Natant
Nylon Nymph

Foam Hopper, Foam Cricket, Deer-Hair Mouse, and Floating Minnow

Ida May, Fair Damsel, Montana Stone, Skunk-Hair Caddis

Montana Stone (Dry)

CHARLES E. BROOKS

THE TROUT AND THE STREAM

Illustrated by Dave Whitlock

CROWN PUBLISHERS, INC. NEW YORK

To Austin S. Hogan,
who coaxed, advised, praised, encouraged, and
helped beyond measure

Library of Congress Catalog Card Number: 73–91522
Manufactured in the United States of America
Published simultaneously in Canada by General
Publishing Company Limited
Designed by Shari de Miskey

Contents

Introduction   vi

PART ONE
TROUT AND THEIR RIVERS

1 Life in Running Water   3
2 The Requirements of a Trout   18
3 Knowing Your Rivers   31

PART TWO
THE PURSUIT OF TROUT

4 Fishing the Water   62
5 The Underwater Fly   82
6 Natural Nymphs and Their Imitations   96
7 Fishing the Artificial Nymph   109
8 Floating Flies   124
9 Fly Patterns and Their Dressings   140
10 Tackle Talk   154

PART THREE
AESTHETICS AND CONSERVATION

11 Developing a Philosophy   174
12 Conservation and Fly-Fishing   179
13 Stocked and Wild Trout   183
14 Stream Management and Improvement   191
15 Reading for the Serious Angler   197
16 Of Streams and Trout, Laws and Anglers   207

Index   213

Introduction

THIS book is not for the serious angler only; it is for one who has determined that he and no one else must be responsible for the future of his trout fishing, if it is to have a future.

This book has *not* been written to appeal to everyone; you will find here some hard truths and some hard language. You can blame the language on me, the truths on the facts of life as we are now coming to know them.

You will find the personal pronoun "I" used in almost every case. If a man has something to say, let him say it, and for God's sake, let him have the courage to say, "I said it, no one else, I believe in it and I am responsible for it." That's how it is here.

That does not mean you should believe everything I say; I'm now and then wrong, but if so, in this book, it is not for lack of trying to find the right answer. Unfortunately, as a fisherman and medical practitioner once said, "There is a disturbing lack of absolutes in fly fishing for trout, as in medicine. We are often right, but we don't know why. Unfortunately, we are more often wrong and we still don't know why."

Most of the information here will benefit the serious fisher for trout whatever his method. But the major amount of information will be about fly-fishing for I have used no other method for over twenty years. I gave up spinning before most people knew it existed.

I condemn no sporting method of fishing. I started fly-fishing because I was curious about it (I was nine years old) and it sounded romantic. I came to enjoy it more than any other style and have found it requires more study and practice in order to be proficient, thus is a greater challenge, while being more delightful, at least for me. This is no apology. As Charles Ritz said, a man should fish only for recreation and pleasure, otherwise fishing would become worse than work.

Nearly all of the theories put forth in this book were mine before I became aware that anyone else had them, and most have been checked by experiment or observation. However, I am still glad that I was able to find confirmation of some of them in some very serious and authentic works. Much of the stream information, insect behavior, life history, and trout behavior, was verified in the following: *The Ecology of Running Water,* by H. B. N. Hynes; *Fundamentals of Limnology,* Franz Ruttner; *Animal Biology,* Guyer and Lane; *Integrated Principles of Zoology,* Cleveland P. Hickman; *Zoology,* Max Silvernale; and *Trout Streams,* Paul R. Needham.

Even so, any work of this kind is a sort of compilation of what one has learned, from others as well as from his own efforts. In effect, every writer of this kind of book stands on the shoulders of every other writer who has gone before him. I found some new ideas, some unexplored information, in Hynes and Ruttner. Where that information was new to me will be indicated in the text. Since this is not intended as a source work, there will be as few acknowledgments in the text as is consistent with proper recognition.

For the past nine years, I have been partially retired, and have been living in the mountains of Southwestern Montana, a few minutes drive from a half dozen of the finest trout streams this country affords. For the last three years, I have been entirely retired, except for summers of teaching classes and stream demonstrations of trout fishing. I have not taught casting, just fishing. Also, for the past three years, when not engaged as above, I have devoted my time to stream, insect, and trout study. Thus, there is little in this book that has not come to me first hand.

Our western streams are much different from streams in other parts of the country. A recent study of one of our mountain streams revealed that there were twenty-five riffles for every pool; naturally, this stream holds few large fish. But most of our streams have few "pools"; what they have is what are better called "runs," deeper water with a still, strong current. Some, having few bottom obstructions, will have little surface disturbance, but will nevertheless have a very definite undersurface movement. This characteristic makes it difficult for fishermen from other parts of the country to find fishing water rather than blank water. One of the things I want to accomplish in this book is to help anglers find water that contains trout of catchable size, wherever they may fish.

A book is like a map; it may help one find one's way through a wilderness or out of a desert, but it cannot *lead* one out of such places. The emphasis will always be on the reader; he must apply himself to the task, or all is lost; neither book nor map can help him.

I have tried to make this book simple, without making it simplistic. I have tried to make it clear, without making it dull. If I have succeeded, readers will let me know. They will also let me know if I've failed.

—CHARLES E. BROOKS
WEST YELLOWSTONE, MONTANA

PART ONE

TROUT AND THEIR RIVERS

*"Most fishermen who decide to learn
more about their stream seem to feel
that learning the identity and hatch
times of the major aquatic flies is the
answer. This is just skimming the surface."*

1

Life in Running Water

DURING my forty years or so of trout fishing, I have become more and more disturbed by the fact that of the hundreds of anglers I met along the stream, most seemed to have no knowledge of anything in or about the stream except the trout, and often they knew very little about them. Most anglers seemed to think that all that was necessary for good fishing was to have the state stock more trout.

This attitude apparently is common, and results in poor fishing, not from lack of fish but lack of know-how. Just recently I attended a meeting of my state Fish and Game Commission; it was brought out that angler success on one of the state's Blue Ribbon trout streams was less than 40 percent. The chairman of the commission, an intelligent and forthright man (but no fisherman), said that this did not seem to him to be very good odds, whereupon the chief of the fisheries division pointed out that when live wild trout were stocked in a tank and experts tried to catch them out, they were never able to catch more than 40 percent of the fish in the tank, no matter what bait or lure was used. Thus, he said, a river that delivered 40 percent success to all who fished it was a first-class stream indeed. He was right.

So, no matter how much you know about trout fishing—or how many trout fishermen there are—all the trout in a given stream will never be caught. But I'm firmly convinced that a trout fisherman can definitely increase his catch rate by learning more about his stream and intelligently applying that knowledge.

Most fishermen who decide to learn more about their stream seem to feel that learning the identity and hatch times of the major aquatic flies is the answer. This is just skimming the surface.

To know a stream well, you have to start with at least a fair knowledge of its watershed, then go to the water itself and find out what qualities it has.

The basic requirements of life are light, water, oxygen, and minerals. All but light are found in a more usable state in water than on land. Therefore, in a serious study of a stream, you start, not with life in that stream but with the requirements to support life.

The first requirement, of course, is water. A good, pure—or reasonably so—and fairly regular supply of water is a must. Not all streams in which trout live or are stocked meet this requirement.

A spring-fed stream is one where the supply of water is generally regular and steady. Such trout streams exist but are not plentiful. The Letort and Big Springs creeks of Pennsylvania, Henry's Fork of the Snake River in Idaho, the South Fork of the Madison River, Armstrong and other spring creeks of Southwestern Montana are the only ones that come readily to mind.

The Deschutes River of Oregon is considered by some a spring creek because of a good constancy of flow, due to a peculiarity of its geologic strata. The upper Deschutes runs through peculiar volcanic formations that can only be described as spongy. The riverbed cuts through this spongy material which slowly gives up a steady supply of cool, pure water well supplied with minerals.

Fluctuation in the volume of streams is one of the most serious deficiencies, other than outright pollution. All streams fluctuate somewhat, but some, because of the shape and structure of the bed and bottom, are less affected than others. Some salmon and trout streams have *most* of their beds covered, even with only one-eighth

Cutthroat rising
to mayfly.

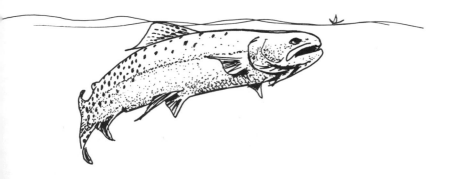

of their average yearly flow. Such streams can survive both serious drought and serious flooding.

Fluctuation causes damage and destruction to life in a trout stream in several ways. Flooding causes severe mortality of every living thing in a stream, by rolling and tumbling gravel and stones in the bed, scouring the stream bed and destroying both plant and animal life; it carves away at banks and bars, causing siltation, by sweeping downstream the brown and green algae that is the basis of all life in running water; and it changes the temperature of the water so that some creatures perish.

Fluctuation of volume is not always caused by drought or floods. Man has thrust his benign hand into the heart of many of our trout streams; the development of dams and irrigation projects is undertaken with such thoughtlessness that destruction of basic stream life is so extensive as to preclude growth and reproduction of trout.

However caused, by man or nature, or both, such fluctuation is the most serious cause of loss of trout-stream mileage, and of course man cheerfully labors to further the damage by excessive or poorly planned timber cutting, overgrazing, bare-ground farming methods, highway building, and channelization—all in the name of progress. Progress to where? The desert?

Drought, if not actually caused by the above activities of man, certainly is aided and abetted by them. Man robs the stream of water for his own use, for power, for irrigation, leaving vast stretches of stream bed dry and barren, exposed to summer sun and winter frost, all its beneficial organisms dried up, burned up, or frozen.

Man channelizes streams in the name of flood control, making a straight chute out of a formerly beautiful meandering trout stream, hustling the water out of one area to throw it in more violent and devastating flood on the area below, and bringing drought above when all the water has gone down the chute leaving a trickle.

He logs off the timber, grazes off the grass, has floods one year and droughts the next, and then wonders why his streams grow smaller and more barren year by year. Without ground cover to hold water where it falls, and meandering streams to throw the water back upon the land, floods and drought are as certain as death and taxes.

Light is necessary for all living things, animal or vegetable. In clear streams with abundant minerals, light will enable that stream to produce four or five times as much green plant life per acre as the richest soil—and green plants are the source of all other life. To quote the old stockmen's adage, perfectly correct, all meat is grass. And in a trout stream that saying can be correctly paraphrased by saying all fish flesh is green algae. Green algae is the bottom link in the food chain, the broad base of the food pyramid which has the trout at the top. And green algae cannot survive without light.

Light enough to promote algae growth is not usually a problem in most trout streams; if the water is clear, there will usually be green algae present. It should be remembered, however, that running water transmits less light than still water, clarity being equal. Therefore a trout stream will not support as much green plant life as a cool clear pond of equal richness, with noted exceptions.

Green algae, called phytoplankton, is eaten by minute organisms called zooplankton, which in turn are eaten by larger creatures, they by something still larger, and finally, the top of the heap, the trout, which is sometimes eaten by man.

Some scientists estimate that it takes ten pounds of food consumed to make one pound of the creature that consumes it. Or, in one example, 100,000 pounds of algae produces 10,000 pounds of zooplankton, which produces 1,000 pounds of aquatic insects, which in turn produces 100 pounds of fish. The "closer to grass, the more efficient the creature" is reflected in this, and is also shown by the fact that carp, which eat phytoplankton and zooplankton directly, will put on weight four or five times faster than trout in the same waters.

Under ideal conditions, plankton in ocean waters has produced forty tons of food per acre of bottom. Birge and Juday, doing research in Wisconsin in the twenties, gave two tons of food per acre as the very top for a trout stream. This would include *all* food, not just plankton. The two estimated such a food supply would support 240 pounds of trout per acre. They found no such stream that approached this maximum, for reasons which will be brought out later.

It can be seen that water is far more capable of producing an abundance of food than any other element. And while Birge and Juday found no stream that supported over 4,000 pounds of fish and fish food per acre, recent studies of the Klamath River near Hornbrook, California, have indicated certain areas of that stream hold over 5,000 pounds of *fish food* per acre, making it one of the richest trout streams on earth.

In Alaska, I found streams in remote mountain areas that appeared to have everything a trout could want but with few or no trout in evidence. These streams were pure, clear, had good mineral content, high oxygen content, excellent spawning areas, good holding water, few predators, and no angling pressure. Still no fish, or very few, rather small fish. Why?

Two things apparently caused these streams to be barren, or

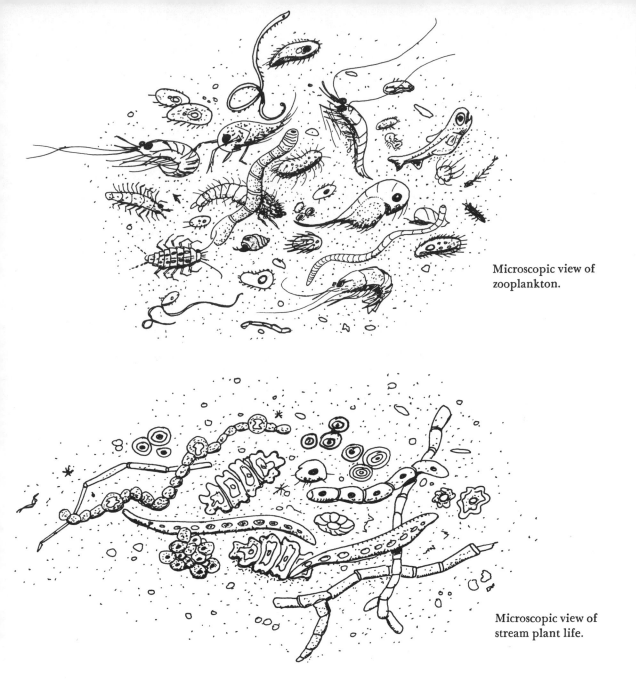

Microscopic view of zooplankton.

Microscopic view of stream plant life.

nearly so. One, terrible spring floods scoured the bottom until it was as clean as freshly set concrete. Spring spawning rainbow and grayling eggs were torn from gravel and destroyed. The job of destroying both green plants and spawn by spring floods was so complete that few algae or fry survived. The algae that did was finished off in the winter by anchor ice which formed around rocks on the stream bottom, floated them loose, and sent them tumbling downstream to destroy nearly the last of any surviving algae. Without algae, other life is doomed, and so some of these streams held no living thing.

A fisherman who beheld these streams only in summer, when water levels and temperatures were ideal, would be baffled by the lack of fish. Only if he knew enough to look beneath the surface, to mile after mile of stone and gravel bottom scoured so clean as to be sterile, would he be able to guess at the truth.

Some streams in this part of the country are almost as badly affected by the same factors. One of them is the West Gallatin River, a few miles from my home. The Gallatin has been heavily stocked in the past but in its upper reaches where the flood scour-anchor ice syndrome prevails, it hosts only small fish because the food supply is desperately short.

A study of this river in 1959 revealed what the problem was. The report indicated that heavy flooding in May and June scoured about 85 percent of the algae from the bottom. The stream remained very cold through July, some algae growth was detected in August and early September, then cooling temperatures and lessening sunlight due to shorter days and more cloud cover reduced growth levels. In December and January anchor ice forming in 30-degree-below-zero weather tears away the newly formed algae. Thus zooplankton has but three or four months of the year to gather algae; two of these are nongrowth months. So the upper West Gallatin remains mostly a small-fish river.

All these factors cause a downstream movement of both plant and animal life, including fish. Downstream where the gradient decreases and the river widens and deepens, there is far more plant and animal food and trout are much larger, five-pounders causing no great excitement.

This condition prevails to a greater or lesser degree in many of our fine trout streams. The Beaverkill and Neversink of New York are somewhat affected, and so are most streams in the north or northeast part of the contiguous forty-eight states. Such a condition may be suspected if lower portions of a stream carry consistently larger fish. It is true that the larger the fish the larger volume of water he requires, but first he requires sufficient *food* to make him large. The very largest fish in a lower stream will invariably be found in large, deep eddies. Such stream sections act as giant traps, holding vast quantities of algae torn loose from the stream bed above. Where the algae is, there also is the zooplankton, the tiny organism that dines on algae, and so on up the line to larger trout.

Much has been made in the past of temperatures of trout streams. Late studies seem to show that high temperature is not the great culprit that it has been made to appear. Over the past ten years it has been shown that lack of oxygen, not high temperature, was probably the limiting factor. However, it must be remembered that temperatures in excess of 89 degrees F. are probably fatal to all trout, regardless of the oxygen supply.

While trout can and have survived stream temperatures that fluctuated from 34 degrees F. to 85 degrees F., the same is not true of smaller creatures. Some of these are so sensitive to temperature that they cannot survive a 2-degree change at either the low or high end of the yearly scale. While some of these may appear briefly in trout streams, their tenure is generally too short for the fish to become accustomed to them as an item of diet.

Streams that fluctuate widely in temperature on a daily basis support less diverse insect life than those that do not. Where such variations occur, as they do in most streams, the variation is always less, the larger the volume of water. In spring-fed streams, temperature variations are never as great as in other streams, and this variation declines toward the source. In general, the more stable the temperature of a stream the more stable all other factors, and the better the growth rate of all creatures it contains. Note that the important thing is *stability* of temperature, not the temperature itself.

We all know about oxygen, and understand fairly well how much there is in our atmosphere. Most fishermen do not seem to know that water is different and that the amount of oxygen in water can vary from none to a high of 12 or more parts per million. In order to be a productive trout stream, four parts per million should be the minimum, and that would be a marginal amount for trout survival if the water temperature exceeded 80 degrees.

As water warms, it loses some of its oxygen. Warming of the water also increases the metabolism of trout and causes the fish to require more oxygen. Thus a combination of high water temperature and low oxygen levels spells trouble, not only for trout but for most creatures in running water. Nymphs of some mayflies and most stoneflies are so sensitive to high temperature–low oxygen conditions that many of them go into a state of suspended animation at such times. Trout become very lethargic, and the result is poor fishing. Green plants give off additional oxygen during hours of sunlight and can be of value for this reason. Though these plants reverse the process during darkness, the water usually cools somewhat at this time and oxygen levels generally are not depleted further because of the presence of green plants.

Only in the last four decades has the importance of minerals in water been recognized. Of course, it was known a hundred years ago that *some* minerals were required in streams to support life, but that was about the extent of knowledge.

Minerals not only provide food for green plants and some lower, smaller animal forms, but they have various other effects, mostly beneficial, which scientists are just coming to know. The elements necessary for life in running water are carbon, hydrogen, oxygen, nitrogen, phosphorus, sulfur, calcium, magnesium, potassium, and iron. Most of these are required only in trace amounts. The important ones in *all* trout streams are oxygen, carbon, and calcium. In some streams sulfur is important. Carbonates greatly exceed all other mineral salts in fresh water, and in most cases the carbonate is calcium bicarbonate, the form most readily used by most creatures. Calcium bicarbonate is formed from the action of oxygen and carbon dioxide on calcium carbonate. For those of you who like formulae, the process is: H_2O plus CO_2 equals carbonic acid, which acts on $CaCO_3$, calcium carbonate, turning it into $Ca(HCO_3)_2$, calcium bicarbonate, which is the form most easily used by most life forms in water.

Waters rich in calcium carbonates are generally referred to as alkaline. Chalk and limestone streams—chemically the same—are very rich in this mineral and as a result are very rich in green plant life, in fish food, and in fish.

While the other minerals listed are necessary in trace amounts, many studies have indicated most streams have more than enough of them, and no one has suggested that they are ever deficient enough to significantly affect plant growth.

As to the importance of the carbonates, dozens of studies have shown a direct relationship between carbonate content of a stream and green algae production, other factors being equal. In a stream with less than 5 parts per million of carbonates (very soft or acid water) one study group was able to find only 3,200 green algae per square meter, while in a nearby stream with 30 parts per million of carbonates, the count was over 13,000 green algae per square meter. All life in water, as previously stated, is directly related to green algae production. One peculiarity of green algae not generally known is that these plants are more efficient in fast water. Not only do swifter currents bring the minerals to the fixed plants at a higher rate, but plants in some manner utilize the minerals more effectively in fast water, and release oxygen at a faster rate—another reason why faster water is better oxygenated. This factor also makes running water of a given carbonate content richer than still water of the same content because a new supply of minerals is being constantly carried to the algae and oxygen being carried away. Thus, current promotes respiration and food intake due to food and oxygen being brought to the organism, plant, or animal with little or no effort required to obtain it.

Carbonates in streams (that is, calcium carbonates) have two other effects not generally known. They favorably affect the respiration rates of fish, causing them to use more oxygen when it is abundant, *but allowing them to use less when it is scarce.* Also, calcium carbonates in the water speed up the decomposition of dead organic material, prevent overaccumulation of such matter, and accomplish all this with less usage of oxygen. Thus, calcium-rich water offers other important benefits besides just higher green algae growth.

I mentioned earlier that sulfur is an important mineral in some streams. The Au Sable of Michigan has much of its bed and banks composed largely of gypsum, a fine sandy material (the formula is $CaSO_4$) the form of sulfate most readily used by microorganisms. The only other usable form of sulfur that microorganisms can use, that I know of, is hydrogen sulfide, H_2S, which is found near the underground thermal sources that abound in Yellowstone Park. Hydrogen sulfide is converted into usable sulfates by microorganisms found only in these warm, sulfur-rich waters. These organisms convert sulfates into protein at a high rate, are eaten by zooplankton, which are eaten by insects—and the result is an animal life high in body-building protein.

The same process takes place in the Au Sable, and is responsible for that stream's amazing productivity. The process is simpler here, because the sulfur is, to begin with, in usable sulfate form. This is extremely fortunate, for the Au Sable, with a sand-silt bottom, does not have a diverse insect structure. But the Au Sable is rich in calcium as well, and the prevalent insect forms prosper greatly as a result.

Some of the silt in the Au Sable is the result of logging operations, and many other streams have been so affected. Some of these streams, being rich in calcium, have been able to survive and become extremely productive. These, like the Au Sable, do not have diverse insect structures, but harbor many large burrowing, organic-material-eating insects, which are large, meaty, and plentiful. These include the *Ephemera* and *Hexagenia* genera of mayflies, the very largest; at least one large species of stone flies; and of course dragonflies and damselflies.

The two mayfly types, while feeding the fish, sometimes frustrate the fisherman, because both are burrowers, and seldom come out where the trout can get at them, except at night or when hatching.

Hexagenia nymph.

Ephemera nymph.

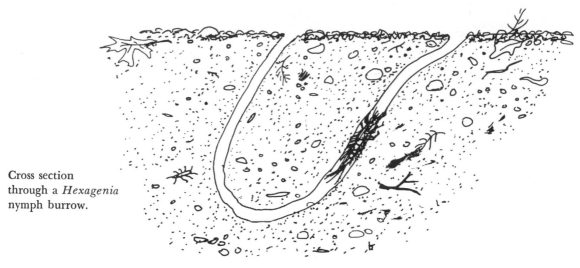

Cross section through a *Hexagenia* nymph burrow.

Insects in streams are not only dependent on the factors we have discussed, but also on bottom type. Most aquatic insects in the pre-adult stage are so dependent on one particular bottom type that they cannot survive in another no matter how favorable other factors may be.

Generally, there is a direct relationship between the size of an immature underwater insect and the particulate bottom matter. Two exceptions are noted, the two mayflies mentioned above, which are quite large in the immature stage, but which dwell in silt, and dragonfly nymphs, some species of which are the size of the first joint of a man's thumb, but which like fine bottom material. Both require fine bottom material because of their feeding habits. The two mayflies eat decaying organic material in much the same manner as an earthworm, and so can only live where such material is found in a finely powdered state. The dragonfly nymphs are predacious and strong swimmers. The nymphs they feed on are more easily seen and captured when there are fewer places for them to hide. There may be other exceptions to the small insect and small-size bottom material, but those are the only ones I am aware of at present.

Again, generally, immature insects that dwell in weed beds are of very small size, and one is apt to associate this with the bottom matter, which is usually silt or earth. But I've come to believe the real reason is different; no matter what the size or structure of a particular weed, the hiding places it provides are small and the boundary layer—the area where the current is slowed to a livable speed—is thin. Therefore, larger insects would find it difficult to survive due to exposure and constantly having to fight the current.

The type bottom thought to hold most insects—and so indicated by most studies—is rubble. Rubble is composite bottom: some sand, some gravel, coarser stones, larger stones, and perhaps boulders—all intermixed. Investigations have shown that rubble bottoms have produced five times as many insects as plain gravel, thirty times as many as sand silt, and over one hundred times as many as plain sand. But green plants—mosses, weeds, filamentous algae, and the like—harbor more insects per unit of area. The reason: vertical use, or volume. A square meter of rubble bottom harbors insects in a layer a few inches thick. Weeds or green plants may be in a layer six feet thick. However, such weed beds harbor only a few *kinds* of insects. Rubble bottoms harbor the most diverse insect structures to be found anywhere in the stream. To put it simply, the more complex the bottom structure, the more complex the insect structure, and the more species in a given area.

Many insects are adapted by shape for their environment. Some nymphs are flattened to allow movement *over* stones on the bottom of swift streams. Being only a few millimeters thick, they can remain in the boundary layer, where surface tension produces a thin layer of completely still water. Others are similarly flattened for a different purpose—so they can live *under* stones. Such insects probably never expose themselves to trout except when they move to the surface to hatch.

A cross section through a rubble-stream bottom.

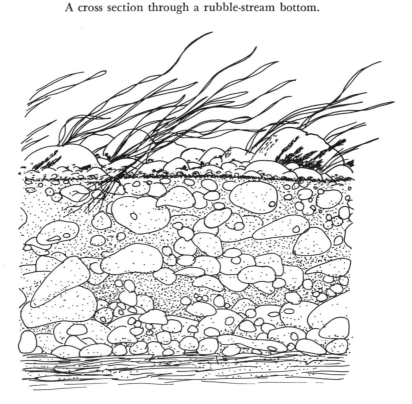

Sowbug (*Ascellus communis*) crawling.

Bottom type is not the only factor that controls the insect species present. Current speed is another, and large changes in current speed over a period of time will cause a complete change in a stream's insect structure. A change of temperature over a period of time will cause the same thing.

Another factor is oxygen content. Even in a stream which has an oxygen content of eight parts per million or higher (considered the saturation level) some stone fly nymphs will be found only in the faster, rockier parts of the stream. These creatures have such an inefficient respiratory mechanism that they cannot survive in slow water, even when it is saturated with oxygen; they must constantly have a new supply brought to them and the products of respiration swept away. When immature, these nymphs are quite small, and they have a more favorable surface-to-volume ratio than they do when they become larger. Thus, such insects may survive in less-oxygenated water for a time (some spend three years underwater) but would never survive to become adults. I make this point because I have found immature stone fly nymphs in water where an adult was never seen.

The stone fly species mentioned above will also be found only in areas of a stream where stones are volleyball size and larger, and the bed is composed of stones upon stones. Scientists have been unable to determine the reason for this. It could be because of their oxygen demand—fast water beating over a rough stone bottom contains more oxygen than the same current moving over a smooth bottom; or it could be these insects require larger areas in which to live, cavities and crevices in and around such rocks. I favor the latter view because these nymphs are clumsy crawlers and are constantly being swept away by the current when they expose themselves.

Water temperature has a definite effect on the life histories of aquatic insects. Warm water (65–80 degrees F.) insects tend to have more than one generation per year; colder stream insects (50–64 degrees) usually have only one generation every year—sometimes only one generation every two or three years. This is most important for the fly-fisherman; the dry-fly fisherman, generally, will find far more hatches, and more often, on a warmer stream.

Some insects are hardier than others with regard to temperature. Most trout stream insects can survive a temperature range of 35–65 degrees F.; some can survive to 75 degrees or higher; and others can survive being frozen. Generally, the smaller the insect the narrower its range of temperature tolerance.

Creatures other than insects have their favorite areas in streams also. Whether this is because of environmental adaptation, or because of a lack of it, is not known.

Some minnows, dace for instance, are not strong swimmers and generally will be found in quieter, less turbulent areas of the stream. In fact, very few trout stream forage fish are strong swimmers. Those that are will usually be found in very rocky areas where areas of dead water exist because of the blocking effect of large stones.

Sculpins (*Cottus*) which, in this country, are always found in the same waters inhabited by the largest stone fly nymphs—that is, very fast, rocky waters—are *not* strong swimmers, but have a structural adaptation that allows them to dwell in such sections. Their pectoral fins are very broad, flattened on the bottom into almost a sucking disc, and are slanted downward back to front. This design makes fast water a help instead of a hindrance: it presses down on these broad, angled pectorals, causing them to function like diving vanes, keeping the little creatures anchored to the bottom.

In summary, we have covered most of the things a *good* trout stream requires, as well as some things that are harmful. However, many streams inhabited by trout cannot be called good, or even fair, trout streams. Where this occurs, there are reasons, and we should be aware of them.

Certain streams can never be trout streams because of too many adverse factors. For instance, most green algae depend entirely on sunlight and dissolved mineral salts to exist. Where the water is too

Sculpin.

muddy to transmit light, or where dissolved salts are too low, there will be few or no algae, thus no zooplankton, and no other creatures.

Trout fry depend entirely upon only a few life forms. Where these do not exist, trout cannot grow to maturity, although they can survive if they are mature when stocked. No reproduction would be possible, but such a stream can be stocked with hatchery catchable-size trout with absolute assurance that this is the only method of making a trout *fishery* out of it. This will usually be a stream in which few green algae can be found. The abundance of all life in fresh water is tied directly to the quantity of phytoplankton available.

This chapter was written for a specific purpose: to acquaint the trout fisherman with the requirements of the organisms other than trout which inhabit or should inhabit his streams. The reason he should know about these factors is not only to enable him to deal more intelligently with the agencies responsible for the management of his streams, but also to make him a better fisherman.

In the past three years, acting as spokesman for the Southwestern Montana Fly Fishers, an organization of which I am secretary, I have made several appearances before meetings of the Montana Fish and Game Commission. These meetings are always crowded with representatives of other groups, all importuning the commission to do this or that or the other to save or improve the fishing.

Almost without exception, these groups were long on emotion and short on facts. They tried to make their point by demanding, by banging the table, by haranguing. The commission listened to them politely, but skeptically, then destroyed them with a few well-chosen questions that quickly revealed that the would-be improvers had little idea of the true nature of what they were asking.

On the other hand, our group has presented five suggestions to the commission, four of which have been adopted outright, and the fifth will be when money and manpower become available. One of our suggestions, immediately accepted and implemented, was for a study to determine the impact of the practice of stocking hatchery catchable trout on a wild trout population. Two years of that study are complete; I have the data, which will be presented later. Two more years of study are in the works. The chairman of the commission, when the program was adopted, made this statement:

"For fifty years our biologists have told us that stocking hatchery catchables was the only way to provide good trout fishing. Now, on the basis of the information provided by this interested group, it appears as if we have been in error. However, before we scrap a program of fifty years' duration, I want a thorough study of the matter, and wish to examine all the facts before making a decision."

No one can, I believe, quarrel with the above statement. However, if our group had not had sufficient valid information, the statement in all probability would never have been made. Having the facts, gathered by our members well beforehand, studying them, then making a quiet factual presentation, made the difference. Our group is presently gathering information on whether fishermen would rather catch fewer wild trout or more hatchery trout, and also how fishermen feel about present limits. When we have the information and have assessed it, we will decide whether to go before the commission with a request to do something. Our group is small, and it has no political clout; but every time we have spoken to the commission they have listened and reacted favorably. I'm sure they would have reacted the same way to a request by any group that could demonstrate it knew what it was about.

If you are one of those who have the attitude, "let the government do it," or feel that it is not up to you to do anything about the present or future of your trout fishing; if you feel that taking without giving will get you where you want to go, then neither this chapter nor this book will do you one damn bit of good, and you will, in my opinion, deserve the kind of fishing you get.

On the other hand, if you are interested and concerned and want to help, you can do a much better job if you know something about the subject, and how and what facts to gather. You may say that it is up to the Fish and Game Department biologists to know about these things. This is true to an extent, but consider this: Most states have less than a dozen fishery biologists. Yet most states have miles and miles of streams. Wisconsin and California have about 9,000 miles of *trout* streams; Michigan has over 13,000; New York has over 17,000, and Montana has more than any of these. It's not possible for department biologists to know *all* about every mile of these streams. But if you can convince them there is something wrong with some of those miles, and give them an idea of what should be done to handle the situation, you have a very good chance of getting their cooperation. And I think you'll get a great deal of pleasure and satisfaction out of it, besides.

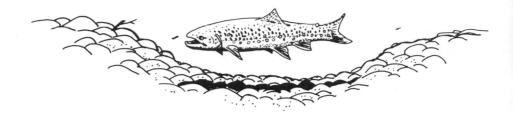

2

The Requirements
of a Trout

TROUT in streams require waters which have a temperature range within their limits of tolerance, a percentage of dissolved oxygen that must be higher, the warmer the water temperature, an adequate food supply, security from predators, and relief from current force and from angling pressure. These they must have to survive; to reproduce they also need large areas of gravelly spawning riffles—otherwise they will have to be artificially stocked in order for there to be a continuing supply for the fishermen to catch.

I do not fish for hatchery trout, and I am opposed to stocking streams that can support a wild trout population. Many streams cannot, although they can provide trout fishing on a put-and-take basis. Some streams can be improved so they *will* support a wild trout fishery. When they cannot, then stocking catchables does provide some sport where none existed before.

The two trout requirements that are of most concern to fishermen are security from predators and relief from current force. These will indicate to the fisherman where the trout will be in a stream, so that he may spend his time fishing where fish *are,* and not over barren waters.

18

When I speak of trout and fishing for trout in this book, I am talking about trout of a catchable size. Trout of this size are different in habit and habitat selection from smaller fish. One of the first things an angler should learn is where small fish are, so that he can avoid fishing such areas.

Studies have shown that in swift streams, fish exhibit growth rates in direct relation to the amount of shelter from the current, not only for the trout, but for *all* the organisms. The more shelter the higher the growth rate.

H.B.N. Hynes says bluntly that in running water, trout lurk downstream of obstacles and the larger the obstacle the larger the fish the angler may expect to catch from behind it. Defense of territory is a characteristic of all *Salmonidae*, he says, and the faster the current the more prevalent this characteristic. Thus, trout tend to school in slower waters, but are individually located in faster waters. In a contest for shelter, the larger fish invariably wins, and the best shelters will be taken by the largest fish.

Brown trout form a slight exception to the above statement. They are more aggressive than other trout, and both Hynes and Ruttner agree that a smaller brown trout will drive out and take over the shelter of other members of the family, including Atlantic salmon. Thus brown trout will dominate all other species of trout of equal size in a stream and be in the best shelters. This characteristic is one reason why brown trout survive nine to one over other trout when planted in the same stream in equal numbers.

If there are too many fish for the available shelter, the smaller fish will be chased continually, driven out into the current until they either leave the area, die from exhaustion, or are captured by predators. This is precisely what happens when several hundred or thousand hatchery catchables are dumped into an area all at once.

It has been learned, mostly within the past decade, that the above factors are the ruling ones in determining the population of a trout stream, and that food, and even angling pressure, do not have as much effect on *numbers*. In fact, where there is enough shelter, angling pressure, no matter how heavy, will not deplete the number of trout in a stream. It will reduce the average size of fish, and if heavy enough, with high enough limits, it will reduce the stream to the point where nine-tenths of the trout are under ten inches. (This will be taken up at greater length in Chapter 11.)

So the angler should have in mind that the first requirement of the trout he wishes to catch is a suitable shelter to give him relief from current force. The angler should also know that if a sizable trout is out from behind his barrier, in an open area, unprotected from the force of the current, he is undoubtedly feeding.

There is an exception to the statement that trout lurk downstream of an obstacle. In very swift streams, a very large rock or obstruction will create an area of still water just upstream, due to back pressure, and trout will lie just upstream of such obstacles, as well as downstream of them. So when you are fishing such a spot be sure to give the area in front of the rock as close attention as that behind it.

The first thing I do when I fish a strange stream is to walk along the bank, upstream on one side, downstream on the other, and look for obstacles in the stream. In swifter streams, I look for a broken surface that will tell me that the obstacle is there, even if I cannot see it. In streams of slower flow, I look for deeper areas, for if a trout does not have a broken surface above him, he looks for deeper water to give him security from attack from above.

Other obstacles in streams are not so readily seen. Sometimes the fish lying behind such a barrier can be seen, sometimes not. These are depressions in the bottom, only a few inches deep, from as large as a washbasin to as big as a living room. In streams with sand-silt, or gravel bottoms, most fish will be in such depressions. I recall seeing, last summer on the Firehole, a trout of about twenty-two inches, lying in such a bottom depression, only a few inches longer than it was.

I was conducting on-the-stream demonstrations for a group of doctors. I called the attention of Dr. Clint Pace to the fish, and he worked over it for half an hour, with dry fly, wet fly, and nymph, but was unable to move it, although smaller fish of fifteen to seventeen inches were feeding throughout the area. This is typical of the behavior both of larger fish and of fish lying in the bottom depressions. I find them more difficult to catch than fish that have their lie behind a rock or some other obstruction. I don't know why.

Where there are sufficient barriers to the current, trout prefer faster waters, because the disturbance created by swift currents beating around obstacles causes diffraction of light and gives the fish a greater feeling of security. Also, faster currents displace crawling or swimming nymphs and larvae and bring the food past the trout for his inspection and selection. For this reason, trout in fast rock-filled runs will quite often average larger than elsewhere in the stream.

Weed beds are one of the best trout shelters. Weeds slow current by the effect of friction on innumerable small surfaces, and this effect can be great enough so that a sizable trout can lie over a weed bed that extends almost to the surface, and be practically free from current force. In the Firehole, Upper Madison, and Henry's Fork, it is common on any given day to see large numbers of trout lying over such weed beds. Nearly all the spring creeks I know contain trout that may be seen just above beds of weeds.

Such a location gives the trout several advantages in addition to not having to fight the current. He is secure—at the slightest hint of danger he has only to sink into the weeds and out of sight. He also has a view of both the surface and the interior of the weed bed ahead of him. Any insect that appears within his line of vision can be taken in an instant.

The fact that such a trout can be seen, and seen to be feeding, does not mean that he can be caught, or even hooked. Such trout are extremely wary and their view of the surface allows them to see any above-surface danger. If you've been taken in by the old story that a trout's view of things above the surface shrinks as he rises in the water, due to narrowing of his "window," forget it. In the Summer 1972 issue of *Trout* magazine, two scientists, Drs. Robert L. Butler and R. D. McCammon, exploded this old wives' tale. Their article was full of scientific findings, sines and cosines, units of diffusion and diffraction, angles of incidence and reflection, but for us nonscientists, the two doctors put it in succinct plain English: When the surface of the water is perfectly smooth, a trout can see *anything* that protrudes above the surface—and if the angler can see the fish, the fish can see the angler, unless he is directly behind the fish.

Thus a trout in a place of lessened current pressure can often be seen, and sometimes the reason for his being there can also be seen. Most of the time both the trout and the obstacle will be hidden

Trout holding over
a weed bed.

Same trout seen
from above.

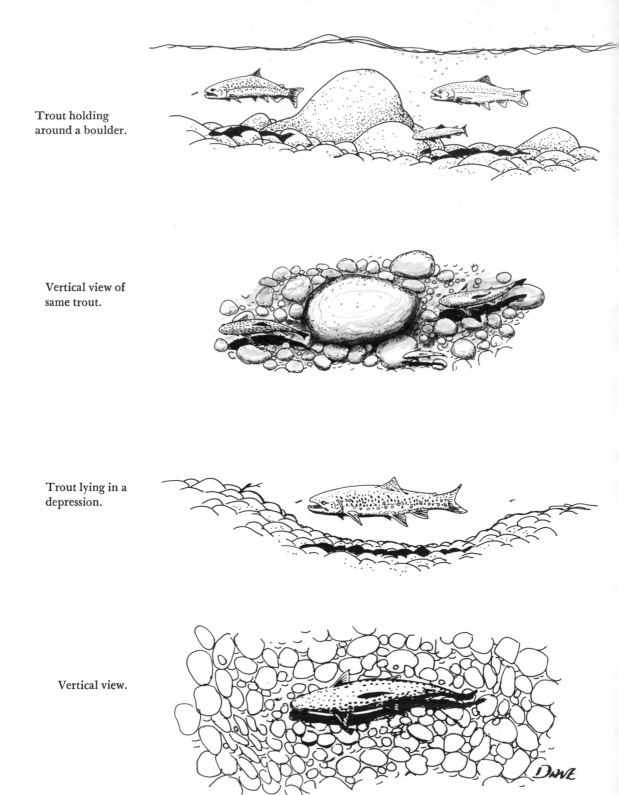

Trout holding
around a boulder.

Vertical view of
same trout.

Trout lying in a
depression.

Vertical view.

and the angler must look for indirect signs of his trout. Broken water, two feet deep or more, will generally contain trout. So will smooth water over four or five feet deep, and sometimes the fish cannot be seen here because of a variety of conditions, including unclear water. Where you cannot see the bottom for any reason, suspect the presence of trout.

There is such a spot on the Firehole. Here, a small section of the stream has cut away from the main river, to return about a quarter mile below. The small stream has a more powerful current than the main stream, which it enters almost at a right angle. The current of the smaller stream has thrown a curving bar of gravel across the Firehole, almost to the surface. The downstream edge of the bar is an abrupt drop to a depth of four feet or so. Because of the mingling currents of the two streams, the bottom of this curving depression cannot be seen *unless* the light is exactly right.

Over a period of twenty-five years I had taken and released any number of two- to three-pound trout from this area and knew that it always contained a fish or two of that size.

One day while giving a student a demonstration tour, I stopped at this spot as being typical of a hold which always contained fish, but where the fish were difficult to see. When we arrived, the light conditions were perfect and we could see the bottom of the depression fairly well.

My student had a good eye. We spotted two trout of eighteen to twenty inches lying on the very bottom at the lower end of the depression. Near them was a long narrow rock.

"There's a much bigger fish just beyond them," said the student.

"That's a rock," I replied, knowing that a fish that size would not likely be in so small a hold. Then the rock moved. It was a trout I estimated at twenty-six inches.

I told a friend of mine, Bob Holmes, of the University of California, about the fish. Bob is a dedicated fly-fisherman who, like me, seldom keeps a fish. We exchange notes on large fish all the time.

Bob shook his head. "I know that hold well," he said. "I'll give him twenty-two, maybe twenty-three inches. But no longer."

A few days later, in an icy drizzle, Bob came to find me on the stream. He was grinning from ear to ear.

"Charlie," he said, "he *was* twenty-six inches!"

"You caught him!" I exclaimed.

Bob shook his head. "I made the mistake of going after him with 2X, because I didn't believe you. He broke me on the second jump, but I had two good looks at him broadside in the air. He'll go twenty-six easy."

The student with me that day gave us an incredulous look.

"You mean even you experts make mistakes?" he asked.

"In the field of fly-fishing for trout, the only expert is the trout," said Bob. "You may get to where you'll have an improved catch rate, but you'll never see the day some fish won't make a monkey out of you."

In the fall and spring trout will run up small streams to spawn. They will also move into such streams in summer if they are better supplied with oxygen, or if the main streams become too warm for comfort. At such times, large trout will not be in what would be thought of as holding areas. Instead, they'll be in resting places, usually located where they can see a long distance in all directions. They are very wary at such times and fishing for them is a stalking proposition. It will often be necessary to kneel or crawl to approach them within casting distance. This is one of the few times it is useless to "fish the water," no matter how well you are able to read and identify holding water.

If shelter and relief from current force are number one in a trout's scheme of things, food will always be number two, except when the fish is frightened or spawning. As a friend of mine once said, a trout has only three things on his mind in a lifetime, and can only entertain one of these thoughts at a time—feeding, spawning, and nothing. (Safety, he said, was an instinct and didn't require thought.)

A trout with nothing on his mind, he went on, is one for which it is useless to fish, unless you can wake him up and convince him it is time to think about feeding.

The above was meant to be humorous, of course, but there is more than a grain of truth there. If a trout is feeding, he can often be seen while doing it, and he can also often be caught. When he is not feeding, obviously the angler is up against a tougher proposition.

Trout in streams feed largely on underwater forms of insects. They vary their diet in direct relationship to the availability of suitable sizes of different species; therefore, as will be brought out in the chapter on nymphs, this habit is more or less controlled by the life history and growth pattern of the insects they feed on.

Selection of food by trout, then, is based on availability; those insects most active, exposed by habit, or which are large will be the ones most often taken. Only if such are in short supply will the trout turn to hiding and burrowing types, unless, as is true in some cases, these come out at night, and are large enough to be seen and taken at this time.

The second thing I do on a strange stream is to go to work with my insect screen. This is a square yard of screen wire, tacked to two

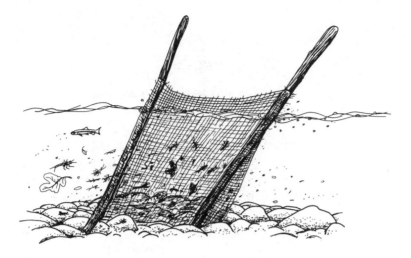

A stream screen
in position.

poles four feet long. I thrust the two poles into the bottom just in front of my feet, then lean over and rake the bottom material around with my hands as far as I can reach upstream of the screen.

I do this in waters that I intend to fish at a later time. Insects will vary according to bottom type, so be sure to do your looking where you intend to do your fishing.

After I've moved all the bottom material I am able to, I lift the screen, bottom first, upstream. Then I carry it to the bank and lay it down for a close examination. This is necessary since the screen will have considerable debris in it—sand, fine gravel, sticks, algae, and so forth—and it is easy to overlook even a fairly large insect.

I make at least three samplings of the bottom in different areas of the hold, to make sure I get a representative sample of the insects in that stretch.

Quite often you will find creatures in your net not profitable to imitate with an artificial. Snails, clams, hardshell beetles, and even angleworms are some of the things I frequently find. It wouldn't be possible to imitate these in an artificial "fly." Or would it?

I took my wife, my brother Ken, and a former student, Jim Mitchell, up to Biscuit Basin Meadows on the Firehole one time. I was teaching my brother, since this was his first try at fly-fishing for trout. Also, I was attempting, at the same time, to teach Grace about holds.

After I got Ken located and fishing, Grace and I walked downstream a way.

"See that tree that has fallen along the bank, in the water?" I asked, pointing.

She nodded.

"See where the roots pulled out, leaving a notch in the bank just upstream of where the roots are now?"

"Yes, I see it."

"There should be a trout of at least eighteen inches in that notch," I said. "There are roots just downstream a couple of feet for security. The current moves well along that bank, which is what caused the roots to wash out and the tree to fall. So a good supply of food will be coming to the fish without his having to work for it. Let's go see if he's there."

We circled away from the bank so that we could come straight to the spot where the notch in the bank was. There was a tree there about five or six feet from the notch, just even with it.

We crept up, using the tree for cover, and peered out from behind it. In the eddy caused by the damming effect of the roots below, and the notch itself, was a nice trout, about a foot under the surface, balancing himself easily with his fins in the slight, uneven current.

I directed Grace to kneel down and crawl to a spot about eight feet upstream from the trout, and about three feet back from the bank.

"Just have your leader through the rod tip," I said, "and drop the fly on the water about two feet up from the notch and a foot out from the bank. Lower the tip slowly, and the fly will come right down to him, ahead of the leader."

The size of the fish had intimidated her, and she refused to try for him.

"I type all your stuff," she said, "and you're always saying how easy it is. So, you catch him."

So I did, exactly as I had instructed her. The instant he hit, I leaned on him hard, and swung the rod tip out and upstream with all the pressure I thought the 2X leader would stand. I caught him by surprise and had him out of his root-guarded lair before he knew what hit him.

While I was all intent on getting the fish out of his lie and safely upstream, Grace had snatched my big net off my back and was kneeling on the bank, trying to net a very green and fighting mad trout. As I watched her slamming and slashing away at the fish, scaring it out of its wits, a picture flashed through my mind, the exact same incident as related by John Taintor Foote in his marvelous short story, "A Wedding Gift."

I managed to retrieve the net before she knocked the fish off the hook, and landed it without any trouble, a fine rainbow nineteen inches long.

As I was working the hook free, Grace called my attention to the fish's sides and belly, which had a distinct knobby appearance.

"He's been eating rocks!" she exclaimed.

Intrigued, I killed the fish and opened it. In its belly were forty-four snails the size of large grapes. They made a double handful when I had extracted them. The shells were a dull, gray-green color.

"What I want to know," said my wife, after we had got over the strange contents in the trout's stomach, "is how you knew how big he'd be? I know that you can tell where fish are because you're always showing them to me. But how can you tell just how big they're going to be? Explain that." Aye, that's the rub.

I made an artificial, of gray-green wool, in a cone shape, small at the bend, large at the eye. I got the spiral effect by cinching oval gold tinsel tightly from bend to eye. One turn of dark grouse hackle, for the mantle and foot, finished the fly. It was a number four, 2X long. I weighted it with fifteen turns of .030″ lead wire. In areas where snails form a portion of the trout's diet, it works very well. Whether the fish take it for a snail, I know not.

To return to our insect screening, when you have made three samplings and looked them over you should know which insects it would be most profitable to use. If you have a very mixed bag, as is sometimes the case, simply apply the criteria listed earlier—those most active, most exposed by their habits, or large. Generally, I start with large.

My constant use of my insect screen in the area around my home has led to numerous jokes, the most common being that I don't catch trout, I net them, and other snide remarks.

Once I was collecting samples for study in a long riffle on the Madison in Yellowstone Park. I was busy netting away, a short distance from shore, in one of those spots where the highway was right along the bank. I heard a car horn, and looking up, beheld a friend, Joe Fraser, the sub-district ranger for that area.

Joe leaned out the window and bellowed, "Don't you know this area is fly-fishing only?"

"I'm only fishing for flies," I yelled back, leaving Joe without a comeback.

When I have finished sampling a mile or so of stream, checking only those spots I feel from my earlier walk along the stream will hold good trout, I am ready to start fishing.

I will move either upstream or down, depending on where I finished sampling, but I prefer to work downstream on one side, then back up on the other. I usually wade very little going down, to prevent spooking the fish. Wading upstream is hard work, but usually necessary.

The order of importance of insects to the trout that feed on them will vary with the stream, sometimes with each stretch of stream and always with the season. Further, insect structures in a stream will almost invariably change over a period of years. For this reason I consider my insect screen the most important of all my gadgets and gear.

Of course, while walking the stream to look for hold areas, I always keep an eye out for insects hatching, for terrestrials, and for noninsect food items—frogs, minnows, mice, and so forth. I do not confine myself only to insects for making my artificial lures, and I nearly always favor the larger items simply because I prefer to fish for trout of a pound or over. In the last fifteen years, at least 95 percent of the trout I've caught have been a pound or larger, and I have little interest in smaller fish. This is the major reason I live where I do.

Using large flies isn't all that's necessary to avoid catching small trout. You must learn to identify holds apt to contain only trout of fifteen inches or larger. How to do this? As I said earlier, that's the rub.

We can use the rule, the larger the obstacle to the current, the larger the fish we may expect to find behind it. This will not be an invariable rule, but it will be generally true for a given stretch of water. Variations in depth or current speed affect any hold. For a ridiculous example, you wouldn't expect a five-pound trout in water only four inches deep even if there was a rock there big as a house. And in slow current, a rock only as big as a softball might be enough of a barrier to shelter a three-pounder from the current force. So one must use his judgment and apply certain criteria to every hold. Things to be considered are size of obstacle, current speed, depth, clarity of water, amount of surface disturbance, location in regard to deep water, and perhaps other factors.

The distance from safety in the form of quite deep water is a very important factor. For instance, there is a riffle on the Madison in the Park that is nearly two miles long, and seldom, in midsummer, more than fourteen inches deep. There are pocket holds in it, some perhaps fifty feet long, half as wide, and two or three feet deep. Although these holds have rocks and logs in them, and are ideal in most respects, they seldom contain a fish of two pounds. The reason is that most are some hundred yards or more from any deeper water, and a fish larger than two pounds just doesn't feel safe in such a small hold surrounded by shallow water. Sometimes a bigger fish, passing through, will rest in such holds, but he will not live there.

So volume of a hold, or the area enclosing a hold, is an important thing to look for. I've found three-pounders in a hold not over four feet long and wide, and perhaps three deep, but these places are always located where there is some deep, secure refuge nearby. Spot holds in fast deep runs are common. A large trout doesn't mind a small tight lie *if* there is a volume of water nearby to give him running and hiding room. But he steers clear of even very good lies surrounded by shallow water.

Of course, there are times when deep water isn't required to make a trout feel safe. If there are ledges or logs to get under, weeds to hide in, crevices or hiding places into which a trout can wiggle and get out of sight *from above,* then he will not be so concerned with depth or volume. But there must be a "security hold" or "hide" of some sort for there to be sizable trout nearby.

The lack of such security holds is what causes an apparently ideal piece of water to host only average fish. I know stretches on the Firehole that have everything a large trout might want—barriers from current force, a nice depth of water, varied bottom, plenty of food; but because they have no real hiding places, the trout seldom reach a pound.

The fact is, the larger a trout grows, the more he requires a security hold, and the larger such a hold must be. He may not live *in* the hold, but he will never be far from it.

A trout will not share his living place with another, except in rare instances, but a security hold is like a bomb shelter, and all trout in an area, regardless of their size, will share a security hold when trouble threatens. They will not take food while there, however, except in those cases where a trout lives in such a hold.

The above factors cause a constant migration of trout in a stream. As a trout outgrows his hold, which he does often in the first four years of life, he will constantly be on the lookout for larger living quarters, and if he finds one that suits him occupied by a smaller fish, he will force it out and take its lie. As trout grow larger, they generally move to areas of deeper water; this usually means moving downstream. By the time he is five years old, a trout will usually have reached the area of a stream where he will remain for the rest of his life.

What will he have found that causes him to remain here? A sufficient depth and area so that he does not feel crowded. A secure hold, either where he is living, or nearby. A good food supply, either in the hold itself (preferred) or in a nearby riffle. And not enough angling pressure to cause him to give up and move downstream to bigger, deeper water.

I look for such places continually, spending more time doing this than I do fishing. Many of these spots will attract a "club crowd" —that is, a number of trout of about the same size, which share the area in perfect harmony. I know several such holds on streams nearby that hold over a hundred trout of over two pounds, none of which can be seen from the surface.

How do I find such places?

Well, I look for the factors above, then when I find an area that fills the bill, upon surface examination, I put on my face mask and breathing tube and go below for a look.

If this seems going a little far, well, I'm not a casual fisherman, and I don't care to fish for small fish. If one wants to catch larger trout, he *must* spend more time finding what their requirements are, and thoroughly studying those places that seem best. And if you ever expect to be able to say, with accuracy, "There should be a twenty-inch trout in that hold," you may have to spend some time under-water with the fish.

At least, that's how I do it.

3

Knowing Your Rivers

PERHAPS the most important single thing a fisherman can know is the character and quality of the streams he fishes. I don't mean casual knowledge, such as might be gleaned from a state tourism pamphlet; I mean deep and abiding knowledge of the stream, from watershed to water quality to characteristics of the banks and bed, the weeds, ledges, logs, rocks, and holes that shelter fish, the insects that feed the fish in the stream, the temperature, rainfall, and climate that affects it—in short, all and everything about it.

It is impossible, in the short span of a lifetime, to obtain that kind of knowledge about more than a few rivers. When I first decided, some twenty-five years ago, that this was true, I also decided to apply myself to the rivers on or at the edge of the Yellowstone plateau. Since then, whenever it was possible, I have stuck doggedly to coming to know the rivers of that area. It was not always possible; of those years, I spent two in Alaska and two in Africa.

The area I speak of stretches about one hundred miles from the Yellowstone River at Gardiner, Montana, to the Railroad Ranch, Idaho, on Henry's Fork of the Snake, and about one hundred miles from the Firehole at Old Faithful to the Madison at Ennis, Montana.

My home on the side of the Continental Divide in Montana, two miles from the Idaho line at Targhee Pass, is about in the center of this roughly circular area. There are perhaps a hundred trout streams in the area; I have made serious study of only seven of these, although I have fished some fifteen others (including tributaries of the seven) but have not actually studied them. The seven are, in no particular order, the Yellowstone from Fishing Bridge to Gardiner, the Firehole in its entirety, the Upper Madison in Yellowstone Park from its start at Madison Junction to Baker's Hole, the Lower Madison from Hebgen Dam to Ennis, the entire South Fork (of the Madison), the Gallatin from Fan Creek to the mouth of the canyon, and Henry's Fork of the Snake from Henry's Lake to just below Osborn Bridge.

The above comprises some thirty-two miles of the Yellowstone, sixteen of the Firehole, seventeen of the Upper Madison, sixty miles of the Lower Madison, thirty-five of Henry's Fork, twelve of the South Fork, and thirty-six miles of the Gallatin, a total of some two hundred miles of trout rivers.

It is impossible to learn trout streams by reading about them, yet there is no doubt that the learning process can be immensely aided by someone else's account of his experiences and knowledge. For that reason, I offer something of what I have learned of these streams in twenty-five years. Hopefully, these profiles of rivers will also suggest *how* you can study those rivers in your area.

THE FIREHOLE

The Firehole has been called the strangest trout stream in the world by both trout fishermen and geologists, as well as by millions of casual observers. What makes it strange is the fact that it absorbs the overflow from countless hydrothermal features; geysers, hot springs, mud pots, warm creeks, hot gases from seepage, and upwellings from hot-water sources in the stream bed itself.

The watershed is small, but the headwaters lie at the top and in the very heart of the Yellowstone plateau. Snow depths range from six feet on top of the plateau to over sixty feet on the east edge, where the Firehole is born. Spring-fed Madison Lake, considered the source of the Firehole, is above 8,200 feet; there is snow on the north slopes there until August some years.

In the upper watershed, countless small eutrophying bogs and subalpine meadows act as sponges to absorb the spring runoff and release it slowly through the short summer and fall. The flow is kept from fluctuating widely largely due to these essential and most desirable features.

The section above Old Faithful has little warm-water input, and is also low in mineral content. Old Faithful pours about one hundred million gallons of warm, mineral-rich water daily into the Firehole, making it quickly more fishworthy. All told, various hydrothermal features add about three hundred million gallons of water daily to the river, running from 90 degrees F. to over 190 degrees F. These sources also add about two hundred thousand tons of dissolved mineral salts to the stream every twenty-four hours. Fortunately for the angler, about 96 percent of these salts are most beneficial; over 90 percent of the load is composed of calcium carbonates and bicarbonates. Since these two minerals are the principal ingredients of limestone, the Firehole is essentially a limestone stream.

Above Old Faithful the river shows less than ten parts per million of calcium carbonates and bicarbonates. Just below, the figure is thirty parts per million and the river at its richest, just above Firehole Canyon, contains 120 parts per million of limestone minerals.

The oxygen content of the river varies, but in its fishable length I have never obtained a reading of less than 6.5 parts per million, while most of the stream gives a reading of 8 to 9 parts per million. This is generally considered saturation. Trout can survive very well in temperatures of 75 to 80 degrees F. if the oxygen content is above 6 parts per million.

The temperature of the Firehole does not vary as much as one might suspect. Excelsior Spring puts about sixty million gallons of 160-degree water into the Firehole daily. Fifty feet downstream from this input, the temperature of the river seldom exceeds 85 degrees F., while a hundred yards below, the temperature is the same as it is one hundred yards above the spring. Ojo Caliente Spring spills 200-degree water into the river continuously, about ten to twenty gallons a minute. I've caught fat healthy trout no more than fifteen feet below this input.

Conversely, a number of very cold springs and feeder creeks run into the Firehole. While occasionally a small brook trout may be found just below these cold sources, it is only very rarely, in the latter end of an exceptionally hot August, that you will find a brown trout in these areas. Rainbows do not seem at all affected by either cold or hot inputs; they generally will be found in the same areas throughout the fishing season.

The temperature variations in various stretches of the river have some effect on the insect life, but not as much effect as bottom type has. However, the 1959 earthquake caused changes that raised, then lowered, the average temperature of the stream, and the stream is now about four degrees cooler than it was prior to the earthquake.

Some very small flies that used to hatch by the millions are no longer in the stream. These include one very tiny mayfly, at least two species of true flies, and one very small caddis.

The bottom of the Firehole is, for the most part, different from that of other trout streams. Kenneth B. Armitage, writing in *Ecology*, in October 1958, says there does not seem to be any parallel for the bedrock formation in the Firehole. The bedrock is rhyolite lava, which is very irregular, has many cracks and crevices, and often has projections or humps. Thus, there can be a great variation in the bedrock bottom due to these features.

Even where the bottom is sand, sand silt, gravel, or gravel rubble, as it is in various areas, this material is nearly always thinly deposited over bedrock. There *are* areas, near slow-moving, hot-water inputs, where the deposit of silt from the thermal feature may be several feet deep. One must be careful in wading into such muck; it

Ojo Caliente Spring, one of the many thermal features that pour their hot water into the Firehole River, making it the most unusual trout stream in the world.

is easy to go over your waders in some of these spots and a smelly inundation it will be, as well as troublesome to get out of.

Mostly, however, the Firehole is easy to wade, the lava bottom is more even than rubble, and there are few places where the current is swift enough to cause concern, except in the last mile or so above the canyon.

It is the variance in insect structures the fisherman needs to be concerned with. These have a direct relationship, not only to the feeding habits, but to the size of the fish. (The Firehole is restricted to fly-fishing only; the limit is two fish, which must be sixteen inches or over to be legally kept.)

From Old Faithful to the bridge above Morning Glory Pool, the river contains few insects, and few fish of any size. The stretch from fifty to one hundred fifty yards below the bridge is good, for fish up to seventeen inches. The insects are plentiful, though there are only a few species—*Brachycentrus* and *Rhyacophila* caddises, and *Baetis* in the mayfly group. The two caddises are better fished as larval or pupal imitations (see Little Gray and Little Green Caddises in Chapter 9) and are good from early in the season up until August. Then one can begin to have some fine sport with a size sixteen or eighteen Blue Wing Olive dry, until late September.

From two hundred yards downstream of the bridge, to the next roadway bridge, above the mouth of Iron Creek and the Little Firehole, there are a few pockets that hold good fish, but they are some distance apart. You will not be bothered by other fishermen in this stretch, which is about a mile of river.

Some good fish move into the area around where the creeks enter the main Firehole, but they are not there all the time. Generally, one can find a good fish or two here in August or early September, prospecting with a big spider or variant, or a grasshopper pattern.

Commencing fifty yards above the Biscuit Basin footbridge at the parking area, the river begins to be more fishworthy. Here, too, a change in insect structures begins. One will find *Ephemerella grandis* nymphs in gravelly sections, until 15 July or so, when the hatch will be over.

There are some stone fly nymphs in this area all season, and a size eight black nymph; Whits Stone, Martinez Black, Ida May, or even a Zug Bug, will be taken at times throughout the season.

From the footbridge, the next mile and a half of river, through Biscuit Basin Meadows, is one of the finest stretches of trout stream anywhere in the world. It contains any number of two- and three-pound fish, some larger ones, and hosts a veritable horde of fish up to twelve inches, which are more difficult to catch than they are else-where.

This stretch of stream is not so easy to fish as these next para-graphs will make it appear. The fish have been much fished over for years and have become wise and wary. One can leave the stream here any day with the knowledge that he has earned any fish he has caught, and if he catches none, that also puts him in good company. The latest study shows that only 18 percent of all fishermen catch any fish on the entire river, and only 5 percent catch trout of sixteen or more inches.

In the Biscuit Basin Meadows stretch, there are several bottom and water types, which cause a difference in insect structures. Basi-cally, however, our two old caddis friends are present (*Rhyacophila* and *Brachycentrus*), both *Baetis* and *Ephemerella* mayflies are here, and there are some few *Hesperophylax* caddises in gravelly sections.

In the weed bed areas, there will be large numbers of midge and blackfly larva, as well as scud and snails. Although I am not positive, I believe that the midge is *Chironomus lobiferous,* which hatches throughout the season. This is a black-bodied fly with pale gray wings, about size eighteen. The blackfly I cannot identify as to species, but a good dry imitation is made with a body of black fur or polypropylene, rather humped at the thorax, and an upright wing of a tiny clump of white deer hair. Tying the wing on first, then wrapping the body material over the wing butt gives the correct humped shape. In sizes eighteen and twenty, this fly is the only thing the trout will touch when the natural is hatching.

Generally speaking, one will have best success throughout the meadow section by using a caddis larva or pupa imitation, fished with either the Rising-to-the-surface or Leisenring-lift methods. If there is a hatch on or the trout are rising very steadily to some natural, observe *very* closely what flies are on the water. There will generally be more than one kind.

If both the Blue-Wing Olive and one of the caddises are hatch-ing, in all probability it is the caddis that is being taken as it comes to the surface to hatch. If midges and blackflies are both hatching, it is the slightly smaller blackfly that will be more often taken. You *must* determine exactly what is going on, or you can cast your arm off and never catch a fish though they are rising by the hundreds all around you. Nearly always, it will be the smallest of the hatching naturals that the fish are taking, though I haven't the faintest knowl-edge of why.

If the fish are up over the weed beds, but not rising, either a nymph, larva, or dry imitation of any of the insects heretofore men-

Three views of a deep, slow curve in Biscuit Basin Meadows on the Firehole River. This section hosts more large trout than any place I know. Down trees, weed beds, depth, and hanging ledges provide security and current relief. (See overleaf.)

tioned will probably work. This calls for delicate casting and long, fine leaders. I prefer to cast cross stream if at all possible; it is almost impossible to cast to such fish from below without spooking them.

Fishing this section requires stalking the area to be fished, and fishing from the bank whenever possible. Quiet, slow movement, and dark-colored, non-light-reflecting clothing are all necessary to avoid spooking the fish. One must be a good caster, and everything that happens must be closely observed, else you are wasting your time. I doubt if 2 percent of the anglers who fish this stretch catch a keepable trout, usually because they violate one or more of the above precepts.

Below Biscuit Basin Meadows there are about two miles of riffles and shallow runs. These contain mostly ten- to fourteen-inch fish,

and are not really difficult to fish as long as the angler proceeds carefully and uses small flies or nymphs.

Just above the upper iron bridge (now closed to traffic) on the old Fountain Freight Road, there is a long run that produces some nice fish. At the upper end of this stretch, there is a short cascade section, above which is a fine gliding run containing some very good fish. This stretch is flanked on the left by a steep bank of whitish rock material. Use the same flies and tactics as indicated for Biscuit Basin Meadows.

Below the iron bridge is a series of riffles and runs for a quarter mile or so. Fast-water tactics with size eight black nymphs—or in August, a grasshopper pattern in size six or eight—will produce fun fishing.

The last of these fast sections slides along a little island into the head of a long oxbow glide, locally known as Muleshoe Bend. This is one of the most reliable pieces of dry-fly water I have ever seen. There will be one or more good hatches almost every day throughout the season, and fish of twelve to seventeen inches will dot the area with their rise forms.

It is at once a pleasant and somewhat frightening place to fish. There are numerous geyserettes, hot pots, hubbly-bubblies, and other thermal features, the crust is thin, the ground hot in some places, and one proceeds with caution, like Agag, lest he tumble in and be fished out well done. Also, some of these things spout off with startling suddenness and noise, causing the contemplative angler to leap out of his waders or into the river. It has happened to me many a time.

Cover is along undercut banks, in weed beds, and in potholes in the bottom. On the highway side, the bank is steep and high; one can park at the turnout at the very elbow of the bend and wait for the hatch to commence.

Begin fishing at the lower end, just before the breakover into fast water. Our two frequently mentioned caddises are here in quantity, and blackfly and midge also. A Blue Dun in size eighteen in both wet and dry patterns is good. The Fair Damsel nymph cast across and retrieved with short, sharp pulls is good at times.

The larger fish will be in the deeper water out from the bank. If you are a quiet wader, you can wade upstream near the middle of the stream and cast to left and right, covering the water thoroughly.

Fish up to fifteen inches are more easily caught; those larger than that require a bit more finesse. But if you observe well, move quietly, and use the right flies, you should take the larger fish.

Below the rapid stretch at the foot of Muleshoe Bend, there is a quarter-mile-long fast run, sliding along a high bank on the far side. At the lower end, Excelsior Spring pours its steaming flow into the river.

The run produces fish to fourteen inches, seldom larger, often smaller. It is just beside the highway and is pleasant to fish, and there are parking areas at the upper and lower ends.

Below the Excelsior Spring footbridge, there is almost a half mile of shallow, fast water which is not really worth your time. Then commences a three-and-one-half-mile stretch of varied water that is quite good throughout.

There are typical meadow glides, deep or shallow runs, riffles, and at the lower end, some fall-like cascades and plunge pools. At the lower end there is a fast plunge into a deep pool under the lower iron bridge on the Fountain Freight Road. One can get to the stretch mentioned above by entering the freight road from the highway just above where Nez Perce Creek enters the Firehole. All the flies and methods previously mentioned work in this varied stretch, but one must change his method to suit the water.

Below the iron bridge, Ojo Caliente Spring sits on the right bank, and there is a parking area behind it. The big curve below the bridge is a quarter mile of the most productive water anywhere.

Then comes a mile or so of riffles with some slower water in between. Dry-fly fishermen dote on this stretch and you are apt to find one or two such anytime somewhere along this piece of water.

Just above and below the mouth of Nez Perce Creek is a series of shallow runs and riffles. Look for the larger fish in the deeper water.

Now comes the broads of the Firehole. The river here is wide, smooth, fairly even bottomed, and eminently fishable for about three miles before getting into the faster water just above the canyon. The highway runs beside this stretch all the way.

The fast water with big boulders just before the Cascades, where the highway leaves the river, is pocket water; you have to seek out the pockets and fish them with a large nymph, using the Pot Shooting method outlined in Chapter 7. You can occasionally get a fish on a streamer here or elsewhere in the Firehole. But the portion of the river above the canyon contains only trout; there are no other fish or minnows.

The canyon section is rough—fast rapids, cascades, falls, and very little fishable water. In the fall, the last quarter mile of river before it joins the Gibbon to become the Madison River will sometimes have good fish seeking spawning areas. Other times it is mediocre.

This is the Firehole River. It is a different stream and one which will test you. It is never as easily fished as it appears, yet the fish are there. Finding them without spooking them is half the battle. The Firehole is largely a stalking proposition. But there is no finer river to challenge the fisherman, and the rewards are commensurate to the skills.

THE UPPER MADISON

The Upper Madison in Yellowstone Park has been called the largest limestone stream in the world; it has also been called a chalk stream. It runs above one hundred parts per million of calcium carbonates and bicarbonates, its oxygen content is always high, its temperature is relatively stable. It has much fine holding water and numbers (though few species) of insects.

From Madison Junction through Elk Meadows, past the Big Bend, along Mt. Jackson, through Madison Notch, Nine Mile Hole and Seven Mile Bridge, the Madison is mostly a stream of deep runs, undercut banks, and weed beds. There are a couple of long, medium-deep riffles, and a couple of shorter, faster stretches, but three-fourths of the water is as described.

There are about ten miles of this water, which is flanked, for the most part, by the highway. It is one of the finest pieces of trout water anywhere and I have known expert anglers who, in an evening's fishing with tiny dry flies, have taken and released over twenty trout of eighteen to twenty-two inches. Yet the stream is not crowded; in the past two seasons I've never seen a dozen anglers any day on this ten-mile stretch.

Why, with most of the river in sight from the highway, is it relatively deserted?

It is tough to fish. Only 22 percent of all anglers catch any fish at all. This river, in the Park, is restricted to fly-fishing and the limit is two fish, sixteen inches or over.

About 80 percent of the fishermen are tourists, and have never fished the river before, strong evidence that getting to know the streams you fish is very important for success.

The 22 percent who caught trout did so at a rate of four per hour, with about one trout in six being sixteen or more inches.

Local anglers—from Montana, Wyoming, and nearby Idaho—make up only 5 percent of the fishermen but catch over 90 percent of the fish: again proof that knowing your rivers is mandatory for an increased catch rate.

The flies and methods indicated for Biscuit Basin Meadows of the Firehole are the ones to use in this stretch of the Upper Madison. Quiet walking and wading is a must and good casting is required. As Howard Back says in *The Waters of Yellowstone with Rod and Fly,* this is *kittle* fishing, no game for a novice or a bungler.

In twenty-five years of fishing this water, I've seen but one angler on the Big Bend section. I do not know why, unless the quarter-mile walk from the road across a sometimes boggy meadow discourages them. It is a beautiful piece of water—deep, well weeded, with potholes and undercut banks providing holds for fish that will often run twenty inches, and occasionally better.

In addition to the flies and methods listed for Biscuit Basin Meadows, a Brown Spider, White Hair-Wing Variant (House and Lot), and a Brown Bivisible will work in August and September. A good hopper pattern is great in August, and a deer-hair mouse might get you a four-pounder. This stretch is not bothered by the casual angler, and the fish will take things here that they will ignore on other stretches of the stream.

To get to the Big Bend, note your mileage at the Madison Junction intersection, and then drive west toward West Yellowstone. Around eight-tenths of a mile from the intersection, look for a turnout and parking area on the left. Here is where you leave your car to cross the meadow, and when you get to the river, it will tell you where to fish. Good luck.

While the first ten miles of the Madison is much of a piece, fished much alike, the rest of the river is not. About two miles downstream from Seven Mile Bridge, the deep, weed-filled runs give way to a shallow riffle nearly two miles long. The roadway leaves the river at this point, and does not rejoin it.

Skip the riffle unless you are looking for mostly small fish, or want to search the rare deeper pockets in the stretch.

One mile or slightly less inside the park's west entrance at West Yellowstone, a road turns off to the north—the right if you are coming downriver, as we have been. This leads to some three miles of the finest fast-water fishing anywhere. It is wet fly and nymph fishing for the most part, the water being too fast and broken for the dry fly.

Keeping to the right, one comes to a downgrade of a hundred yards or so, about a half mile in. A road to the right here is closed to visitor traffic. Continue down the grade, across the flat, keeping right, and you will come to the parking area on a low bluff, with a high bank across the river from you.

This fast, deep run is known locally as Hole Number One, and early in June or late in August and September, it provides good fishing. The rest of the season it is heavily pounded by every passing angler and the fish are driven to deeper water.

Upstream from this is Cable Car Run, a long shallow run or deep riffle that produces now and then. You must fish the water.

Below Hole One is another stretch of riffle water, then comes Hole Number Two, a fine, deep, fast hold which contains a very large number of good fish, and a few big ones. You can drive here from Hole One; there is a parking area, and this is end-of-road. From here you walk.

Downstream of Number Two, there is a series of fast riffles, for three-eighths of a mile. Here the river, which has been about two feet deep, and which has been sliding away to your right, now deepens and curves left. There is a rock near the far bank from which a spume of white water breaks, and one just upstream nearer the middle. These boulders mark the beginning of Hole Number

Three, the last of the locally numbered holes. I don't think local people fish beyond here.

For almost two miles more, there is a series of deep riffles and much deeper runs. The deeper water will always be at the outside of an elbow bend, and the larger fish will be here.

All this fast water is stone fly water; both *Pteronarcys* and *Acroneuria* are found here, along with sculpins. The best methods are the Brooks method mentioned in Chapter 7, and the standard streamer methods, using at least a number two streamer.

The big stone fly nymphs are used—Montana Nymph, Montana Stone Nymph, Whit's Stone Nymph, Bitch Creek Special, and big black woolly worms. All catch fish, good fish, and many of them. The three most used streamers are the Dark Spruce, Green, and Brown Marabou Muddlers. You want a big, bulky fly in this fast water.

You must be a strong wader; this is powerful water, and the bottom is rubble and rubble-boulder. A wading staff is a very good piece of equipment to carry along.

Seek out the deeper water, the larger rocks, and cast up far enough so that your *weighted* fly will be deep enough when it comes to the fish; then be prepared to strike with speed and strength. Use strong leaders.

For the most part, especially in the riffles, you are fishing the water. In some of the deeper sections, you fish the hold. But get the fly down, or you will catch mostly small fish or whitefish, which abound in this stretch.

The fast water ends in Beaver Meadows about three and one-half miles below Hole One. Here begins a different type water than is found anywhere else in this area.

These are *deep* meadow pools, fairly quiet water with undercut banks and bottom depressions. The fish run large, five to eight pounds, with not too many smaller fish.

This is a boggy area, difficult to get around in, and it is nearly a four-mile walk from either Hole Number One at the upper end, or Baker's Hole at the lower. There are also grizzly bears in the area and for this reason most anglers give it a pass.

The fishing is with dragonfly nymphs, large streamers or ter- restrials—hoppers and mice being the best bet among the floaters. You will not get much action but your fish should be sizable.

And so we come to Baker's Hole, discussed at length in another chapter. Who Baker was I know not but his Hole is famous locally and a good place to start or finish a day's fishing.

The upper ten miles of this river is much like the Firehole in Biscuit Basin Meadows, and has the same type of holds and locations, though the water is generally deeper; still, the flies and methods given for that section are the best producers on most of this upper ten miles.

One section in this ten-mile stretch is different enough to require different flies and tactics.

This is Nine Mile Hole, about nine miles in from the west entrance and about four miles from Madison Junction. It can be recognized by huge, automobile-sized boulders in and along the river. It is the only stretch where such huge rocks are found in the stream.

A variety of methods are required to fish this stretch. In and around the rocks are deep pockets of eddy water. Here small nymphs work, and at times a hopper pattern will bring up a good trout.

Over the weed beds small dries, ants, and small nymphs will occasionally work, but trout do not come up, or close to the surface in this stretch very often.

The best bet for larger fish is to use a sink-tip line, long leader, and big weighted nymphs in size six or eight, and try to drift this nymph down the deep channels in the weed beds.

You *will* get hung up, so use a strong leader—1X is minimum.

Three views of Nine Mile Hole on the Madison River in Yellowstone Park. Large rocks, sunken logs, weed beds, and potholes in the bottom provide security, and make this one of the most difficult stretches to fish. It holds very large trout. Type 4, run. (See overleaf.)

Some anglers have reduced the hanging-up problem by using Keel hooks; these also produce good hooking because of the up-riding point. Some local shops carry a limited selection of nymphs on these hooks.

One angler I know, Sid Terrell, who has been fishing this area for fifty years, fishes Nine Mile Hole regularly. He uses the method just described, and says that patience is the key.

Keep your fly riding again and again, deep in the channels, he advises. Take your time getting free when you get hung up. Go slowly and carefully, and keep at it. This is Sid's way, and it's the best bet to produce a three-pounder from this stretch.

THE GALLATIN

The Gallatin is somewhat different from other streams so far described. It is a typical mountain stream as far as water types, mostly riffles and runs, with only an occasional pool or deeper spot. It falls somewhat naturally into two sections in the area under discussion.

From Fan Creek to two miles above Karst Ranch, it is largely a panfish stream. The water type is mostly riffles, and the bottom, for the most part, is of gravel and small stones. It is a mineral-rich stream with about sixty parts per million of calcium carbonates and bicarbonates. The potential for food and growth is there but is blocked by the flood scour-anchor ice syndrome, which keeps food production down.

The prevalent insects are small caddises and mayflies, but the latter are scarce. Flies of twelve and fourteen are standard in this section.

For the most part it is riffle fishing—not difficult but not productive of large fish. Three methods can be used with success: the cast across and natural drift, the cast across and hand retrieve during the drift; and the dry fly. Terrestrials can be good after July tenth, and match-the-hatch dries at other times.

The river is easy to get to; it is paralleled by the highway along most of this section, the banks are relatively flat and open, and there are parking areas all along for your convenience.

It is mile after mile of pleasant, not-too-difficult fishing, and you will nearly always be sure of a few for the skillet. The limits and seasons are different for that section in the park and that in Montana. Check them before fishing.

At present, the park section is limited to artificial lures, including flies, and the limit is two fish, with no minimum length. The state-owned waters have different regulations and must be checked.

That section in the canyon from two miles or so above Karst's to the mouth of the canyon is different water.

The bottom is rubble and rubble boulder, the water mostly runs, rapids, and cascades.

The insects are different. Here is found the giant stone fly, *Pteronarcys,* and the nymphs will be present all season, any season.

You'll need sinking lines for the most part, but if you catch the "salmon fly" hatch the last week in June and the first week in July, you'll need a floating line. Also, there are the tails of some runs which offer fair, if challenging dry-fly fishing through August.

Method number ten in Chapter 7 has produced the most and largest fish for me; I would recommend it as a basic method to start with, using one of the big black-stone nymph patterns. Method number eight, pot-shooting, is good in the pocket sections which one finds throughout this stretch.

The occasional deep holes one finds at the base of bluffs and in eddies calls for sinking the fly at the head of the hole and keeping it working in the area as long as possible before picking up to recast.

Big streamers, with standard methods of cast and retrieve, produce good fish at times. It should be remembered that this river does not host many large fish due to food shortage. The larger fish will invariably be found in the deeper water.

One thing that will aid you in making better catches is to cross the river and fish from the side away from the highway. You will find yourself all alone, and the fish, not having been bothered, will be larger and more willing.

You do not need a large selection of flies. The stone nymph is a must, some small standard dries for the tails of runs, streamers, big and bulky, if you care for them, and a hopper pattern or so will get you through the season. In most cases, the big nymph, deeply sunken, and dead-drifted through the fast rocky sections, will get you more action and larger fish.

THE SOUTH FORK

This is another stream different from any other in the area. For most of its length, the South Fork, which in full is the South Fork of the Madison, is a winding, willow-lined brook, extremely clear and excessively cold.

It is largely spring fed, and it runs through bogs and swamps in places; thus its temperature and volume are fairly constant, and its waters not as mineral rich as most other nearby streams.

It runs about thirty parts per million of carbonate minerals, is nearly always saturated with oxygen, and its bottom is sandy gravel in the lower, and gravel to gravel rubble, in the upper sections. It is densely lined with willows, except for the last mile or so before it runs into Hebgen Lake.

The South Fork falls naturally into four sections. The upper one, from Mosquito Gulch down to the old airport road bridge, is five or six miles long, so winding that it is impossible to be more accurate. This water is difficult to describe and more difficult to fish.

It looks like a panfish proposition but it isn't. You may be going along, catching twelve- to fourteen-inch fish regularly, singing a song, happy in the foolish belief that everything is under control, when of a sudden a three-pound brown will smash your fly, run under the twining roots, back out, vault through the canopy of limbs overhanging the water, drop back, and swim away with your fly and leader, leaving you dazed, confused, and uncertain as to what really happened.

The water at the numerous bends is always deeper than it looks, and the pockets back under some of the willow-root mats are more like caves. There are trout of six to eight pounds in some of these root-guarded lairs, and an eleven-pound brown was taken in the pool by the airport road bridge in 1967.

The willows are thicker than sheep's wool, just as entwined, and make both wading and fishing very tough. In early season, this whole upper area is a giant bog; this part of the stream is better fished after the Fourth of July.

The insects are our two so-often-mentioned caddises, two species of *Ephemerella* mayflies, both black, sizes ten and twelve, one stone fly about an inch long (I've not been able to identify this nymph, it has the appearance of *Arcynopteryx,* but that's as close as I can come), and there are two species of *Baetis,* both quite similar.

The upper South Fork is a place for a sink-tip line, fairly short leader, short casts, and luck, in spite of which you'll often be hung up, in front, behind, in the water, in the willows. If you can abide these frequent irritating interruptions, the South Fork can supply excellent fishing, with always the possibility of hanging a really good fish, which, of course, you will not land.

The section between the old airport road bridge and the Highway 191 bridge is about four miles long. The latter two miles run through privately owned land, and I have not bothered to fish this four-mile section for that reason. Some anglers do fish the section just down from the upper bridge and say it is no different from the section above the bridge, except that the water is deeper. They say that the same tactics and flies do the job.

From the highway bridge to a mile from Hebgen Lake is *about* five miles of river. I'm sorry I cannot be more specific, but this is one of the most winding streams on earth and it is impossible to be accurate concerning distances. A dirt road roughly parallels the stream some quarter mile to the east, leaving the highway, looping down to and along Hebgen Lake, then striking the highway again where it runs north out of West Yellowstone. In the first five miles, it has frequent turnoffs that go down to, or near, the stream. These were made by fishermen in bygone days and are indications of spots to approach the stream. There is no other way, because the willows in this section are virtually impenetrable.

The flies and methods quoted for the upper section work here, *but* step up one size number. The bottom material grows progressively finer and the insects smaller as the river flows to the lake.

Do not waste any time in the first half mile of stream below the highway bridge. There is a large campground here and casual fishermen pound this stretch constantly during the summer.

There are fifteen to twenty turnoffs between where the dirt road (it may be oiled in the near future) leaves Highway 191 and where it makes a sweeping right curve to leave the river and follow the lake shore. One may identify this road by a large wooden Forest Service sign at the highway, reading MADISON ARM RESORT and LAKESHORE SUMMER HOMES. This is the route to the lower South Fork.

The last mile of the South Fork before it runs into Hebgen Lake is meadow stream and is fished with meadow-stream tactics, small nymphs, small dries, and hoppers during the season.

In August, there is a steady hatch of a small (size sixteen to eighteen) golden olive mayfly. I've not been able to get it identified, it could be *Ephemerella infrequens;* the size and color as well as the hatching time fit this small mayfly, but it could be some other species.

A number sixteen or eighteen Ginger Quill will sometimes work when this fly is hatching, as will a Ginger variant. I've had best success with a fly with a body of olive-yellow fur, wings of wood duck, and a bright golden badger hackle. I call it Golden Olive Dun. There is a similar fly to be found in some of the shops but I don't know the name.

In the estuary section, the depth of the lake will have a profound effect on the depth in the stream channel. There are times when really big trout circulate in this channel—usually in June and September—and these fish like plenty of depth. A brown of over eighteen pounds came out of this estuary channel, so when I say big fish, I mean quite large. Al McClane reported taking a number of four- to seven-pound fish from this area on one occasion.

The local people take these fish on large Woolly Worms and big streamers. This is slow catching; one may fish all day without a strike, or he may catch two or more fish over five pounds. It depends entirely on whether the fish are out of the lake and into the channel and there is no way to find this out but to go fishing.

HENRY'S FORK OF THE SNAKE

This is a large, varied stream, extremely prolific in insect types and fish production. It is impossible to cover it in the limited space available. It is one of two streams where I believe the visiting angler to be better off with a guide, at least for the first few trips.

One branch of the river rises in Henry's Lake; it flows several miles through meadows, marshes, and bogs. Much of the land is private holdings and one must be careful not to trespass.

Another fork arises at Big Springs, whose 420-million-gallon daily flow makes one of the richest and most beautiful stretches of trout water in the world, though it is quite short, only a half a mile or so long.

After these two forks join, the river is rather large by trout-stream standards, and it is plagued throughout by stretches of private holdings, where the bank belongs to a private citizen or club, although you are entitled to the stream bed.

Below Island Park Reservoir, the Box Canyon stretch is something more than two miles of wild water that offers fantastic fishing in June during the salmon fly hatch. This must be fished from a boat —or at least, you travel by boat—and I would want a thoroughly trustworthy man at the oars.

In June, of course, one uses a floating line and one of the big dries, size six or four—Bird's Stone Fly, the Sofa Pillow, or some such. Take plenty of extra flies, and strong leaders: this will be strong water and strong fish.

During the rest of the season this stretch is fished with big stone fly nymphs, and fast-sinking lines, using the Brooks method in Chapter 7.

Below the mouth of the canyon are mile after mile of beautiful trout water, with the most diverse insect population of any stream I know. Our old caddis friends *Brachycentrus* and *Rhyacophila* are here by the millions, mayflies are represented by three species of *Ephemerella*, two of *Baetis, Callibaetis, Tricorythodes,* and perhaps others; some *Pteronarcys* are found in short stretches, *Hyalella* (scud) inhabit weedy sections, and midge and blackfly abound.

Scud (Hyella).

I once sat on a low bluff above this stream and for three hours witnessed the most incredible hatch I have ever seen. Both species of caddis were hatching, two genera, and three species of mayfly were on the water, midge and blackfly, and even some few crane flies were hatching; the water surface was so covered by floating insects that it took on a smoky gray color. It was just at the close of the salmon fly hatch, the fish were glutted, and only a few small fish rose all day. By my notebook this was 19 June.

Where the bottom is of finer material there will be numbers of dragonfly and damselfly nymphs, and when there is no hatch on, these big nymphs, sunk to the bottom and fished with short, sharp pulls, can produce some good, even big, fish.

This is one of the finest fly streams in the country, but as I said earlier, it is so large, diverse, and so hemmed in by private land, that I would hire a guide for my first few days. Excellent guide service can be obtained in either West Yellowstone or at Last Chance, in Idaho, on the river itself.

THE LOWER MADISON

What I said about guides on Henry's Fork applies doubly to this huge stream. It is entirely possible for a first-time visitor to spend two weeks on this stream and not catch a decent fish. There is just too much river, and too much private land surrounding the banks. The river is over seventy miles long from Quake Lake Slide to Ennis.

Some sections can be floated, but which sections these are varies from time to time. Any guide will be up, not only on this, but on what stream conditions are, what flies to use, and so forth. Some guides have clients on this river nearly every day of the season, and really get to know it.

Guide service can be obtained at either West Yellowstone or Ennis.

The river is fast—runs, rapids, and cascades, the bottom rubble boulder; the dominant insect throughout is the giant stone fly nymph.

The stream is very rich in insect life, but smaller insects are apt to be overlooked in the rough fast water and along the extremely rough bottom.

The river *is* dangerous to wade; it is fast, strong, and often deep. The stones are quite smooth and round so wading requires great care. A wading staff is a must.

Bruce Peeples says that over on the Clearwater there is a warden who goes around once a week, greasing the rocks on the stream bottom. That same fellow works the lower Madison on his off days. If you are going to wade this big, brawling stream, you had better be a strong wader, and fearless.

Getting back to small insects, dry-fly fishermen do not do much matching the hatch; the hatches and hatch times of the smaller insects are not well known, and small (size twelve and under) floating insects just get lost in this rough water.

So big, high-floating, highly visible dry flies are used—Wulffs, Bivisibles, Goofus Bugs, Irresistibles, and others of this sort. Of course, during the salmon fly hatch, one uses the huge dries that are supposed to imitate the natural: Bird's Stone Fly, Sofa Pillow, and Dave's Stonefly, all in number four or six.

The big stone nymph imitations are good throughout the season, for this river is loaded with the natural. I have picked up a handful of the huge nymphs at one screening with my insect screen, at many places on this river. If I were looking for the best day-in, day-out fishing on this river, I would use nothing but my Montana Stone nymph, a fast-sinking line, and method number ten in Chapter 7. But if I were a visitor, I'd hire a guide and take his advice.

THE YELLOWSTONE IN THE PARK

As I indicate later, this river has made an exciting and dramatic comeback under new, stringent regulations. It is restricted to artificial lures, including flies, no fish may be killed, and the river is closed until after spawning, about 15 July.

This is the finest cutthroat trout fishery in the nation; from Upper Falls to Fishing Bridge no other fish are in the stream except suckers that spawn in the area. These are from Yellowstone Lake. Below Lower Falls, on down to Gardiner, one will now and then encounter a brown or a rainbow.

There is a stretch of 6.4 miles, from Sulphur Caldron to Alum Creek, which is permanently closed to fishing. This is a wildlife-study area, and one will see moose, elk, deer, buffalo, otter, geese, rare trumpeter swans, ducks, shorebirds, and many smaller creatures in this area.

The highway from Canyon to Fishing Bridge parallels the river; if you are driving in this section, be very alert: at any time the car in front of you may stop suddenly, the doors fly open, and people jump out to go racing over the countryside to see and photograph some of the birds or animals. No one signals or gives any warning, and accidents are numerous on this road in July and August.

The Yellowstone is pleasant to fish, a wide, easy-flowing river. From the lake to the falls, the gradient is low, about five-and-a-half feet per mile. The bottom in most areas is fairly even, and it is pleasant wading.

The lake, the highest of its size in the world, remains frozen through much of May. Much of its water is melted snow, and the river running out of it is cold even in late August. Hatches occur late in the day, so there is little need to be on the stream before ten o'clock in the morning.

Our two caddises are the major insects, and are the ones to use. Fish the larval or pupal imitations until the adult flies start to flutter over the stream in numbers, then switch to a sedge type dry, or an Adams, a number fourteen Ginger Bivisible, or similar fly.

This is the most heavily fished cutthroat stream in the world and you will be surrounded by anglers most days. But the fishing is getting better, and in two years this river should be fabulous fishing for the knowledgeable fly-fisherman. The evidence is that lures are not too successful.

The best method to locate fish that are feeding is to drive along slowly until you see fish rising. Find a parking place—there are many along here—and rig up with a sink-tip or slow-sinking line. The fish you think are rising are invariably taking caddis in the pupal shuck as they pop up from the bottom. Put on a larval or pupal imitation and go fishing.

Sometime during the day, usually late afternoon, the adult caddises will appear on the stream by the millions. Then it is time to switch to the dry fly, not before.

In early August the riffle beetle larvae become active. If you can detect this happening, or if you are having no success with the underwater caddis forms, switch to a number four, 3XL olive green Woolly Worm and work it slowly over the bottom. This can save the day.

From Lower Falls to the Tower Junction Bridge the river runs through the Canyon. Some areas are reachable, but only if you are a mountain climber. The fish are not more numerous nor significantly larger.

Below Tower Junction in to Gardiner the river is from one to four miles from the road. This section does not see an angler a year for each mile of stream. It is boulder-rapids for the most part, the dominant insect is the giant stone fly, and fish are plentiful. They run from one to two pounds.

If you decide to hike in and fish any section of this twelve or so miles of river, take a compass and a map. You may be able to see where the river runs when you leave the car, but you will be down in gullies, depressions, small valleys, and other low areas where you will not be able to see much of anything. You may not get lost but you can wind up hiking three times the necessary distance.

One time Jim Begley and his son, Dr. Lew Begley, talked me into hiking to the river with them. Our destination was the mouth of Geode Creek, locally known as Jodie Creek. It figured to be about a three-mile hike, and so it was, going in. Coming out, we turned to go around a spring bog, missed our turn back, and walked over seven miles to get to the highway, where we were lucky to catch a ride some two miles to our car. Take my advice, carry a map and compass.

Despite its being only a few miles from the highway, this is as remote and wild as any place in the continental forty-eight states. If you look, you will see deer, bear, buffalo, antelope, mountain sheep and goats, all wild—not the same type of creatures one so often sees from the road. Most of them have never seen a man.

If I were going back to the river in this area, I would pack in a sleeping bag and five ready-to-eat meals and spend the night. I know of no spot where a trout fisherman can find wilderness, an unspoiled stream, and superb fishing so close to a major highway.

The hike in and out is not really rugged; the terrain, for the most part, furnishes good footing. Until you get close to the river, the ground cover is mostly sagebrush and bunch grass. The last quarter mile before the river can be tough; there are canyon stretches which are difficult to get into and out of; but if you like the wilderness and good fishing at a rather small physical price, this is the place.

Which of these seven rivers, and what stretches of them would I fish? It would depend on what kind of fishing and what size fish I wanted.

If I wanted a lazy, easy day of carefree angling, I'd go up to the Gallatin; I'd wear my hippers and fish the riffles, drifting nymph and larva imitations across and down. I'd admire the scenery, enjoy the animals, take my time, and just dream along.

At noon, I'd eat my sandwich and drink my beer, then have a nap. Later on, I'd try the dry fly, fishing back upstream to where I left the car. I'd have had a pleasant day, not too many fish to release, and would be just tired enough to sleep well.

If I wanted to concentrate on placing and fishing the fly, catching mostly fourteen-inch fish, but with the possibility of hanging a very good one, I'd fish the South Fork. You do no dreaming on the South Fork, or you will spend the entire day retrieving your fly from roots and willows. It is the most demanding of technique of any of the seven streams.

If it were a fine day's demanding dry-fly fishing I was after, I'd fish the Firehole in Biscuit Basin Meadows and Muleshoe Bend, and the Upper Madison at Big Bend. There are no more splendid waters to challenge and please the dry-fly man (or woman), and these are beautiful streams as well.

The Yellowstone I reserve for taking guests who have not fished much, especially with the fly. I'd take them to the Buffalo Ford section, along with a big picnic lunch and some refreshments, and we'd make a day of it. We'd catch as many fish as we wished, see many animals, and have a most enjoyable day with both camera and rod.

I'd save Henry's Fork for a day when I didn't know what method I wanted to fish. On this diverse and beautiful stream one can find half a dozen different water types, each of which would require a different fly and technique. I could make it as tough or as easy fishing as I would want, and for any size fish I might want.

I fish the Lower Madison as little as I do any stream in the area. This is a physically demanding stream if you do not float it, and the fish are not more plentiful nor much larger than elsewhere. Some days when I am in a I-can-whip-the-world mood, I go and pit myself against this raging river, but I'm looking for exhilarating physical effort more than I am a pleasant day's fly-fishing.

I do most of my actual fishing on the fast-water stretches of the Upper Madison, in the three or four miles below Cable Car Run. Here I know that my deeply sunken nymph will work, that I'll catch fish mostly over a pound and up to three or four, and that I'll not be bothered much by other anglers. And after twenty-five years, I'm still learning to fish this water.

I prospect much on the Firehole and its tributary streams, spot-fishing for the most part, locating the lies of larger trout, of which there are many. I test out new terrestrial patterns on this stream and

its feeders. And I use it as a pacifier, to soothe me when I'm upset. For these reasons, it is a jewel beyond price.

A great many anglers I have met have expressed regret that there is no grayling fishing left in the continental forty-eight states. These gentlemen were mistaken, and were delighted when I told them that good to excellent grayling fishing could be found in Montana and Yellowstone Park. I have caught them by the thousands in both places, and for those of you who would like to fish for this rare and beautiful fish, I have listed those lakes and streams in Montana and the Park where one may still take grayling.

Grayling Waters in Montana	
Agnes Lake	near Glen
Bobcat Lake	near Wise River
Cyclone Lake	near Whitefish
Elizabeth and Kintla lakes	Glacier Park
Ennis (Meadow) Lake and Madison River	upstream near Ennis
Fishtrap Lake	near Thompson Falls
Big Hole River	near Wise River
Fuse Lake	near Phillipsburg
Froze-to-Death Lake	near Cooke City
Half Moon Lake	near Coram
Hamby Lake	near Jackson
Handkerchief Lake—Groves Creek	near Bigfork

Harper Lake	near Seeley Lake
Heart Lake	near Lincoln
Hungry Horse Reservoir	near Hungry Horse
Hyalite Lake	near Bozeman
Lasalle ponds	near Kalispell
Odell Lake	near Wisdom
Pintlar and nearby lakes	near Wisdom
Red Meadow Lake	near Olney
Red Rock lakes, Red Rock River	in Centennial Valley, Red Rocks Wildlife Refuge
Rough Lake	near Cooke City
Schwinegar Lake	near Jackson
Skytop lakes (3)	near Cooke City
Sylvia, Lone, and Monroe lakes	west of Kalispell
Turgulse Lake	near Cooke City

Grayling Waters in Yellowstone Park

Grebe and Ice lakes	between Norris and Canyon
Wolf Lake	
Cascade Lake	

No grayling may be kept or killed in Yellowstone Park, but Grebe Lake offers grayling fishing that is as good as many lakes and streams in Alaska.

Not many anglers are so fortunate as I, but I am not here by accident. I spent my entire early life working and planning to be where I am, doing what I do. Now that I *am* here, I hope I can share with others some of my learning and enjoyment through this book and others.

PART TWO

THE PURSUIT OF TROUT

"Stop learning and the world will pass you by: this is no less true of angling than it is of anything else."

4

Fishing the Water

WE fish either to feeding trout or to trout that are not feeding. In the former case, our job of getting into position and placing the fly is greatly simplified. We know where the fish is, or should, and all moves are visible. We may make mistakes, but if so we should be able to detect them instantly, and to correct them. Not so with fishing the water. A veteran angler, writing about fishing the water, said that it compared to floating in a spaceship over a continuously cloud-covered planet and lowering a grab hook through the clouds to seize one of the inhabitants, whom of course, you could not see. I don't think it's quite that difficult but it isn't easy.

There are at least three methods of fishing the water. One requires covering every inch of water in a stream capable of holding a fish. This is, in my experience, the most common method and is shockingly inefficient. It requires no thinking, and this probably is the reason it is so popular.

Trout obviously do not occupy all the water in a stream, and catchable trout are to be found in only a few places. Finding those places, and fishing them, is the first step toward angling success with either the sunken fly or the blindly cast dry fly. This method requires considerable study and practice before one becomes proficient in it, and this study must go on throughout one's angling lifetime. Stop learning and the world will pass you by: this is no less true of angling than it is of anything else.

The third method of fishing the water has been called spot-fishing. It consists of learning the exact lie of a fish in a stream and working it thoroughly. In effect, it is similar to fishing for a feeding fish since one knows that the fish is there even if it cannot be seen.

The second method is called fishing holding water, or holding areas—and method three may be thought of as fishing the exact hold itself, an area of not over four feet in any direction.

The two latter methods are the best if one is able to read the water with some accuracy. Without this ability, we are back to method one, chuck-and-chance-it fishing.

Before deciding on the fly or method of fishing the water, it would be well to consider this piece of information from Ted Trueblood, one of the most knowledgeable anglers around: "From a few inches from the top to a few inches of the bottom the water is as barren of trout as a snowbank."

The reason for the above statement is that except when a hatch is in progress, insects that fish feed on are either on the bottom, where they live out their immature lives, or, briefly, on the surface before they fly away to mate. Fish where the food is, Trueblood is saying. And about 90 percent of the time that food will be on the bottom. Not a few inches from the bottom, not in midwater, but *on* the bottom.

So, if we are setting out to fish the water, it would seem more profitable to fish the bottom most of the time. Some anglers say that since you are going to be fishing blind anyway, why not fish on top, which is easier and more fun. These fellows, I expect, are the same ones who bet on inside straights, long shots in the races, and Britain in the America's Cup.

If you are going to fish the bottom properly, you will need proper equipment. A sinking line, weighted fly, and the proper length and strength of leader are required. If you persist in using floating lines, unweighted flies, and long, fine leaders, as a great many do, there will be a great deal of water where you will be wasting your time, simply because your fly will never get within two feet of the bottom during the drift.

All types of water cannot be fished with the same line. It used to be that one had only two choices of line, floating or slow sinking, and much of the water could not be properly fished. In the last five years, fly lines of many kinds have become available, much improved over lines put out by the same companies in the past.

To fish the water properly, one should have—and have *with* him —not less than three types of line: floating, slow sinking, and fast sinking. Sink-tip and Hi-D lines are specialized lines for very limited types of stream fishing, according to my experience. I can fish the slow sinking line anywhere the sink-tip will work, and can use added weight on the leader with my fast-sinking line to get around the need for Hi-D. To each his own, however, as long as the line chosen either floats on top or sinks to the bottom, as needed, in the type of water being fished.

As you proceed up or down a stream in your fishing, you will find that you are faced with different types of water in different stretches of the stream, and if you are experienced you will note that a line that works perfectly in one stretch either sinks too fast, or not fast enough, in other stretches.

It is too much trouble and too time-consuming to change everything from the reel spool out to the fly each time the water type changes. So I fish along with one line, fishing those areas where my present setup works well, skipping those for which it is unsuited. Then, when I reach the point where I turn around and fish back, I change reel spools, putting on a different line, leader, and fly, and fish the places I skipped coming the other way. I may have to pass some stretches with both methods, and of course should a hatch come on, I switch to the floater. But fishing the water, I usually fish one direction with a fast-sinking setup and fish back with a slow-sinking outfit. I can get in more fishing with less fussing using this system.

Limnologists list six water types that can be fished in trout streams. In order of increasing current speed, the six are: pools, flats, riffles, runs, rapids, and cascades. These, of course, will not be so neatly arranged along the stream. In selecting the proper line to fish the sunken fly, one can say pools, flats, and some riffles can be fished with either a sink-tip or a slow-sinking line. You cannot, usually, bottom fish with a floating line except in shallow, very slow water.

Some riffles, runs, and rapids can be fished with a fast-sinking line. Other rapids and cascades require a Hi-D line, for this is pocket shooting, using a very short leader—and line, leader, and fly have to go down *now*. But this last is very specialized fishing.

In wide, big rivers, one will find that the lies of most fish are somewhat isolated from other lies. In effect, this is a type of pocket water, made so not by current speed but by the *volume* of water. Some of this water will be slow, some quite fast; but because there is usually ample room to drop the fly as far upstream as needed to plumb the bottom on the drift, the type of line used here is not as critical as it is in smaller streams. The Yellowstone, lower Madison, and upper Missouri are this kind of water.

When fishing the water, the type of line used is no more important than covering the water. Thus, in the same stretch, the angler may find water that requires a slow-sinking line along the bank, and a fast-sinking one in the middle. The answer here is to treat the area as two different stretches and fish it one way going down and another coming back.

Bottom type usually is not too important a factor in line selection. Sand, sand silt, gravel, gravel rubble, rubble, and rubble boulder are the six bottom types generally considered to hold fish in trout streams. This ignores mud and bedrock, both of which exist, but which are usually not common. If the line is chosen to suit the current speed and depth, bottom type will not affect matters much.

The same is not true for leader selection. A long leader is perfectly all right for all but rubble and rubble boulder bottoms. Here a short leader is required. Why?

Here is how the scientists phrase it: Turbulence caused by water moving with good speed over an irregular bed forms helices about a horizontal axis, which increase in size as they rise and move downstream, and finally reach the surface in a flat upwelling elevation of water. All things adrift in the stream are lifted toward the surface by this action.

In effect, the above says that fast water beating around rocks or other bottom obstructions causes disturbances that rise and grow larger as they are carried downstream, and that they carry all drifting objects upward with them as they move toward the surface. The actual cause is that air is beaten into the water, making an area of less dense water that is forced upward by denser surrounding water.

Whatever the reason, it will lift your line, leader, and fly toward the surface and off the bottom. The heavy line will not be lifted much, but the leader will, and so will an unweighted fly.

Therefore, fast current, rough bottom spells short leader. How short? Never longer than six feet, and in very fast water with basketball-size boulders, four feet is plenty. Trout in such areas are *not* leader shy.

Our long leader usage in such areas is a hangover from the days of silk or nylon lines, where, since the line wouldn't sink or sank slowly, a long leader was needed, or so we thought. It never worked well then and it doesn't now.

Even a short leader will not help in this kind of water if the fly is unweighted.

I have fished such waters with anglers who refused to fish weighted flies. Often, I have seen their unweighted fly thrust to the surface by one of those powerful upwellings that exist in such water. Of course, a long leader did nothing to help the situation.

It is not absolutely fatal if your fly floats up; all things free-drifting in the stream are thrust upward by the action of these up-wellings, natural insects as well as our artificial ones, but the simple fact is, unless he is quite hungry, a trout will not move far in such waters to seize anything. Trout in running waters must learn to exercise economy of motion in acquiring food. Those that do not learn do not survive; therefore this habit is an ingrained instinct of thousands of generations that have survived. This is a major reason hatchery trout of catchable size usually do not survive more than a few months in trout streams.

Once one has chosen his line, leader, and fly, with an eye to their suitability for the water being fished, the next step is to decide upon the method. The water will, to some extent, limit the methods one can use.

Very slow water, with many weed beds? What method shall we use?

This is one of the most difficult water types to fish. No matter what method is chosen, one is apt to get into difficulties. Skill and experience may help, but seldom provide a complete answer, because of variables of depth, current, and location of weed beds.

Since we are fishing the water, not fishing to a fish, we will skip fishing above the tops of the weeds. What does that leave us?

Weed beds are one exception to Trueblood's statement that mid-water is usually barren. I have seen trout at various times, at all levels, grazing on creatures in the weeds. These are usually cress bugs, small snails or clams, and other clinging creatures whose actions it is not possible to imitate. I have never succeeded in taking a fish when they are feeding in such a manner.

To take fish in weed-bed areas you must get your fly well down and move it along the edge of a bed, or in the channels between beds. This is difficult. Sometimes you can cast directly upcurrent in a channel and let the fly drift and sink as it comes toward you, taking in slack the while. I've caught trout not a rod's length away by this method.

To catch fish in this manner, you must wade in, get into position, then wait a few minutes before casting. A long leader is essential to prevent "lining" the fish. A floating or sink-tip line will work if the upper currents are agreeable. If they are too fast to allow the fly to settle well, a slow-sinking line is better. I find small flies of grizzly, badger, or furnace, sparsely hackled, with gray, yellow, or peacock herl bodies better than more imitative flies or nymphs. Also, dry-fly hackle works better than softer hackle, because no matter how skillful you are, your fly is going to be in the weeds some of the time.

I find it best to take a position below (downstream of) the weed beds when starting. Quite often there will be a fish lying under the trailing veil of weeds flowing from the downstream end of the bed, and I work this area first. At times I've taken as many as three fish from such places, but the odds are against it. When they feel the hook, most trout will plunge headlong into the weeds, getting hung up, thrashing around, and scaring all other trout in the area.

Chalk-stream fishermen in France and England and even in similar American streams, such as the Letort, are always faced with the problem of landing trout from such weedy areas. Each has developed a method for his particular stream, some of which seem quite crude.

Skues and Halford have spoken of "kicking them out," wading into the weed beds and booting the hooked fish out. Other writers speak of slacking the line completely and letting the fish come out of his own accord. Charles Ritz and others use strong leaders and haul them out bodily. I've done all of the above. I like the slacking-off method least because it's sometimes half an hour before His Nibs decides to come out into the world.

No matter what method you decide to use, you are going to lose some fish, generally the larger ones. Crying won't help; Grace does it all the time. Stamping your foot while up to your waist in water only makes you feel ridiculous. I swear a lot in such situations, which puzzles Grace. You never keep the fish, anyway, she says, so why are you so upset when he gets away? I give up, why am I?

Deep, quiet pools sometimes host the largest fish in the stream. They are fairly easily fished, although catching fish in them is a sometime thing. We have few such water types in our area, and none where there is not a decided current. This always-present-current limits the methods we can use; our pools cannot be fished as though they were ponds, as can such places in other areas.

Baker's Hole on the Madison is fairly typical of our "pool" type water. It is a stretch some 250 feet long, 70 wide, and 4 to 5 deep. It contains some fish of five pounds, and on two occasions I've seen trout in it I felt would weigh eight pounds.

Most anglers who fish Baker's Hole, and they are legion, do so with the dry fly. They get some fish, for this is an exceptional trout factory. But two-pounders, taken by standard dry-fly methods, are rare. In 'hopper season, larger ones are taken now and then, although such catches are not frequent.

Two views of the lower end of Baker's Hole, a deep, wide pool. This is an exceptional trout factory.Type 1 water, pool. (See overleaf.)

I've had success with only two methods here. One is with large streamer flies, starting at the head and working down the length to the tail or flat, using the standard across-and-down cast, and a stripping, jerky retrieve. This works better in spring and fall.

In summer, I use nymphs, with two styles of fishing, as well as two types of nymph. The method that takes the most fish, although not the largest ones, is to cast up and slightly across, using a sinking line, and immediately commence a hand-twist retrieve. I start at the tail or flat, work through to the head, fishing from the bank, because I've gone over my waders more times in this pool than in all other waters together. Then I return to the tail, cross over, and work back up the other bank. By the time I've finished, I feel that every

Tremendous depth at the foot of the bluff provides shelter and security. A riffle above and a rapids below provide diverse feeding areas for large fish. Type 1, **pool.**

trout in the area has had a chance to see my fly, and to see it behaving naturally. I like a suggestive nymph for this work: Zug Bug, Otter Shrimp, Fledermouse, Hare's Ear, and so forth. You will note that I chose a method to cover the water thoroughly, and this is necessary in pools.

The second method is an unusual one and I use an unusual nymph, my Assam Dragon pattern. I use a Hi-D line, long leader, and the fly size is number four, 2XL. I cover the water with the same casting pattern as the previous method, but when the line sinks to the bottom, as it does very quickly, I retrieve in short, sharp pulls of six inches. The nymph represents the large-bodied dragonfly nymph that is found in this water, and these nymphs swim by jet propulsion, taking in water and ejecting it from the rear, which causes them to move through the water, along the bottom, in a series of short, quick pulses.

This method requires more work to cover the bottom than does the method where the hand-twist retrieve is used, but almost every fish that hits will be hooked. On the other hand, many strikes will not really be felt when using the hand-twist retrieve, because the fish will just suck in the fly and spit it out. This difficulty in detecting the strike makes this, in my opinion, the most difficult of all fishing methods. But once you've mastered the feel or appearance of the take, this is a most productive method.

No one can tell you how to sense reliably when a fish has taken your fly in this cast-up, drift-back-with-hand-retrieve method. Some anglers put a large bright fly on a dropper at the *head* of the leader for an indicator. Some watch the line where it enters the water and strike upon any motion at that point. No one I know has a foolproof method. So, why do we use it? Well, it is the most reliable method there is for inducing nonfeeding fish to take the fly.

In both methods, a thorough coverage of the bottom is what is desired. The casting method will vary with the angler. I like to think of the bottom of the pool as a roof that I am covering with long narrow strips of roofing paper. I start casting about fifteen feet up and about a foot from the bank. Some pools have deep water near the banks and perhaps undercut banks as well. So, I start near the bank on which I am standing.

Each succeeding cast is about one foot farther up and one foot farther out. About forty feet is the maximum distance I try to cast. Then I move up and, starting fifteen up and one foot from the bank, repeat the entire business. I cover one bank, tail to head in this manner, then do the same on the other side. Such a method, on a very wide pool, may leave the center. Personally, I usually leave it; I get so interested and concentrate so hard when fishing this method that I do not look where I'm wading; so I prefer to have a stretch of deep water unfished rather than risk going in over my waders.

Riffles are the easiest of all water types to fish. They do not produce large fish, in most cases, but are the best bets to produce large numbers of smaller fish. This, plus the fact that they are a distinct pleasure to fish, causes them to be worked more than other water types.

A good, bouncing riffle can be covered with almost any method. Since most are under three feet deep, a fast-sinking line need not, in fact, often cannot, be used. If the riffle is around two feet deep, a slow-sinking line, or a sink tip works well. If the water is eighteen inches or less, a floater can sometimes be used.

Riffles, by the nature of their bottoms, usually hold diverse insect structures. Thus choice of fly is not critical, provided we don't go overboard. Almost any standard fly in subdued color will produce. However, I like to refer to my insect screen in riffles and go with what I find in it. This is a confidence builder, mostly, and confidence is a big factor in angling success.

The major points about fishing riffles are to cover thoroughly and not to wade where you have not yet fished. I've seen many anglers step in and start wading up a riffle, scaring trout right out from under their feet, and eventually spooking all the fish. I've seen fish lying in the shallow parts of riffles with their backs out of the water. Such fish are most wary, and the condition is not unusual at all. So, fish through any water where you intend to wade, before wading.

There is virtually no style or method of fly-fishing that will not produce in riffles. Because of the many kinds and types of insects, some are sure to be active almost anytime, and they act differently, according to type. Therefore, dead drifting, hand retrieving, twitching, stripping, skipping, and skittering all work at times. Also it matters little, most of the time, whether you cast up, down, or across. An easy cast and a lively fly will put you in business, although your fish are not apt to be lunkers.

There are some riffles hereabouts that contain pockets of deeper water, and these will contain fair-sized fish. Perhaps now would be as good a time as any to give you my definition of fish size, since it does not agree with that of most other anglers. To me small fish means under fourteen inches, fair fish, fourteen to seventeen, good fish eighteen inches and up, or two pounds and up. Big fish means over three pounds.

When I go riffle fishing, I like to pick a clear, warm day, with only a slight breeze. I wear my hippers, for I'll do no deep wading, and I generally wear my secondary vest, with only a small assortment

This long riffle, with a composite bottom of stones and gravel, provides much food but little shelter. The trout will seldom reach fourteen inches. Type 3 water, riffle.

Two views of a fast, deep mountain run, which holds many large stone fly nymphs and large trout. Rocks and broken surface provide shelter and security. Type 4, run. (See overleaf.)

A long, very deep run on the Yellowstone. Potholes in the gravel bottom provide current relief, depth gives security. A tremendous feeding area, due to gravel bottom.

of goodies. It will be a day for relaxation and meditation, for musing and dreaming, and not concentrating, because the fish will let me know when he has my fly. It is such a pleasant way to fish that it is apt to spoil one, and become an addiction.

This is too bad, for such fishing can halt one's progress as an angler. There is not much to be learned fishing riffles.

Runs are my favorite type of water, and I like them deep, three to five feet, fast enough to border on being rapids, with a rubble-boulder bottom. Some Eastern friends look at the runs I take them to, and do label them rapids.

Such runs, in this country, hold the largest of the stone fly nymphs and also sculpins. They also hold fish up to five pounds.

With the exception of weed beds, they are the most difficult of water types to fish. No one I know is really expert in fishing them and most anglers pass them by.

I started trying to solve the secrets of fishing such waters exactly twenty years ago and the challenge is such that I still keep trying to find the perfect method for fishing them.

You have to fish the water; there may be some spots that signal "fish here," but mostly the broken surface will not give much of a clue. Because I use only large stone fly nymphs in such waters in this area, I'll leave covering them to the chapter on fishing nymphs.

Rapids are pocket water and some of them, where there is sufficient depth, hold fish of very large size. The Canyon stretch of the Madison downstream from Hebgen Dam, the stretch wiped out by the 1959 earthquake and now covered by Quake Lake, had trout in its rapids pockets that *averaged* four pounds. I consider that this was the finest stretch of such water in the Rocky Mountains, perhaps in the world.

It takes a Hi-D line, short leader, short cast, courage, and bold wading to catch fish out of rapids pockets. I consider it the most exciting form of fly-fishing and quite challenging. I never pass a good rapids without giving its pockets a thorough searching.

I want a big fly, with hackle enough to give it life. A big Woolly Worm, number four, 4XL, is a good starter. The fly is going to be in the pocket only a few seconds, I want something to capture the trout's attention at once. They will not pursue anything beyond the confines of the pocket.

Position is critical. Where to stand while delivering the cast is of paramount importance. You need to be close, ten feet is not too close, and you need to be where you can exert some control over the fly. Whether this puts you above, below, or alongside the pocket often has to be determined by trial and error.

Also, to find out how far above the pocket to drop the fly, you must experiment. It is not usually possible to get it right first try. Once you've found the place to stand, and your fly is working the pocket well, make at least ten to twenty casts and drifts before you give up and move on to the next pocket. Do not waste time letting the fly drift to the end of the line, pick it up immediately after it clears the lower end of the pocket and shoot it back to the upper end or above, as needed, in a series of short casts and short, fast drifts. With small pockets and very fast water you will be casting anew every five seconds. Pocket water generally cannot be fished with long casts.

Cascades occasionally have pockets in them which can be fished. These cascades are usually difficult to get to, and go unfished for

Canyon Cascades. Pocket water, difficult of access, but containing good fish. You will excuse me if I do not accompany you. Type 6 water, cascade.

◄

A rapids (not cascades), easy of access, difficult to fish. A large fly, fast-sinking line, and short casts are musts here. Type 5 water, rapids.

the most part. Also, they sometimes hold fish of rather large size, and there are some anglers who seek out and fish such places. I do not, because rather early in my career as an angler, I did a tour as a park ranger, and during my first six weeks, we averaged one angler a week, killed or injured, fishing such waters. The one that forever decided me against fishing such places weighed 280 pounds, and he injured himself two miles up a steep, rocky canyon. We didn't hear about it until nine o'clock at night, it was midnight when we got to him, and it took ten of us four hours to bring him out. So, if you are going to fish such places, go without me. Tell me all about it on your return; I shall be glad to hear it.

So, we return from having fished the water. The important things learned should be that the right kind of line for each type of water is a must, that position to start fishing must be chosen with care, and that thorough coverage of the hold is necessary. We also should know that a different fishing style is required for different types of water, and that we should know something of the insects in the water, their size, shape, and color, and hopefully, something of their activities. If we know this much, then we know that fishing the water is not really a chuck-and-chance-it affair. If we have learned this much, the trip has indeed been worthwhile.   81

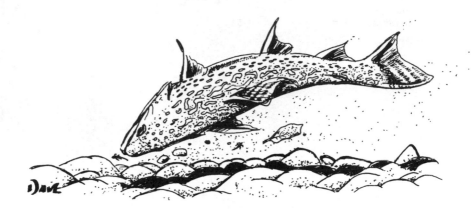

5

The Underwater Fly

THE term "underwater fly" is used here because "wet fly," by tradition and long association, is too limited a concept. By underwater fly, I mean all artificial flies that are not dry flies. Such flies account for most of the trout caught and for nearly all the very large fly-caught trout.

The first artificial fly of which there is any written record is a dry fly. The origin of the wet fly is lost; when first it appears in writing, it is fairly complete and well developed. It bursts on the scene like the heir in a play, of whom nothing was known, until he appears full grown and ready to claim his inheritance.

Since the day it appeared, in the famous *Treatyse of Fysshynge Wyth an Angle* first printed in 1496, although written about 1420 or earlier, the wet fly has been an item of controversy. Was it imitative and, if so, what or which fly did it imitate? Or did it imitate a fly at all? Or anything at all?

When it comes to taking a firm stand on the above questions, color me chicken. I do not have the answer, nor do I have any information that could lead to an answer. What information I have, and it is much, points in all directions, like a pile of jackstraws. So, I take the Fifth and depose not.

I am a wet-fly man, devout and unabashed. But most of the flies I use are not "conventional" wet flies. So to prevent any further misunderstanding in what is already a very confused picture, let us get up a few definitions for the purposes of this chapter.

The "conventional" wet fly, let us say, has a body that may or may not be ribbed, and hackle only at the front. It may or may not have wings or a tail. OK?

The term "streamer" will be used for any longer-than-ordinary fly, whether made of feathers, hair, or the beard of a prophet.

Nymphs will be dealt with in the chapter on nymphs.

Attractors will be used to designate bright or fancy flies not generally thought to imitate insects. These may also be called fancy flies.

"Regular" will be the term for wet flies that may be considered to imitate some aquatic insect in some form.

Palmer-tied wets will be treated as Woolly Worms.

Now that we have some idea, however vague, of what we will be talking about, let's proceed—though in view of a lack of established firmness of direction, feel free to disagree with anything said here.

I like wet flies. I like to tie them, I like to use them, and I like to give them away when they don't work. I don't especially like, however, to have someone to whom I've given a completely useless specimen come back and tell me he caught a three-pounder with it under the drift at the big bend in the south of Hogan's pasture.

The actual fishing of wet flies has been written about with the same clarity that has accompanied their descriptions. Did the early fly-fishers cast upstream? Did they cast downstream and move the fly up? Did they cast at all? Maybe they fished across the stream—who knows?

The downstream-upstream controversy has been raging since long before Stewart in 1857, and largely ignores what seems to me to be an evident fact. Wet-fly users, for the most part, cast neither up nor down stream; they cast across and let the fly swing, with or without some form of manipulation.

Dry-fly fishermen, starting with the biblical works of Halford, have always postulated reasons for casting upstream. But the appearance of Halford's first work, circa 1886, and later works, caused a decline in interest in wet-fly fishing and writing about it. In fact, it was said that after 1900, a wet-fly fisher in England "skulked like a poacher," so great was the influence of the dry fly. Thus, there has been no really definitive work on the wet fly, one which explained why the fly was cast as it was or fished as it was. Even after the malignant influence of the dry fly began to wane, as fishermen regained their senses, no one seemed to have the courage to come out strongly for the old wet fly. Skues and Hewitt after 1900 put some of the emphasis back under water, where it belonged, but they evaded the real issue by bringing out a new type of wet fly, the nymph.

The wet-fly picture in this country has been complicated further by two things—the old fancy brook-trout flies and the introduction of the streamer. The brook trout has long been gone from most areas in catchable size and numbers but the legacy of the bright fly lingers on. And what has been done to the streamer is hardly to be believed.

Let me come out of the chicken house with one positive statement. Any wet fly fished in any manner will, at some time or other, catch trout. But if one wishes to catch more trout more often, then he would be better advised to skip fancy flies, including that old standby, the Royal Coachman.

Hurrying on to avoid the attack I know is coming, let me say that the wilder the fly pattern the less important the method of fishing it. If it looks like nothing so much as a microscopic Christmas tree, then it little matters how it is presented. It is the fishing of this kind of fly by any method that has caused the dry-fly man to look on it with contempt and regard it as a chuck-and-chance-it business.

However, there are more things going on beneath the surface than the dry-fly man knows or cares about, and there is good reason to believe that the conventional wet fly does imitate, to an extent, some creatures found in the water. Let's take a look at one fly and the nymphal form of one insect.

In England, where it all began, *the* Mayfly is *Ephemera danica*. Other members of the family are present but don't hatch in May and are therefore called something else. *Ephemera* nymphs generally have three long tails, a body that increases in breadth and depth toward the head, and prominent dark fuzzy gills along the back and sides. This nymph swims, and it does so with its rather noticeable legs folded back toward the rear, streamlined. It swims with an undulating motion that gives the appearance of proceeding in an irregular manner. It is a dark nymph with blackish brown appendages. Its wing cases are dark gray to black when it approaches hatching time.

So, let us design a fly with tail of hackle fibers, body of peacock herl, tapered and full, wings of a gray duck primary, and soft hackle, brown or some dark color—Leading Coachman, perhaps. The Brown Hackle Peacock lacks wings and tail, but the tails of naturals get broken off, and the wing pads are not prominent at certain seasons.

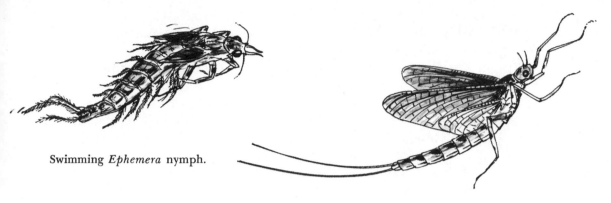

Swimming *Ephemera* nymph.

Ephemera dun.

In any event, the Brown Hackle with peacock body, cast across stream and retrieved with a standard hand-twist retrieve, looks and acts considerably more like an *Ephemera* nymph than it appears to at first glance. The Black Hackle would probably work even better. Thus, two of the oldest wet flies known seem to have come about in an attempt to imitate a prevalent nymph in English waters. Further than that we cannot go.

The method of casting across and retrieving with a hand twist or weave gives a drift to the artificial that is quite representative of swimming nymphs. We have at least three genera that swim in this country, the aforementioned *Ephemera, Ephemerella,* and *Isonychia.* None are strong swimmers, so when they swim out into the current, they are carried downstream as they proceed toward the opposite bank in a long arc much like the standard wet-fly drift.

I discovered the above a few years ago while sitting on a bank above a long glassy stretch of Henry's Fork. For most of the day, *Ephemerella grandis* nymphs were taking off from my bank and swimming toward midstream. Where they were going or why I don't know, and the trout didn't care. They would rise to intercept them as the nymphs crossed their lie, then drop back into their pothole lies in the bottom with a little wiggle that Ray Bergman used to say denoted satisfaction.

Though I had been a wet-fly user for years, it was this episode that put me to studying underwater insect forms seriously and trying to associate what I learned with common methods of fishing the wet fly.

I am more fortunate than most trout fishers. My entire work, if it can be called that, for the past several years, has been with trout and trout streams. I spend about a hundred days a year on the water.

Mostly, I do not fish. Many days I carry no tackle, just binoculars, a face mask, chemical testing kits, note pad, and so forth. I have spent a good many hours on the stream bottom, studying what goes on down there. It has been rewarding.

One method of wet-fly fishing, possibly the oldest in this country, is a hangover from our brook trout days. At least, I used to think so. Now, I'm not so sure.

This was a short cast method, twenty or thirty feet. Then the flies (two or three were generally used) were retrieved by an upward, jerky movement of the rod. When the flies came out of the water, they were cast again, across and down, with the angler proceeding steadily downstream, a step between casts. This would work only with bright flies and unsophisticated fish, I thought. I was wrong.

There are mayfly nymphs, which, when they are about to hatch, act in such a manner. They cling to a rock on the bottom and puff themselves up with air. Then they release the rock and head for the surface. But they never make it on the first try. Like a farm girl on her first date, they've never done this before, and do not take on enough air. So, it's back to the bottom, puff up some more, then try it again. Sometimes it takes as many as four attempts before they finally pop out, split the nymphal shuck, and fly away. Meanwhile, the current has been carrying them downstream as they go up and down, and the trout have been eating those they can get.

Thus the upward jerk, followed by slacking the line to allow the fly to sink, then repeating the act all over, is a pretty good method for imitating the above actions. I've found that if you use two or three flies of the same type, you may be creating your own little hatch. Doubles are not uncommon, and two fifteen-inch brown trout on the same cast will bulge your eyeballs. At least, they bulge mine.

What patterns? In my experience, the simpler, the more drab, the better. I prefer wingless wets, though I must admit I've caught almost as many trout on the downwing kind. Colors should be gray, black, brown, or olive; body material fuzzy fur, yarn, or herl. Hackle must be soft and sparse.

Good patterns would be the Gray and Brown Hackles, the Black Hackle, Cahill, Blue Dun (one of the best), and various nymph types such as Zug Bug and Otter Shrimp. A Gold-Ribbed Hare's Ear is one of my favorites. Sizes should be ten, twelve, and fourteen, and I've had good success by using one of each size, all of the same pattern, on one leader. Put the smallest on the bottom.

An old-timer some years ago taught me a wet-fly method that, though it worked, seemed not to imitate anything in nature. He called it skimming. He used two or three thin-bodied, sparsely tied flies, fished only in riffles or fast shallow runs, and covered the water with many casts.

He used a long rod and a short cast, directly across. Then he would bring the rod rather swiftly to the upright, twitching and bouncing the flies in the surface film by shaking the rod tip as he retrieved.

Since I started observing insects more closely, I've noticed crane flies dipping and bouncing over riffles in this manner, with trout leaping and lunging at them. What these flies are doing I don't know. Information on crane flies is scarce, and what I have seems to indicate this is not the manner in which they lay their eggs. Nevertheless, they act this way and the fishing method described will take fish. Patterns? I don't know any standard patterns that seem to fill the bill. Flies that work best for me have thin bodies and long, soft, sparse hackle. Colors can be on the bright side; orange or red for bodies, with grouse, guinea, or wood duck flank hackle serves well. Sizes six and eight, 2X long seem best. (See Striders in Chapter 9.)

Not all wet flies are as consistently as successful as the Woolly Worm. I have never failed to take at least one fish with this pattern in any waters where I have fished it. Though I always thought of it as nonimitative, I must have been wrong. In February, 1972, *Field & Stream* magazine conducted a survey to find what were the most productive flies being used in this country. Six dries, six streamers, and six nymphs were chosen. The Woolly Worm was listed as a nymph. They might be right.

This past summer, my sister Vallie and her husband, Red James, of Cedar Hill, Missouri, came out for a visit. Vallie and Red are dyed-in-the-wool fishermen. We went over to the Yellowstone in Hayden Valley to fish. I explained to them that this section of the river contained mostly small insects, and sizes ten and twelve were best. We started fishing. Vallie and I, and nephew Ron did nothing. But Red commenced hauling them in, cutthroats of fourteen to seventeen inches. I walked down to him.

"What's the secret?" I asked.

He grinned. "I couldn't see that itty-bitty fly you gave me," he said, "so I put on this one."

"This one" proved to be an olive green Woolly Worm, size 4, 4X long.

"You can't catch fish on that," I said skeptically.

"I know it," Red agreed, releasing another sixteen-inch cut-throat, "because you told me so."

Ron came up and I gave him a couple of big Woolly Worms, meanwhile trying to figure out what on earth the fish could be taking them for.

"Say," Ron called, "what is this thing?"

I went down to where he was, in the edge of the water, and looked where he was pointing. Crawling out of the water was the

Riffle beetle larva.

biggest, ugliest underwater beast of the insect family I'd ever seen. It was about three inches long, a dark greenish brown, segmented from end to end, and sprouting appendages in all directions.

We looked farther and found them all along the bank, crawling out and burying themselves in the mud. This, then, was the reason for the success of that big Woolly Worm.

I've since identified the "beast" as the larva of the riffle beetle, genus *Dytiscus*. Most trout streams, I've found, have these larvae as well as the adult beetles. This creature undergoes complete metamorphosis and when it comes time for them to pupate, the larvae crawl to the bank and bury themselves in damp sand or mud. That's what they were doing on the Yellowstone that day, by the thousands. My family and I, using big olive green Woolly Worms, took and released about 150 trout, running from twelve to seventeen inches. Most people nearby caught either nothing or small fish. I believe it was because they were not using the right fly. So, is the Woolly Worm a nymph? Well, riffle beetle larvae are not, but then, maybe there's some other "beast" down there I haven't met yet.

There are fishermen around here, darn good fishermen, who say that if you can't catch fish on the Woolly Worm, you might as well give up. One fellow I used to know, now deceased, used nothing but this fly, in three sizes and four colors. He caught as many trout as any of us, and as many big ones. George used brown, olive green, black, and orange Woolly Worms, in sizes four, six, and eight, all 4X long, all weighted. He said he never felt a need for anything else. He called dry flies "feather dusters." Spend more of your time fishing the water, he would say, and less sorting through your fly box and you'll be a lot better fisherman.

For fishing deep eddies, where many big fish lie, I've had much success with an unusual wet fly. This fly, called a Sprite, is, I think, original with me. It has neither body, tail, nor wings, just two turns of soft hackle in the center of a number fourteen 2X short hook. Hackle should be long and soft, about suitable for a size eight. I prefer badger, grizzly, and furnace, in that order.

This thing is simple to tie and simple to fish. Using a sinking line, cast into the far side of the eddy and let it circle the eddy. Try to give a little slack but not much. After five or six circuits, pull it out and cast again. For some reason, fish hit this fly hard; I've been broken on the hit so many times in the past that I never go below 3X on the leader anymore. I don't use this fly in ordinary trout-holding water because it attracts too many six-inch fish. The fly is similar to W. C. Stewart's "spider" flies, except mine have much less hackle.

Although I know of no definitive work on the wet fly, it has had some staunch defenders. G. E. M. Skues, probably the best all-around British fly-fisherman to write on the subject, put the matter in proper context when he said: "There are days and hours when the wet-fly has not a chance against the dry-fly, and there are days and hours when the dry-fly has not a chance against the wet-fly."

John Waller Hills in *A History of Fly Fishing for Trout* admits that in spite of a bias for the dry fly, he recognizes that wet-fly fishing is not a dub's game. We do not always know why the trout takes our fly, he says, but there are flies and methods that work better than other flies and methods, and it takes a great deal of skill and experience to sort the good from the worthless, both in flies and methods.

The truth is, Hills says, that the wet fly is not always taken for a just-hatched fly, or a drowned one. There are more things in running water than just mayflies, and perhaps our wet fly is taken for a nymph about to hatch, for a shrimp or a scud, or some other aquatic animal. Some of these swim or move through or against the current and the fly is taken while doing the same. There is much still to be learned.

This was Hills's thought in 1921 and it is as valid today. The fact is that none of us are fishermen; we are still learning to be fishermen, and always will be, as long as we fish. There is much more to be learned about wet-fly fishing than is left to be learned about dry-fly fishing because wet-fly fishing has not been studied to the extent that dry-fly fishing has, and it is far more complex and difficult.

Just as the origin of the wet fly is lost in antiquity, so is the origin of the streamer. A friend says the streamer and bucktail were both being used by Indians hundreds of years ago. Perhaps so, but they did nothing to develop it; the Swiss lake dwellers used metal fishhooks in prehistoric times, but there is no record that they improved it or developed a sport based upon it. The artificial fly was invented by the Greeks in the third century of the Christian era. What do you read nowadays of Greek fly-fishing? It is not as important which people invented a thing, I think, but who did something with the invention.

Current knowledge of the streamer fly goes back only to 1905 or thereabouts. Some fishermen used deer-hair devices called "bobs" perhaps a hundred years earlier, but the record is bare on any development of same.

When first used, for landlocked salmon in Maine, the streamer was two white saddle hackles bound to a hook so that they would trail in the water. That simple tie will take fish today. But today's streamers are a far cry from just a couple of feathers. As to whether the modern tie is more effective, the record is moot; one man's opinion is as good as another's.

That the long fly is effective, especially in taking larger trout, is not really debatable. It takes trout and it takes large trout.

In spring, when waters are high and fish voracious, the streamer stands high, also in fall, when most hatches are gone and the fish are hungry. What about summer, though, when insects should be plentiful? Well, if I were after a really big fish, I'd be more apt to try a streamer than a fly that imitated some insect. The fact is, as trout reach maturity they turn toward meaty items when they can get them, and are alert for a large mouthful that can be obtained without too much risk or effort. A streamer, at least the kind we use out here, fills the bill.

In some trout-fishing books, about Eastern trout fishing, the writers speak of using streamers in sizes ten and twelve. If I were a trout, I wouldn't get too excited over a size ten minnow. A trout can be in a feeding groove and suck in maybe 500 flies with less effort than it would take to capture one such tiny minnow.

I wondered about those small streamers until an Eastern friend told me about the state of some of their trout streams. They had been turned into a series of pools and riffles by blocking them with hundreds of low rock dams and weirs. The pools, he said, were like shallow ponds; if the water was clear, it took a small fly to keep the fish from detecting it as a phony.

Our streams are free running or as one Easterner said, "free roaring." Our streamers are larger. How much? Well, most of our local experts, and we have several in the streamer field, consider a size four as small, a size two about right, and a 2/0 as being a shade large for clear water, all being 4X long.

Dick McGuire, a fishing guide on the Madison, starts where the others leave off. Dick's flies will be at least five inches long, as big as most tarpon flies. They are bulky as well. But Dick will catch more four- and five-pound brown trout in a year than most fly-fishermen catch in a lifetime.

One of the favorite streamers of big fish anglers hereabouts is a green Marabou Muddler. Two and 2/0 are preferred. A description will be found in the chapter, "Fly Patterns and Dressings." A brown Marabou Muddler of the same design is also a favorite. This one does not look anything like a minnow or small fish. It looks, instead, in the water, like some sort of small animal.

My wife and I were fishing one October at Hole #1 on the Madison in Yellowstone Park, using big stone fly nymphs. We had taken only a couple of fish, of fifteen inches or so. We were joined by

Bud Lilly, who runs The Trout Shop in West Yellowstone, his son Greg, and Barry Schaplow, one of Bud's guides. They were fishing brown Marabou Muddlers.

Barry and Greg went down through the run—deep, fast, rock-filled—without raising a fish. Then Bud stepped in at the head of the run and commenced to cast. He used the standard method, a long cross-stream cast, sixty feet or so, retrieving with pulls of a foot or so as the fly swung downstream. When the fly came into the shallows below, Bud would retrieve upstream until he had only twenty or so feet of sinking line and weighted fly out, then pick up and recast.

A tourist, apparently lost, came stumbling down the bank from the bluff where we parked our cars.

"What's he doing?" he asked, indicating Bud.

"Fishing," I replied.

"I *know* that," he said, "but what's he using?"

"A fly," I replied briefly.

"It doesn't look like a fly," said the dude, "it looks like a musk-rat."

The instant he said it, I had one of those instant flashbacks. Several years earlier, on the Firehole, I had taken a two-pound-plus brown, the belly of which was padded out in a heavy bulge. I killed the fish and opened it, and found therein a baby muskrat. (Muskrat or what-have-you, Bud caught a three-pounder just after the new-comer left.)

Trout of large size in streams are more aggressive, less cautious than those under two pounds. Their diet is different, larger items being the rule rather than the exception. Such trout vigorously guard their holds against incursion, not only from smaller fish, but from terrestrial creatures that incautiously invade their lairs, and they will eat any invader that they can swallow.

If you know the exact lie of such a trout, you can now and then lure him into striking a large and outlandish fly when smaller lures have failed. A 3/0 streamer with a trailer hook, both well bulked out, snatched rapidly through the hold several times, will sometimes provoke a strike. The lure must be moved rapidly at all times when it is in the area of the hold, so that the fish does not get a good look at whatever is so bold as to challenge him repeatedly.

The above is one theory of using streamers. Another is the help-lessness, or injury, theory. I've often seen minnows and smaller trout swimming literally under the noses of larger fish, apparently fearing no harm. Let something happen to one of the little fellows, however, and the larger fish will be on it like a tiger.

The best example of this I've ever seen came about while I was dry-fly fishing. It was in Biscuit Basin Meadows on the Firehole. The weather had been calm and clear for several days and the fish were very spooky. So wary were they that it was almost useless to cast unless a vagrant breeze ruffled the water.

I had been watching a pair of browns of two and one-half pounds feeding steadily on small dries, out in midstream, and waiting for a breeze. It came, and I immediately dropped my fly just above the rise form of the nearest fish. Bang! The strike came the instant the fly touched the water. Startled by such instant response, I jerked the rod tip violently upward and a little trout of four inches came flying through the air to land in the water at the edge of the bank on which I was standing.

The line had wrapped around the rod tip so that the little fish was stranded, half in, half out of the water. As he thrashed there, while I tried to clear the mess and get him off, a brown of five or six pounds shot from under the bank and engulfed the little fellow.

The Firehole had just been restricted to fly-fishing only. As I stood there for what seemed like hours, but could have only been seconds, tethered to the larger fish by the smaller one, my mind raced. Was I, however inadvertently, bait fishing? What if the rangers came along? Could I convince them I was "clean?" Would the size 18 hook, imbedded in the one fish, hold the other?

Finally, I gave a desperate yank, hoping to break the 5X leader, but only succeeded in yanking the fatally injured smaller fish out of the gorge of the larger. I came back later and tried to imitate the frantic actions of the little trout, using a streamer, and while I was unsuccessful there, I've used the technique with good results many times since. If you know exactly where the trout lies and can get into position where a very short cast can be used, this method is deadly. My favorite pattern for this kind of fishing is my own Floating Streamer. (See Chapter 9 on "Fly Patterns and Their Dressings.")

Any large, bulky streamer with lots of flash should work in the above situation. The fly must be slammed on the water, then worked and skipped about in a small area to create a surface fuss that will delude a large trout into thinking a small fish is in trouble.

The standard method of streamer fishing, mentioned earlier, not only imitates terrestrial creatures, but when a flashy, minnow-like streamer is used, it represents a small fish fleeing to escape, and this also stirs up the killer instinct in big trout. It reminds me of Jack London's stories of wolf packs in the far North. As long as a wolf was healthy, or not panicky, the rest let him alone. The instant something happened, the rest of the pack would leap on the un-fortunate one and tear it to pieces.

Flashy or fancy flies, however tied, attract by their flash, I think, and are more effective, at least for me, when treated as a streamer.

But a fancy fly in size eight or ten has seldom brought me a trout over a foot long, however used. I don't know why this should be, since the same patterns in four and six have produced steelhead up to thirty inches.

I recall once, in Alaska, standing in the same spot, at the confluence of two small streams, and catching sixteen sea-run trout on fancy flies in a four-hour period. These fish ranged from twenty-six to thirty inches and a size six Parmacheene Belle was like caviar to them. But sea-run trout, as far as I can see, have a different life plan and different emotions. It's a mistake to apply steelhead methods to resident trout except in spawning time—late fall or early spring.

One thing must not be overlooked in the use of any fly, and that is confidence on the part of the user. If you have no confidence in the lure on the end of your line, you might as well be strawberry picking.

This is reflected in the attitudes of fly-fishermen, most of whom know this, even if they are not conscious of it. Watch them picking out flies in the shop, or selecting a pattern on the stream. It is most informative.

Take the fellow who protests that the wet fly imitates nothing in nature. Does he just go to the display case and grab a handful of whatever pattern he first comes across? Ha! He'll spend half an hour picking out a dozen flies, muttering and complaining that they're too bulky, overwinged, bodies too thick, or the colors all wrong. If they imitate nothing at all, why do these details matter?

There is the fellow who insists all fish are color-blind. Does he, too, just grab any color of fly that has the right silhouette? You know the answer to that one. The Light Cahill body must be the palest fawn, the hackle the brightest ginger, and should the wing be dyed mallard instead of wood duck—horrors! He wouldn't touch such a fraud with a ten-foot pole. It all boils down to the fact that if the fisherman doesn't think his fly is just right, it isn't.

The man who uses regular wets should stay with the duller patterns. If these are of the downwing type, he will have better success in waters that do not have complicated currents. The thing about wet-fly fishing that makes it the more difficult art is that it is a three-dimensional affair, while dry-fly fishing is two-dimensional. It's the difference between plane and solid geometry.

The wet-fly line and leader, being sunken, are acted upon, not only by currents between rod and fly, but by currents between the surface and the level at which the fly is drifting. These pluck, pull, turn, and twist the line and leader, imparting not only false motion to the fly but turning it upside down on occasion. From down on the stream bottom I have seen trout repeatedly refuse to take a downwing or other winged fly when it was acting thus, only to smash it lustily a few casts later when it did not act in such a manner. On the other hand, a plain hackle fly or a palmer type was taken almost every time they appeared to be drifting at the same speed as the current they were in.

If I'm going to use a winged wet fly, I do it in areas where the water is relatively smooth and free from crosscurrents. Maybe it isn't necessary, but I have more confidence in this system.

I do not believe in exact imitation, such a thing being an obvious impossibility. But I'm much happier if my fly has some of the elements that give the natural insect its character. Body shape, size, color, and a tendency to look, when wet, something like the form of the natural, are what I look for.

G. E. M. Skues said that some wag opined that an artificial fly was generally a caricature and that caricatures caught the most fish because there were so many of them. Maybe artificial flies are caricatures of the naturals, Skues said, but if they were tied with skill and intelligence, and used with these same qualities, they became something much closer to nature. I'll buy that.

Give me a fly that has some of the elements of identification with the natural, and let me fish it as nearly as possible in the manner in which that natural conducts itself, and I will be more at ease with myself—and will also catch more fish.

That leaves us with only three methods of fishing the regular wet fly—that is, only three methods that will work consistently.

The first method, mentioned earlier, is to cast across, or across and downstream, retrieving line by weaving it in—by rotating the fingers in the standard hand-twist retrieve. Slow retrieves work better in faster currents, and faster retrieves in slower currents, according to my experience. Varying the speed of the retrieve on different casts will often reveal which is the taking speed.

Ray Bergman was most meticulous in timing the retrieves so that he would have the correct one. Twenty-eight completed hand movements per minute might be the correct speed on one day or stream, while eight or forty completed movements per minute might be required on other days or streams. Generally, I just experiment until the fish start coming and try to maintain that speed of retrieve thereafter. Make no mistake, it is important—but why, I do not know. It probably has something to do with the maturity of the nymph or other creature we hope we are imitating, but one cannot be certain.

The second important wet-fly method has also been discussed.

This is where the flies are cast across, with a short cast, then re-trieved with a short upward jerk, the rod tip lowered, the flies allowed to sink briefly, then the tip jerked upward again—the whole thing being repeated until the flies must be lifted out of the water and recast.

Timing of the sinking period is important here. I usually count "A thousand and one, a thousand and two, a thousand and three," and so on. Most days, a count of three works best. But I've caught fish some days when a count of only one was required and at other times have counted up to eight. When the quick count is the taking one, action is usually fast, with the fish coming one after the other.

The third method, the one that works most often, is at the same time the simplest and most difficult of all wet-fly methods. This is the old stand-by, the natural drift—and it is the most effective.

I usually start fishing this method with a cast of not over fifteen feet, then lengthen each succeeding cast about two feet until casting maximum distance. In this basic method the fly is cast across and let drift without any motion at all, with the fisherman extending every effort to see that contrary currents do not act adversely upon either line or fly. When the fly comes straight below, I use two methods of retrieve and pickup for the next cast.

The first method is just to strip the line in foot-long pulls until the fly is in easy pickup distance. The second method involves letting the fly drop back two feet or so after every third pull.

The natural drift is the most taking method, the largest portion of the time. When it is not, try the other two methods. But give this method a good long try before abandoning it. It's the basic wet-fly method. The three methods together about complete the tactics of the pure wet-fly fisher, he that fishes regular wets but not nymphs and streamers.

For the streamer man in western waters, only two methods are required. One, the standard across-stream cast and jerky retrieve, is for fishing the water. The second, spatting the fly down and jerking it around on the surface, is for fishing for a particular fish in a known lie.

If I fish the streamer, I do so for the purpose of trying to raise a good fish. I find streamer fishing both tiring, from the endless casting and retrieving, and boring, because it is essentially a me-chanical method, requiring little thought. But it is the fly-fishing method that will bring larger fish more of the time. Regular wet-fly fishing will produce more action from average-size fish, and requires a great deal more thought and skill. At least, that's what I tell myself.

6

Natural Nymphs and Their Imitations

THERE has been little research and identification of underwater forms of most caddises and stone flies, and some mayflies, for the benefit of the trout fisherman. Scientists who do such work are seldom interested in putting the results of their studies in usable form for laymen.

Even trout fishermen who have done such research have tendered little of value on underwater forms; the main thrust of their work has been of value only to the dry-fly man. The reason, in most cases, is that the adult form must be on hand in making the identification in many species. Very few persons had either the time or the inclination to capture the immature form and raise them to maturity. This requires large numbers of aquaria with strongly running water of high oxygen content, which must be free from purification chemicals. The species must be segregated and a close watch maintained on the hatching process.

This is expensive and very time-consuming and few persons have done it. Doug Swisher and Carl Richards did some work along this line and have, in *Selective Trout,* contributed information not previously available. Ernest Schwiebert has made the biggest contribution with his recent work, *Nymphs.* So, while interest in nymphs

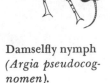

Damselfly nymph (*Argia pseudocog-nomen*).

is improving and growing, it will be some time before we reach the stage of information on nymphs that presently exists on dry flies.

The nymph fisherman is going to have to do the bulk of the work himself for some time to come. Our streams are many and varied; they host the most diverse insect structures of those anywhere in the world. North American streams contain at least four hundred species of mayflies, four hundred species of stone flies, six hundred species of caddis flies and eight hundred species of dragon and damsel flies. Since no one could possibly make a stream-by-stream study of them, it behooves the angler to study at the source.

You don't have to have any scientific background or training to do this. You don't really need to know that the brown-and-tan mottled damselfly nymph which is prevalent in the riffles of your favorite stream is *"Argia pseudocognomen";* all you really need to know is how to make a representative artificial and how to fish it so that it acts like the natural.

Of course, if you are writing or discussing it with some other nut, knowing the scientific name is the only reliable way of being sure you are both talking about the same insect. But for fishing, "brown damselfly nymph" will do just fine.

Your insect screen, mentioned earlier, will do most of the work of collecting underwater forms. If you don't have one, make one. Get a couple of dowels four feet long and one inch in diameter, along with a square yard of window screen, from your lumberyard or hardware dealer. You can lace the screen to the dowels with string or fine wire, or you can roll it around the dowel one complete turn and tack it. I use the latter method. Also, if you can, get nonrusting material. Mine is fiberglass, but aluminum is just as good.

Leave two inches of dowel protruding at the bottom to thrust into the stream bed. The top ten inches make convenient handles and the whole thing rolls up and stores nicely. I consider it my most important piece of equipment.

You must have some order in collecting stream insects or you will be wasting your time. A notebook is a must, so that you can write down a description of your find, unless you use kill and collecting bottles. Still, each insect type must be labeled as to what kind or which piece of water it was found in. As I said earlier, you must catch the insects in water you intend to fish for it to be of direct value. If you are merely studying to acquire knowledge, you can seine your insects anywhere.

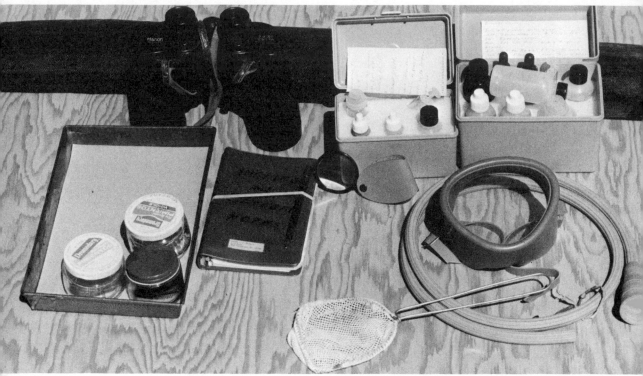

The tools of a working angler: Insect screen, binoculars, alkalinity and oxygen test kits, pan, kill and collecting jars, notebook, magnifier, face mask, breathing hose, insect net.

One other piece of equipment is desirable—a shallow pan such as a cake pan. If you can obtain a white enameled pan, good; if not, give the bottom a couple of coats of white paint. When you have captured some nymphs, fill the pan with water and drop the insects in for study. You will see a little of how they behave, and if you look closely you will notice they *do not* look the same in water as they did in the net, or in your hand.

The buoying effect of water brings out their form and shape, and causes their gills to appear. These are so prominent on some species that when they flare out in breathing, the nymph looks like a completely different creature. It is important in such species to imitate the gills in the artificial. Peacock and ostrich herl are used for this, although on some fur-bodied nymphs, they are unnecessary.

Another thing I do with my pan is to drop my artificial into the water along with the natural, and compare the two. This is a very valuable step. An artificial that appears to resemble the natural quite well when dry may look completely unlike it when in water. Because of this, I am constantly redesigning my nymph patterns;

they are quite different now from what they were several years ago.

I should like to make clear that my study of underwater forms is always for the purpose of creating a better artificial with which to fish. I like knowledge for its own sake, as long as it is obtained as a fringe benefit in study for some practical application.

It is this fringe benefit knowledge that led to the discovery, through reading Hynes and Ruttner, that fish activity is largely geared to that of the insects they feed on, that insect activity is closely linked to their feeding habits, and this, at the end of the scale, to the activity of zooplankton, which feed on phytoplankton, and that these are activated by light, although a conditioned response due to day length still takes place on dark days. Thus, the amount of light and length of the day have a profound effect on underwater insects, and thus on fish.

Dry-fly fishermen apply this information to determine hatch times; they generally use water temperature as an indicator but recently have come to realize that day length, the amount of light over a period of time, is the major factor. A dark, cloudy spring will result in delayed insect hatches, and also in less activity of underwater forms. Conversely, a succession of clear, warm, cloudless days will speed up insect activity and make for earlier hatch times.

Thus the amount of light over a period affects the growth of nymphs, and it is a simple fact that nymphs become more active—thus more available to the fish—as they grow larger and more mature. It is this information that is of value to the nymph fisherman.

Something else of value to the fisherman that cannot be obtained by use of the screen is knowledge of the life histories and habits of insects. This can usually be achieved only by reading scientific works, and in order to be sure of what you read you must be able, somehow, to identify the nymph you wish to know about. It is this latter information that is difficult to come by, and it is this that has held up progress so far.

Why do you need this kind of information? Well, suppose the fly known as Hendrickson (*Ephemerella subvaria*) hatches around the first of June in your area. On the Fourth of July you journey to the stream, tie on a nymph to imitate this species, and fish away. You have a nice day, not too hot, a light breeze. Water levels and temperatures are ideal. But you catch only a few small fish. What was wrong?

When a particular mayfly hatches out, it usually depletes the stream of that nymph in any size for up to five months. There were no *subvaria* nymphs left in the stream and the trout were geared to the taking of other species.

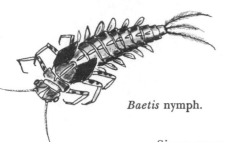

Baetis nymph.

Since most mayflies and caddis flies have only one generation per season, when any of these species have hatched, they are gone for that fishing season, and the angler must go to something else. Some mayflies (*Baetis*) have two or sometimes three generations per season, therefore *Baetis* nymphs will be good ones to use throughout the season *if* they are present at all in your stream.

One of the great values that large stone fly types have is that they have only one generation per two, three, or even four seasons. Thus, these nymphs will always be in the stream in edible sizes and numbers, whereas a stream that hosts mostly mayfly types will have greatly depleted nymph stocks in late summer and fall.

The so-called "salmon fly" of this area of the Rocky Mountains is *Pteronarcys californica*. This fly has a life span of four years from egg to hatching adult. Thus, even when the hatch has just been completed, the one-, two- and three-year-old nymphs will still be in the stream in large numbers. *Acroneuria,* another large genus beginning to appear in quantity, has a three-year life span; it hatches at a different time, but occupies the same waters as does *Pteronarcys.* Together these form the bulk of the trout diet in waters where they live and provide nymph fishing through the entire season.

In streams in this area, certain nymphs or larvae appear in most streams; there are also nymphs and larvae that appear in some streams but not in others. In this chapter, remember that I am speaking only of those nymphs and larvae worth the fisherman's time to imitate and use.

In mayfly species, only one of fair size appears in most streams. This is *Ephemerella grandis,* the western Green Drake. It is a size ten when completely mature. I imitate it with my Ida May nymph in sizes eight and ten. Why larger than life? Experience has shown that a nymph slightly larger than the actual nymph it represents has a better chance of being taken than does one a size or two smaller. Scientists call this the "exaggeration theory," and liken it to a little boy automatically selecting the largest piece of cake on the plate.

The Ida May has tails of grizzly dyed dark green, body of fuzzy black wool, tapered and full to just back of the hook eye, ribbing of peacock herl reinforced with fine gold wire, and one and one-half turns of soft hackle, grizzly dyed dark green, at the front, just back of the eye. The hackle is tied to slant backward, streamline fashion, because the natural swims with its legs folded back along the body.

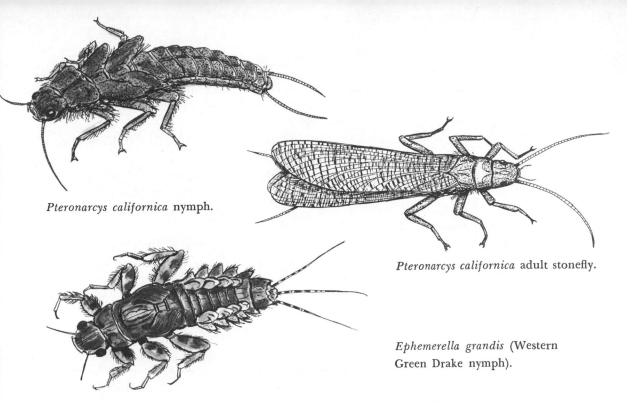

Pteronarcys californica nymph.

Pteronarcys californica adult stonefly.

Ephemerella grandis (Western Green Drake nymph).

The natural looks all black in the hand, and its gills and prickly back are not evident. Put it in water and it takes on a dark bluish-green shade, with gills and prickles quite visible. Peacock herl over the black body imitates gills and prickles quite well, adds life to the artificial, and gives a good dark blue green color.

Some anglers pooh-pooh wool as body material, preferring fur. Wool is just a type of fur, or hair, and while it is not very good material for dry flies because it soaks up moisture, it is fine for sunken flies for the same reason. I prefer fuzzy wools, and some of these have other materials mixed in to give a fuzzy appearance. One of my favorites has 75 percent wool, 15 percent angora, and 10 percent acrylic. It has an added advantage in that the angora and the acrylic are different colors, and both are different from the wool color. One that I especially like has black wool, green angora, and dark orange acrylic. The overall appearance is very dark green with lots of life.

Where do I get such lovely stuff? In knit shops, which I haunt with great regularity. A six-foot, two-hundred-pound man lumbering around among the bins, fingering and fondling the different colored skeins draws sly glances and snickers from the salesgirls. I

A brown "bulging" for emerging mayfly nymphs.

bear it with much equanimity because one can find some really terrific wools for body materials in these places, especially among imports from Italy and Switzerland.

The natural of this nymph hatches between 10 June and 15 July in this area; it has but one generation per year, so it would seem not to be worth while to fish this nymph after 15 July. However, there are stonefly nymphs not too much different in some stretches where this nymph lives, and also some very dark blue damselfly nymphs, so this fly is good all season.

The nymph swims with an undulating wiggle, and is carried along by the current as it does so. This type of action is imitated by method number nine, live nymph method, in the next chapter.

All our worthwhile trout streams in this area contain two genera of caddis-fly nymphs. These are *Rhyacophila,* the little green caddis, sometimes called the naked caddis because the larvae build no case, and *Brachycentrus,* the little gray caddis, which builds a case of bits of bark laid crosswise. The case is unique in that it is square in cross-section. One species of this caddis is called Grannom in the East; the western caddis of this genus is very little different and may be the same species.

Main phases of *Rhyacophila:* larva, cased larva, pupa, adult.

These larvae are abundant in most streams in our area, and are the number one trout food most of the season. They do not occur in silt or sand-silt bottoms, and only around the edges of rubble or rubble-boulder bottoms. They prefer cold, quite swift water with a gravelly bottom, and in streams that meet these conditions, such as the Yellowstone in the Buffalo Ford area, and gravelly stretches of the Henry's Fork, these larvae are incredibly abundant.

They have a delayed hatching cycle; all do not hatch at one time, as do most other aquatic insects. Thus, *Rhyacophila* hatches all through May and June and, in very cold waters, into July. *Brachycentrus* hatches through June and July and, in cold waters, into August. By late September and through October, *Rhyacophila* that hatched in May will be three-quarters full size, and in October, *Brachycentrus* that hatched in June will also be. These caddises, then, provide larvae of edible size for trout from May through October, or later. Therefore the artificial is of value through the entire season.

When these creatures pupate, the larvae seal themselves inside their case (*Rhyacophila* makes a pupal case of stones at this time) and turn into an adult, which may take two weeks. Then it chews

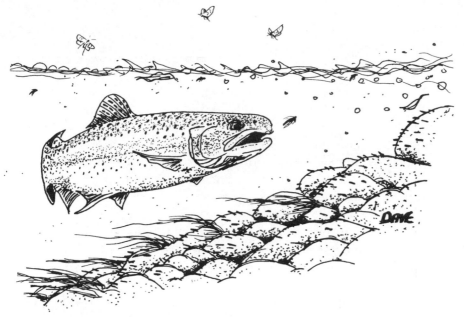

A rainbow hybrid working at a riffle dropoff taking emerging caddis pupae.

through one end of its case and emerges full grown, but enveloped in an air-filled membraneous sack, except for one pair of legs.

The air-filled sack causes it to pop upward toward the surface, at a rate of one to three feet per second. Also, since it is carried downstream by the current, this rising arc downstream is well imitated by the Leisenring lift. Just under the surface, the sack splits and the full-grown caddis flies up and off the water like a shot. Its hairy wings are waterproof, and the adults require no drying-off period as do mayflies and stone flies.

Unless it is *very* windy, you get to imitate them only with a dry fly when they come back to lay their eggs. If there is a strong wind, then a dry imitation is a killer. But a larval or pupal imitation is good anytime.

My Little Green Caddis larvae and pupae are very good all year, and so is the Little Gray Caddis. Descriptions will be found in the chapter, "Fly Patterns and Their Dressings."

The proper method for fishing the larvae is method number three, the Hewitt method, in the next chapter. Fish the pupae as in method number six or seven, the Rising-to-the-surface, and Leisenring lift methods. Both simulate the rising of the pupae (adult, really; though the insect is still in the pupal shuck or membrane, it is full grown and ready to fly away) to the surface, where they burst through flying and are immediately gone.

Two large and one smaller stone fly are prevalent in *certain stretches of certain streams* in the West Yellowstone area. The smaller, as mentioned earlier, is adequately imitated by the Ida May nymph. It is found in similar waters, hatches late in the season, and makes that artificial a taking fly into August at least.

The two larger nymphs are *Pteronarcys californica* and a species of *Acroneuria.*

Californica is, just prior to hatching, from one and one-half to two inches long. In most waters, it is black, with brown showing at the abdominal and thoracic segments and at the bases of the legs, and underneath. The nymph is round in cross-section, *Acroneuria* is flattened. *Acroneuria,* just prior to hatching, is about one-quarter inch smaller than *Pteronarcys,* and is brown mottled with dark yellow. The two nymphs occupy the same waters; *Acroneuria* hatches some two weeks later than *Pteronarcys.*

As mentioned, *Pteronarcys* has one generation every four years, *Acroneuria* one generation every three years. As a result, there are at least two- or perhaps three-year classes of these nymphs in the stream at all times.

Pteronarcys can be compared to the classes in a high school. When the seniors graduate (hatch) in June, the junior, sophomore, and freshmen classes still remain in school (stream), thus one cannot go wrong in using an imitation of those left.

Both of these stone flies require very fast, well-oxygenated waters, and rocky bottoms of stones on stones. Where these conditions are met, the number of nymphs one can find with his insect screen is unbelievable. I have taken as many as three dozen nearly full grown nymphs from one screening—a double handful.

Pteronarcys is found in large numbers in that section of the Madison River in the Park from the Barns to four miles below, in that section between Hebgen and Quake lakes, and in the entire river from the foot of the Quake Lake slide to below the Bear Traps, a distance of nearly a hundred miles, riverwise. They are found in certain rockier stretches of the Yellowstone from below Tower Falls to some miles below Yankee Jim Canyon, in the entire canyon section of the West Gallatin, and in the Box Canyon stretch of Henry's Fork, as well as other less well known stretches of that river.

Where they are found, there is no other nymph that begins to compete with them as trout food. Their size and numbers are only one factor; these are crawling nymphs and when they stir around in search of food, which they do at least once, and sometimes twice a day, they become available to the fish and cause feeding spells by trout that last for an hour or more. The amount of light (day length) triggers this but I have not yet found out how to predict the time of this happening accurately.

These nymphs dwell in midstream when mature; at hatching time they commence to crawl across the stream bottom toward the bank. They crawl out on the bank or upon rocks or logs that protrude above the water, split their nymphal shuck, dry off, and fly away. During the time they are crawling to shore, which takes up to twelve hours, thousands are swept away by the swift current and are eaten by trout, and thousands more are picked off the rocks of the bottom and are also eaten. However, they still hatch by the uncounted millions and the salmon fly hatch is carnival time in this area.

Several artificial nymphs have been developed to imitate *Pteronarcys*. Locally there are the Montana and Bitch Creek nymphs, Dave Whitlock makes a fine black stone fly nymph (Whits Stone Nymph, black) and I have my pattern, the Montana Stone Fly Nymph. All are good. Some anglers prefer one, some another, some use all patterns indiscriminately, as well as the Black Woolly Worm. Cal Bird's Stone Nymph and my Yellow Stone Nymph are the only *Acroneuria* imitations I know of. I prefer mine because it looks more like the natural, at least to me, but Cal's nymph catches lots of fish. Bird's Stone Fly dry is the best commercial imitation of the salmon fly, although more anglers use the Sofa Pillow. Dan Bailey's mossback nymphs are used for both *Pteronarcys* and *Acroneuria*, but, while these look real, they also look dead, like an empty shuck.

Gills are quite important on these nymphs. They are found at the bases of the legs, and when the nymph is in the water, are quite prominent. You will note that in my Montana Stone Nymph pattern, the gills are represented both by ostrich herl and undyed grizzly hackle. Since the first noticeable difference between a live nymph and an empty shuck, in the water, is these gills, I want them prominent on my artificial.

I have never found it profitable to imitate midge or blackfly larvae in streams. These wormlike creatures, about a half inch long and little thicker than a toothpick, are plentiful in backwater areas of some streams, the Firehole especially, the upper Madison, and Henry's Fork. I've caught trout below such areas that were literally stuffed with these larvae, but all the fish I've caught in these back-waters have been under eight inches.

Chironomus larva.

They are a taking lure in some spring-fed ponds. The Widow's Pool (Culver Springs) in Centennial Valley is loaded with large rainbow and brook trout, and it is also loaded with the larvae of *Chironomus modestus,* the little green midge. I've taken trout of two pounds and up on larva imitations in this and other spring ponds. I no longer use them in streams.

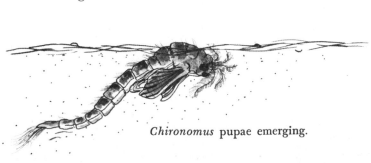

Chironomus pupae emerging.

I've had good success with my Assam Dragon Nymph (Grace's favorite fly) a generalized version of the larger dragonfly nymphs such as *Libellula pulchella*. Dragonflies are found on nearly every stream; their nymphs will be found in certain areas of those streams where the bottom suits the habits of the nymphs. In general, these nymphs prefer sand, sand silt, and gravel bottoms. Since they are strong swimmers, current speed is not usually a factor. These nymphs and those of damselflies, which are found in the same waters, swim by taking water in and ejecting it forcefully at the rear.

They are predacious and live on other nymphs, larvae, small minnows, and even trout fry. They can find their prey more easily in areas where the bottom material is fine, thus providing fewer large hiding places.

To fish a nymph of either damselfly or dragonfly, one needs a sinking line and a long leader. One can cast up, down, or across and fish the cast out with short, sharp pulls of six inches to a foot. Since these nymphs and the artificials that imitate them are large, do not allow them to dawdle on the retrieve lest they be detected as frauds. Use them only in areas that have one of the three bottom types mentioned.

They are takers of good-sized fish; I've never taken a trout of less than twelve inches on my Assam Dragon, and nothing much smaller with the Fair Damsel. At least 95 percent of the trout taken on either fly have been fifteen inches or over.

There are large caddis larvae in some of our streams, and these are also found in other parts of the country. *Hesperophylax* is one of the larger ones; the cased larva is imitated, even if poorly, by my Skunk Hair Caddis pattern. I have spent over twenty years trying to develop a better imitation, and so have a great many other anglers.

This insect makes its case of sand grains and tiny stones, building a larger case as it grows. At maturity, just before pupating, it will be an inch to an inch and a quarter long, and as large as a goose quill in diameter. They are quite a meaty item, and trout eat them regularly in areas where they occur, case and all.

They like faster currents, and bottoms of packed gravel, bedrock, or the edges of rubble-bottomed stretches. They are never off the bottom, so a sinking line and weighted fly is a must.

In some California streams—the Yuba, Truckee, Merced, and Feather—I've seen these creatures so abundant you could scoop

Dragonfly nymph *(Anispotera)*.

them up by the handful. In these areas it is just about useless to use any other artificial; the fish eat these caddises almost to the exclusion of other species. Like most damselfly and dragonfly nymphs, these caddises spend two years underwater, and are always available to the trout.

Some anglers are so frustrated in trying to make a suitable imitation of this cased caddis worm that they resort to catching the natural, removing the worm, and slipping the case over the eye of the hook that has been weighted with lead wire. They then stuff the case with cotton soaked in glue, add a turn of black hackle at the front, and finish the head large with black tying thread.

These lures do catch fish and good fish, and in areas where the bottom is literally covered with the natural, it's about the only thing that works.

My feeling is that nymphs form the meat-and-potatoes of a trout's diet, and that adult aquatics, terrestrials, and other foods are like caviar—welcome, but not too regular a component. So, I spend most of my research time studying nymphs and most of my fishing time using artificials to imitate them. I know I will catch more fish the more I know about the nymphs they feed on.

In chalk streams, especially those of England and France, studies have indicated that some nymphs are often found at midwater, free drifting. Two unrelated things cause this—overpopulation, which forces out the weaker individuals which are carried away by the current, and feeding by the nymph on drifting plankton. Both activities occur only in rather slow waters very rich in minerals. Both types of activity are much the same; the nymph simply drifts along about midwater at the same speed as the current. Fish station themselves along the line of drift and feed continuously as long as the condition lasts.

Streams in this country where the above takes place are few and scattered, but they exist. The Letort in Pennsylvania, Hat and Hot creeks in California, Silver Creek and some sections of Henry's Fork in Idaho, and the Firehole in Yellowstone Park are some such streams. Spring creeks in southwestern Montana also have this characteristic.

When this type of activity is taking place, the feeding of the trout will be the same in most respects as when feeding on a dry-fly hatch, except that the trout will be hanging about midway between top and bottom. The fish will move slightly right, left, up, or down to intercept a drifting nymph but he will not move far; he is in a feeding groove and will remain there until the drift of food has ceased.

You fish for such trout with the Sawyer method, and you can have a fantastic day if you hit such a period and are prepared to take advantage of it. Use small nymphs—sizes fourteen and sixteen —since large nymphs do not exhibit this activity. A close imitation is not usually necessary; trout are less selective on these occasions than when feeding on the floating fly.

If you are going to fish artificial nymphs, you should know the habits and habitat of those you are imitating, and a good representation of the natural will be required in most cases. You will not be able to rely much on shops to provide you with your imitations because nymph patterns have only just begun to become standardized.

This is one of the main reasons nymph fishing has lagged; the non-fly-tying angler could not obtain the proper patterns for his stream or area. Nymph patterns are more difficult to standardize than the dry fly, and most anglers will not know what nymphs occupy their streams. Progress will be slow, until we get enough anglers who will study and identify the naturals, then work out a good, easily reproductible pattern. It will take time, just as it does for any good imitative fly. The Cahill was known about 1890 but was not available in the shops until about 1920. This will be true of any recently developed nymph patterns, but things are accelerating. I expect nymph fishing to be as fully developed and standardized as dry-fly fishing by 1990. I hope to be around to assist in the development and practice because this is the coming thing in fly-fishing.

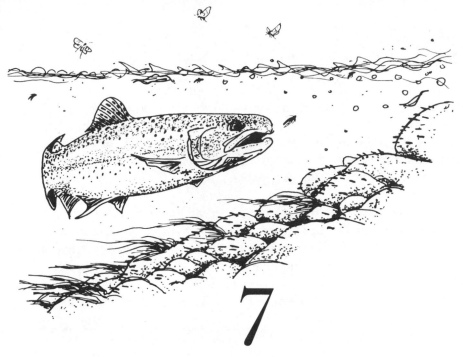

7

Fishing the Artificial Nymph

IN the past seventy years or so that the artificial nymph has been known, its use has been surrounded with more hokum than a P. T. Barnum publicity project. The result is that most anglers have either been scared off by the alleged difficulties, deluded by the secrecy that clouded its use, or put off by misleading statements as to its effectiveness.

In essence, *consistently* catching trout on sunken artificial flies requires knowledge of three things: where trout live and feed, what insects are in that stretch of water that the trout feed on, and how to fish a representative artificial in a manner that will delude the fish into believing the artificial is live and real.

What keeps the above from being simple is the fact that the artificial is attached to a leader and line and these are acted upon by currents nowhere near to those that act upon the fly, and which never affect it in the same way.

However, the difficulties can be overcome, and while nymph fishing will never become really simple, it can be mastered with practice.

How effective is the use of artificial nymphs in the hands of an   109 experienced nymph fisherman? Let's see what some fine, knowledgeable anglers have to say.

"The angler talented in fishing nymph and larva imitations is the man who will take trout consistently throughout the season," says Schwiebert in *Matching the Hatch*. "He can accomplish this because he is fishing patterns suggestive of the bulk of the trout diet. Any angler versed in nymph fishing is aware of this, and it is rare indeed that trout do not respond to this deadliest of trouting techniques." *

Charles Ritz, one of the world's great anglers, admits that he would rather fish the dry fly but that the nymph is deadlier more of the time. He cites stomach studies of chalk-stream trout, wherein there are more, and more regular, hatches than on any other type of stream, and says that the studies consistently show that two-thirds of the insects are underwater forms, with only one-third being in the winged state. From this, he draws the conclusion that trout spend at least 80 percent of their feeding time gathering nymphs, since the winged insect is generally captured in large quantities in a very short time during a hatch.

Ritz also asks the rhetorical question of confirmed dry-fly fishers: Why view with contempt the use of the same fly without wings and hackles, since nymph fishing is a more difficult form, requiring quick sight, more study, a sense of anticipation, and expertise to the maximum? Most dry-fly fishers, he concludes, have neither the know-how nor the desire to fish the nymph.

The key element is desire. If you want to become a skilled nymph fisherman badly enough, you will acquire the know-how. After that it's a matter of practice.

I've spent the last fifteen years becoming a nymph fisherman. In that period I've read all the books on nymph fishing, and on natural nymphs, that I could find. I've screened thousands of yards of stream bottoms. I've tied scores of trial patterns of artificials, and I've fished artificial nymphs at least 80 to 90 percent of the time. I've spent several hours on the stream bottom with plastic mask and breathing tube, observing the actions of natural and artificial nymphs. I'm still learning.

One of the first things I learned was that there were a lot more ways of fishing the nymph than I had first thought. I'd imagined that there were no more than three or four ways of fishing nymphs. But I've come up with ten separate and distinct methods. The name

---

* Copyright 1955 by The Macmillan Company. Used by permission.

given the method is not necessarily that of the man who originated the method; it may be the one who developed it.

1. Skues Method: This, perhaps the earliest of all methods, differs from dry-fly fishing only in the type of fly used. Dry-fly tackle is used from rod butt to leader tippet; only the fly is different.

The fly should be chosen to match the underwater form of a natural that one knows to be in the area being fished. In order to be specific, say that the stretch contains *Ephemera guttulata,* the Eastern Green Drake, and that though a hatch is expected sometime during the day, only a few flies are in evidence.

If the water is smooth, the tactics are exactly the same as would be used if one were fishing the dry fly. The cast is made up and across, so that the fly drops just upstream of the rising fish. The fly should be size ten, tails of grizzly hackle fibers dyed dark green, body of medium green fur, ribbed with peacock quill, wing pads of gray primary fibers, hackle, one turn of soft grizzly dyed dark green at the front of the fly.

The drift should be drag-free and one watches *both* the point of the floating line and the spot where the drifting nymph should be. At any sign of motion of the line tip or a rise in the area where the nymph should be, strike. The strike should be quick, but not violent; firm, but gentle. Some slack should be held below the fingers of the line hand and if one feels a strong resistance to the strike upon striking, some few inches of slack should be allowed to slip through the fingers of the line hand to avoid breakage. Breakage on the strike is the most common reason for losing fish in nymph fishing.

A size ten artificial nymph is about as large as one can get away with in smooth waters, and the fraud will be detected at times with this size. Though a few mayfly or caddis imitations require a size ten, most will be twelves or fourteens, and these are generally more effective than larger sizes in *smooth* water.

If the water is somewhat broken, or there is a fair current, it may be necessary to dress the leader with floatant to within eighteen inches of the tip to prevent the nymph from sinking too far. This is almost a surface method of fishing the nymph, and it is not too effective if the nymph sinks too deeply. It is the method to use when you are expecting a hatch, but do not know exactly when it will come. It is the most effective method for most mayfly types just prior to the time of the actual hatch, and including the first few minutes of the hatch. Then one switches to the dry. It's quite easily done; just remove the nymph and tie on a matching dry.

Since this method is used mostly during prehatch periods, and since these sometimes produce highly visible activity, one can often see the fish roll or turn as it takes the artificial. This is a great aid in timing the strike, and at these times one hooks more and loses fewer trout than at most other times. Skues, writing of such periods, described the flash of a taking fish as, "that cunning brown wink under water," one of the most endearing descriptions in angling literature.

2. Sawyer Method: This is a bit more difficult than the Skues method, although some consider it only a further development. The nymph must sink a foot or two, and is sometimes weighted slightly in order to do so. A floating or sink-tip line is used and the leader should sink. This method is not used during prehatch unless the water is more than three feet deep; if fish can be seen turning and flashing, or bulging the surface, the Skues method is better.

The method was developed by Frank Sawyer, a river keeper on the Wiltshire Avon, in England. It is not a blind casting method; Sawyer cast only to fish that he could see. This requires rather smooth, clear water; if the water is not of this character, one of the other methods will probably work better.

One should be in position almost directly across from the fish, only very slightly downstream. The distance the fly must be dropped upstream of the fish is determined by his depth and the speed of the current. The fly should drift by the fish on the angler's side and on, or just below, the level of the fish. It requires great precision and considerable practice.

The artificial should represent a nearly mature nymph of a type found in the stretch being fished. The drift should be as drag-free as possible. If it appears that the nymph has not been taken, which can usually be detected by the fish turning toward the angler, then facing back upstream, a slight upward motion of the rod tip may induce a strike.

Generally, the angler will not be able to see his fly when using this method. Therefore, in order not to be fishing entirely blind, he *must* see the fish, and be able to observe its actions. During the drift the rod should be parallel to the water and pointing straight down the line. The drift must be mended if necessary. To strike, move the rod tip *downstream* in a smooth swing, and take up slack with the line hand at the same time. As always, if the strike comes up against a very firm resistance, let some line slide through the fingers of the line hand.

3. Hewitt Method: This is a further development of the Sawyer method, though it was earlier developed by Hewitt. It is used in

faster water, and one does not, usually, see the fish. Therefore, the cast is made above a known lie, and again, the fly should be dropped on the angler's side of the fish.

A floating or sink-tip line is best, and a long, fine leader is an asset, as in the Skues and Sawyer methods. The fly should represent a natural nymph known to be prevalent in the stretch being fished.

The cast is fished out as in the Sawyer method, but here, if one gets a strike he should be able to feel it. The rod is held parallel and low over the water, pointing down the line at all times. The line must be mended, possibly more than once. Strike by moving the rod tip in a downstream swing, controlling the strength of the strike with the line hand, releasing or taking in slack as needed. Your answering strike must be very quick.

Some see no difference in the Sawyer and Hewitt methods. The differences can be compared to an ordinary game of handball (Sawyer method) and playing the same game blindfolded, striking to the sound of the ball hitting the floor. It's almost that difficult until you've learned to strike by feel.

4. Continuous Drift Method: This is an unorthodox method, and some anglers consider it unsporting. I don't know why. There are two phases of this method, the bank walking and the stream wading. Both employ the same principle but use different means of achieving the desired drag-free drift.

The bank-walking phase is easiest, although tiring. One uses whatever line he happens to have on the rod and a six-foot, 2X leader. The fly should be representative of the largest mayfly nymph in the area.

With only the leader extending through the rod tip, and the fly about a foot below the surface, the angler walks the bank downstream at the same speed as the current. Arm and rod are extended, the angler keeping back from the bank edge as far as possible, while keeping the fly close to the bank. A quiet stealthy tread is necessary. When the fish hits, it will usually be hooked without the need for an answering strike.

This phase works only along undercut banks, or where the water is deep along the bank. Where this is not the case, the wading phase is used.

In this phase, the angler needs a sinking line and a long leader tapered to 3X. The angler takes a position at the head of a shallow run or a long riffle, casts across and down with a long line, then wades downstream, quietly, at as nearly the same speed as the current as he can manage. Only when the line comes straight below, or when he runs out of fishable water does he pick up and recast.

When done with skill, so that the fly is neither pulled nor drags, and when the angler is a quiet wader, this is a surprisingly effective method. It also has the advantage of allowing the angler to cover a lot of water in a short time. The method is called "roving" when a live minnow is used instead of a nymph.

5. Upstream Method: This method is used almost entirely in weed beds or upstream of drifts. All tackle is the same as that used for the dry fly, except the fly. If one can see the fish, then the Sawyer method is used—cast up and just to one side of the fish. If no fish can be seen, one casts up, then retrieves slack at the exact speed that the line tip moves toward him.

Since in most cases the fly cannot be seen, this is a most difficult method. The line tip must be watched closely, and concentration must be fierce, else you will never detect the strike. The rod should be low over the water, parallel to it, and pointed directly down the line. If the line tip moves, pauses, or hops, bring the rod tip smoothly to the upright, controlling the strength of the strike with the line hand. Any hesitation is fatal.

The method is deadly if done right. One must start from below any spot where fish are suspected to lie, and approach with utmost care. The first cast must be short, and in most cases, in weed beds, directly upstream. Each cast is lengthened by about two feet, until twenty-five or thirty feet of line are out. Then the angler must seek a new position. Always commence casting short so as not to "line" the fish.

Fishing over log or brush drifts calls for a little different technique. Here only short casts are used, since the fish is expected to be under the drift. A short, fine leader is best. The first cast is made directly upstream from below unless there is an obvious reason for not doing so. Then, the next cast can be made just right or left of the first spot, and this is continued, casting fanwise, until the area in front of the drift is covered. One need not lengthen line.

The fly will come downstream to the drift just slightly faster than the line tip. Thus, when the line tip reaches the drift, the fly will still be just a little above it. The slack should be taken in by raising the rod tip, and the cast should not be so long that slack cannot be handled in this manner. As always, the rod should point to a spot above the line tip.

When the line tip reaches the drift face, only a foot or less of line should be on the water. This is critical if one does not wish to get hung up. Wait about two seconds after the line tip reaches the drift face, then snap the rod tip sharply forward and down. This is a variation of the roll cast, and if executed smartly and at the right time, the rolling line and leader will pluck the fly from under the drift and send it upstream.

Here the fly can be dropped to start a new float, or it can be picked up with a normal backcast and placed wherever desired to start another float. Trying to pick up the fly over a drift with a standard backcast will get you hung up more often than not.

6. Rising-to-the-Surface Method: This is an imitation of the actions of some nymphs at hatching time. The tackle needed is a sinking line and weighted nymph. The cast is quartering upstream and the fly allowed to sink. If it will not, because of current speed, you need a faster-sinking line. The fly must sink to the bottom in this method.

When the fly reaches the bottom, raise the rod tip slowly and smoothly to the eleven o'clock position. Lower it back to just over the water and parallel to it, at the same time stripping in the slack with the line hand. Do not move the fly by this stripping action. Then raise the rod once more, and repeat the entire process. This is continued until the fly comes to the surface.

In order for this method to work, the water must be three or more feet deep, and the current not too fast. And, of course, there must be trout in the stretch being fished.

This is one of the easier and most productive methods of nymph fishing. The fly should be either a definite mayfly type or a caddis pupa.

7. Leisenring Lift Method: This is the deadliest of all nymph fishing methods, provided the exact lie of the fish is known and the currents are not too complicated. A floating or sink-tip line is used.

The lie of the fish must be known exactly. The cast is up and across to drop the fly straight upcurrent from the lie. It must be far enough upstream so that the fly will be on or below the level of the fish when it reaches him.

Let drift without drag until the fly is only a foot or so upstream of the fish. At this point raise the rod tip with a slow upward lift. By the time the rod tip reaches the eleven o'clock position, the fly should have either been taken or be well beyond the fish.

In all nymph fishing methods, one follows the drift of the fly with the rod tip, which should be pointed straight down the line *or* at a spot directly above the fly, or line tip. The rod is parallel to the water until such time as it becomes necessary to move the fly or to strike.

The Leisenring lift will take fish that are not feeding more often than any other method, provided the lift raises the fly smoothly toward the surface at just the right time, and provided the fly is representative of a natural in the area.

Jim Leisenring used this method more than any other, and he was extremely adept in locating the fish and getting into exactly the right position so that the drift and lift could be timed just right. Mostly, this method requires that the lie of the fish be somewhat isolated from other fish, and that the barrier which shelters it from the current not be so high that it forces the lifting nymph too far up in the current to clear it. Bottom depression holds are ideal for the Leisenring lift. The fly can be either a caddis or mayfly, depending on which are found in that stretch of stream. Many of Leisenring's wet flies were actually imitations of hatching caddises and were perfect for this method.

8. Pot-Shooting Method: This requires pocket water, with very fast current above, below, and on all sides. A sinking line, short leader, and weighted fly are required. A short cast—ten or not over fifteen feet—is a must.

The fly is cast directly above the pocket, the rod tip parallel to the water at the finish. As the fly races downstream and through the pocket, the rod tip is kept pointed at the spot where the fly should be. When the fly clears the lower end of the pocket, it is immediately picked up and shot back upstream.

The above is repeated ten or fifteen times in rapid succession. When the strike comes, swing the rod tip sharply downstream, and pull with the line hand. The line should be taut or nearly so throughout the drift, and hooking should be easy.

This type of water should be stone fly water, but in any case, one wants a large nymph imitation, so that it may be seen during the short trip through the hold, and it also should be big enough to tempt the fish to take it. Number eight is the smallest that should be used and I often use number four, 3 or 4X long. In this type hold the trout cannot be bothered with small stuff.

9. Live Nymph Method: One of the easier methods, and the one used by more anglers than any other, this is only slightly different from some regular wet-fly methods.

A slow-sinking or sink-tip line is required, a fairly long leader of not coarser than 3X, and a mayfly nymph that imitates one of the three swimming types—*Ephemera, Isonychia,* and *Ephemerella.* A damselfly nymph can also be used.

Ephemerella nymph
swimming.

Swimming *Ephemera*.

Swimming damselfly nymph.

The cast is across or slightly down—a long cast, to the opposite bank, if possible. Or, on wider streams, wade the middle and cast first to one bank then to the other. An immediate hand-twist retrieve is commenced, and kept up throughout the drift. When the fly comes directly below, continue to retrieve in the same manner until a quiet, easy pickup can be made. Take two steps downstream and repeat.

On every other drift, when the fly is being retrieved from straight below, let it drop back a foot or two once or twice during the upstream retrieve. This will sometimes induce a strike from a following fish.

Should you get a strike on the downstream drift, swing the rod upstream, parallel to the water, and pull with the left hand. The strike must be quick, but not violent, and the line hand must always control the strength of the strike.

10. Brooks Method: My name is on this method because I have never known a fisherman who used it until he was taught it by me. It is for fast, heavy, deep runs only, and most fishermen do not seem enthusiastic about fishing this kind of water. The tackle required also is a factor; many fishermen either don't have or won't use such equipment.

A long rod is a must—eight feet is minimum length—and it must be powerful, although not a wrist-breaker. A very fast-sinking line, a leader not over six feet and testing not less than eight pounds, and a large weighted fly complete the rig. It is not a pleasant outfit to use.

The angler commences fishing at the head of the run, from the bank, if possible. In this method, one casts upstream, but *fishes* down. Start with a short cast, fifteen feet up and a few feet out, then lengthen two feet on each succeeding cast.

I call it five-phase fishing. Phase one: the angler chooses his position at or above the head of the run so that when his first drift is finished, it will be above (upstream) of the expected lie of *any* trout. You will work down to him on succeeding casts. Phase two, casting phase: the angler casts upstream fifteen feet and a few feet out. The rod tip should finish low over the water, parallel to it, and pointing down the line. Phase three, sinking phase: As the fly moves downstream, it and the line should sink very rapidly. Also, since the fly is moving toward a position opposite the angler, slack will develop. This is controlled by raising the rod tip, and if the cast is a long one, by raising one's arms overhead. On a cast of thirty-five feet, I will have my arms over my head as high as I can reach, with the rod pointing straight up.

A friend says the only way to hook a fish, if it strikes while you are in this position, is to fall over backward. If you get a strike while in this position, you have goofed on phase one; you should have commenced farther upstream.

Phase four is control phase, where you commence to take in a little slack and to feel for the fly. If you have done right in the preceding phases, this should take place from about ten degrees upstream to about ten degrees downstream of directly across. Phase five is the fishing phase, and it should be in the area of from ten degrees below you to directly below (downstream). Throughout the drift, your rod has been kept lined up with the line, even when pointing straight up, and you have pivoted as the fly moves downstream so that you end up facing across and somewhat down. Control slack by lowering your arms and the rod tip until the rod is low and parallel over the water and pointing directly down-current.

The fly will *always* be trailing the line, no matter how skillful the angler. This is because the line cuts through the faster water to the surface, while the fly is in the much slower bottom layer. As a result, when the line comes directly down-current, the fly will still be several feet farther up-current.

The pull of the current on the bow in the line and leader causes the fly to move down and across current in a smooth rising arc. Expect most of your strikes here or just before this action commences. Also, wait at least five seconds after the line becomes straight below before picking up to recast. This is to allow the fly to be straight below.

The hit, when it comes, will usually be hard and very fast. You must react instantly and your strike must be violent. This is the reason for the eight-pound-test leader. Do not think you can get by with leaders of lesser strength by metering your strike.

A few years ago, my brother Ken brought along his family doctor and his son when he came out to visit me. Pete Cook, the doctor's son, was an ardent fly-fisherman from Michigan, and he stayed on to fish a few days after Doc returned home.

Pete, Ken, and I made up some leaders for the fast-water nymph fishing the night before I introduced them to it. I usually make my six-footers in two steps, from .017 of an inch to .014, then to .012, but I could not convince Pete that such stout leaders were necessary.

"In Michigan," he allowed, "we never go stronger than four pounds on the tippet for sunken nymph fishing."

I argued but in vain. When he, Ken, and I stepped into the fast deep run on the Madison known as Hole Number Three, the next day, Pete was equipped with four-pound-test leaders.

The fish must have heard he was coming. Within fifteen minutes he got at least ten strikes, all from fish of a pound or larger, and missed every one. The frustration was driving him up the wall, and he began striking more and more violently, trying to set the hook.

Then the inevitable happened.

His violent strike on a much bigger fish hooked it—and broke it off. But his lusty heave brought the trout to the surface and rolled it, a brown of nearly five pounds.

Pete came down to where I was for another big stone fly nymph, and tied it onto his frail leader.

"Better go to eight pounds on that leader," I counseled.

"I'll be easier with the next one," he replied grimly.

But he wasn't. Within five minutes he rolled another fish of about the same size, and snapped it off.

This time he went into a state of shock, gasping and reeling, waist deep in raging water.

I thought he was having a heart attack, and got him to shore and laid him down. It turned out he hyperventilates when he gets excited or upset, and boy, was he upset. But I had no further trouble getting him to use stronger leaders.

If you fish this method in the fast deep runs where it is most effective, use strong enough leaders or you may wind up in shock!

One October I took a friend, Jack Kiely, and three friends of his, Bob Karwel, Ted Herlyn, and Jed Holtzman, to fish a fast deep stretch on the Madison with this method. The men were from the East and had not fished such strong water before; only Jack had any experience at all in western waters.

When we reached the head of the fast, powerful run where we were to start fishing, I explained the five-phase method to them.

"The casting and controlling slack are a little difficult to explain," I said, "so, I'll give you a quick demonstration. I won't go all the way through the range, from fifteen to thirty-five or forty feet; I'll show you a couple of short casts and drifts, then a couple of long ones. If I choose my first position right, I should be upstream of the fish, and if I get any hits, they should come on the longer casts and drifts."

I waded in, demonstrated the short cast and drift, then immediately went to a cast of forty feet.

"This is how it's done," I yelled over the rush of the water, holding my arms and rod high to control the slack.

The fish hit just as I spoke and my violent reaction hooked it, a brown of seventeen inches.

"Pretty impressive, Charlie," Jack commented, as I netted the fish.

"Do you guarantee me I'll get one that size?" Ted asked.

"No guarantees," I said, "but the fish are here and the method works. The rest is up to you."

The four were experienced fishermen and that and the two following days produced several fish larger than the demonstration fish. Then I had to go to Ogden, Utah, for a couple of days.

When I returned, I called Jack to inquire about the fishing.

"We tried the Firehole and Upper Madison with dries and streamers," he said, "but we took nothing over twelve inches. This afternoon we went back to your big nymphs and fast water."

"How'd you make out?" I asked.

"Fine," he replied, "we took several good fish, and are kicking ourselves for not sticking with it. Frankly, it's the only method I have any confidence in for taking good fish."

I wish to reemphasize that the strike is all-important in this method of fishing. No matter how skillful one is at controlling the slack, there will always be some slack between rod and fly, and it requires a fast, powerful strike to set the hook. I strike by throwing my hands wide apart, the line hand snatching the line to the left, my rod hand throwing the rod hard to the right. It can scarcely be done too swiftly, or with too much motion. That is why you must have a strong leader, and for me, and most people I've fished with, eight-pound test is minimum.

No matter how you strike you will still fail to hook more than one out of three hits. Some anglers cannot abide this and refuse to fish this method after giving it a try. They agree that it produces more strikes and generally bigger fish than most other methods, but the frustration of missed strikes is too much for them.

When you first start out, you will probably not hook one fish of six or eight that hit. But as you continue your practice you'll begin to know the area where most of your hits will come and can gear yourself to be more alert at this point. Also, simply by practicing you will become better at striking and your hooking percentage will pick up.

The deeply sunken line and weighted fly cause many anglers to have casting problems. This is usually because they attempt to pick up and cast in a more or less normal manner. This will sometimes not work at all, and it will be exhausting even when it does work.

The reason it sometimes won't work is the fact that one may have twenty feet of line down deep in two or three feet of water. When you try to pick this up with an ordinary back cast, the fly will never come to the top of the water, and you will find yourself with your rod at the one o'clock position and your line and fly still sunk.

Some anglers try to get around this by retrieving enough line so that a normal pickup can be made. Then this line has to be worked back out and upstream in a series of back-and-forth casts, tiring, and with the weighted fly, sometimes dangerous. There's a better way.

Suppose you are on the left side of the stream, you are a right-handed caster, your drift has finished straight down-current of you, and you have forty feet of line and leader out, at least half of which is deeply sunk.

When you reach this position you should have pivoted to face across and slightly downstream, your casting arm should be across your body, and your rod should be low over the water, parallel to it, and pointing down the line. You are in perfect position to lift line and fly from the water and drop the fly back upstream in one easy, continuous movement of your rod arm, aided by a pull with your line hand.

Reach to the stripping guide with your line hand, grab the line, and give a smooth accelerating pull toward your left hip.

At the instant you start the line pull, raise the rod smoothly to shoulder height, but *keeping it parallel to the water*. Keep your rod arm fully extended, and as the leader-line joint comes to the surface, make a smooth, powerful full-armed swing out over the water and upstream. The rod does *not* come upright, the cast is only slightly above horizontal, and the motion is much like a powerful tennis backhand.

This is difficult to explain but easy to do and in the course of a day's fishing it will save you hundreds of false casts to pick up and redirect your cast. I had one student, an experienced and skillful angler, who said learning this one cast was worth the entire fee for the day's teaching.

To use this cast on the right side of the stream (right-handed caster), you must reach across your body with your line hand to give the pull and, of course, the lift, cast, and swing are like a tennis forehand. Remember that right and left sides or banks of a stream are defined facing downstream, the way the current flows.

If you wish to extend line on either the backhand or forehand casts, simply strip it off prior to making the line hand pull, then shoot it when the line straightens out upstream.

While this cast, coming with the line extended downstream, is as natural as slapping a mosquito on your bald spot, it takes some time to break the old pickup, recast, redirect, and recast-some-more syndrome of ingrained habit.

That's not the only habit that's hard to break. Some anglers, especially steelhead fishermen, hand retrieve or strip in continuously during the drift. This is wrong; the fly must drift drag-free, without motion. It has sometimes taken me all day to stop a student from doing this, and in one case of an angler who had been fly-fishing forty years, I was unable to get him to break the habit. It should be noted that all my students were already skilled fly-fishermen, with an average of seven years' practice. That's long enough to develop quite strong habits.

Fishing the deeply sunken, dead-drifting nymph for utmost success involves locating holds that contain larger trout and in using an artificial that represents the largest aquatic insects that inhabit the stream in that area. Since no aquatic insects that live in strong, swift waters are swimmers, the drag-free drift is best for imitating the actions of the nymph.

All methods of nymph fishing require that the angler know something of the types and kinds of natural nymphs in the area he is fishing, and he must know enough of their habits to fish a representative artificial in imitation of the actions of the living nymph.

Some knowledge of bottom and water types is necessary, so that one doesn't fish stone fly nymphs in smooth-bottomed glides or gravelly runs. Conversely, do not fish small mayfly types in fast, rocky runs. Recognize that each nymph type requires a particular bottom and water type, and while there may be several genera of nymphs in the same area, it is because they require the same habitat.

Generally, mayfly nymphs will be found in pools, riffles with gravel bottoms, in glides where the bottom matter is small and the current not too swift, around weed beds, and sometimes in silt or muck.

Caddises of different genera range widely in streams, but generally, the case-making type or the naked caddis, *Rhyacophila,* will be found, not in the swiftest water, but along the edge of such fast currents. Where caddis and mayfly larva and nymphs are found in the same area, the mayfly will be easier to imitate because of its actions.

It is the complexity of the above that causes most anglers to feel that nymph fishing is beyond them. Still, except for the differences in actual fishing method, not a great deal more knowledge is required than the dedicated dry-fly man must have. It's a little harder to

Rhyacophila in case during pupation.

acquire because most of it is hidden below the surface, and I believe this is the reason no one has dug deeply into it.

Another factor causes the nymph fisherman some problems. There are very few standard nymph patterns available in tackle shops. Orvis has come out with a line of eight nymphs, but these are quite general in nature. Dave Whitlock and Polly Rosborough have good series for the West and Northwest, but few shops carry their flies. So, the nymph user is just about restricted to rolling his own at present. Indications are that things are looking up in the artificial nymph field.

Fish can be as selective to nymphs as to dry flies, although this situation is rare. All trout have periods when they feed indiscriminately, both on the surface and below. In fact, I think they feed this way more often than they do selectively, though I have no way of proving this.

A friend of mine who is very well rounded in the field of trout fishing said this: "Most trout fishermen only catch fish when the fish are feeding indiscriminately, because these people have given little or no thought to what insects inhabit the stream where they are fishing, nor to the behavior of those insects. Both their flies and methods are nonimitative of any insect, so it stands to reason that they catch only those fish which will grab anything that comes along." It's a fair statement.

Though the feeding habits of fish are largely conditioned by the insects they feed on, there must be times when the fish wish to feed but the insects are uncooperative. One such time is when fish move into riffles and actively grub for nymphs. Another is when they cruise up and down the stream, looking for any kind of insect activity. Both of these feeding activities can be seen by the angler, but there must be many more times when fish actively seek food but where they cannot be seen.

These would be the times when the average angler does well, and skill and knowledge are not much required. All who are on the stream at such times are favored by such a condition, which I am convinced, exists a large part of the time.

The rest of the time, an angler with knowledge and skill in fishing nymphs will do well, and this, with some small attention to dry-fly fishing, will make a well-rounded fly fisherman and one whose "luck" is always good.

8

Floating Flies

IT'S unfortunate that when floating flies were first brought to the notice of the general reading angler, it was done in a manner that resulted in a cult of the floating fly. Largely, this was due to the conviction of Halford, who first wrote extensively on them, that here was the ultimate method for taking trout. He was a convincing writer, and succeeded in persuading so many anglers that dry-fly fishing was the only sporting way of taking trout that many streams in England were closed to other methods, and thousands upon thousands of anglers came to regard any other method as unsporting.

Dry-fly fishing as practiced by Halford is not the difficult, esoteric, and successful method of fly-fishing his converts have long preached. It is the easiest to learn, easiest to practice, and the least successful on a day-to-day basis, of all methods of fly-fishing. I am speaking here of dry-fly fishing as practiced by the Halford cult, not as it is generally practiced in this country.

Halford limited himself to imitating adult aquatic flies, mostly mayfly types, although he gave lip service to caddis (sedge) flies. His followers became so obsessed that many of them got to the point where they would use only artificials imitating mayflies, and in some

124

cases, in England and this country, there are fanatics who use not more than two patterns to imitate two stages of the same fly.

I've no objection to anybody using as few or few kinds of flies as he wishes. But anybody who does so and then tries to tell me I'm being unsporting because I choose to imitate a great variety of creatures is simply signaling me that he has neither the talent nor ability to be a complete fly-fisherman. Nor am I about to undertake his education. If ignorance is indeed bliss, bless the blissful.

A great many of this country's fine, complete fly-fishermen prefer dry-fly fishing, not because of any form of prejudice, but because they find it more fun. No one can argue with this position, because pleasure in its practice is the *only* reason for fly-fishing, or any other fishing.

Some of our angling writers in the past have hinted that there was more to dry-fly fishing than the use of a few aquatic imitations. The first to come right out and say so, and make a logical case for using other floating flies than those designed to imitate aquatic insects, was Vincent Marinaro, in his splendid *A Modern Dry-Fly Code*.

Marinaro made the point that trout take all kinds of floating insects, many of which are not aquatic, and that these frequently appear when aquatics are not hatching. The joy in using the floating fly is that it floats upon the surface where all moves are visible, and that it fools the trout into believing it is a real insect. Therefore, any fly which floats and is taken by the trout as food is legitimate for the angler to imitate and use, says Marinaro. This is the dry-fly code that most anglers in this country subscribe to, and it is a most sensible one.

My conversion to using terrestrial imitations began long before Marinaro's work appeared, and has a wider scope. I started using grasshopper imitations in 1931, the year I became a fly-fisherman, and I also started using deer hair mice the same year. I used them then for the same reason I use them now: they are two of the best lures of any kind with which to catch, not only a fish, but a sizable fish.

As a matter of fact, all of the largest trout I've ever taken on floating flies, save one, were taken on artificials designed to imitate terrestrial creatures. The one exception was a six-and-a-half-pound rainbow taken on an imitation of the adult stone fly. I have taken far more trout over three pounds on terrestrial floaters than I have on conventional dries.

So, if it floats, and is taken by trout while doing so, I imitate it and use it, including imitations of injured or dying minnows (Floating Streamer). Here let me define my attitude toward "imitation" as it refers to artificial flies. Art is in the mind of the artist, not necessarily in the eye of the viewer. There is no such thing as "exact imitation" of any fly in nature, but if the angler has a particular creature in mind when he makes up a fly, as far as I'm concerned, that's an imitation. Whether it looks anything like a natural to you or me is completely immaterial. I am not trying to fool you and me, I'm trying to fool a trout, and if he consistently takes my imitation, I am not going to concern myself with whether he thought it was what I think it is.

I recently read two studies concerning floating flies and trout streams which I believe are of interest. These studies were made by the use of drift nets, and stomach examinations. They involved one stream in the East and one in the West.

The drift nets supposedly trapped all floating creatures in a certain area; underwater forms were ignored in this survey. To trap aquatic insects hatching all along the stretch under survey, nets were set every three feet, and creatures were removed every few minutes, to limit escape.

The kinds and amounts of creatures in the nets were then compared to the kinds and amounts in the trout's stomachs. In the course of the season, as it progressed, a change in preference by the fish was noted. Early in the season, the aquatic insects accounted for over 80 percent of the insects both in the nets and in the stomachs. By midsummer, the ratio had changed; aquatic insects accounted for 70 percent of the insects in the nets, but only 40 percent in the stomachs.

By fall, the ratio of net contents to stomach contents had balanced again, and percentages were in agreement. However, terrestrials accounted for over 70 percent of the totals in nets and stomachs.

The conclusions reached by the study groups were: (1) Over the year, terrestrial insects outnumbered aquatic insects on the study streams. (2) When aquatic insects were at a peak of hatching (spring), trout took them in almost exact proportion to their availability. (3) When terrestrials were at their peak (early fall), trout took them in almost exact proportion to their abundance. (4) More terrestrials were taken in the course of the season because they were available more hours of the day than were aquatics, which hatched sporadically.

The above reinforces the earlier statement that availability is the prime factor in selection of insects by trout. Since terrestrials can be found on the surface of almost any stream, from late spring to early fall, anytime during daylight hours, it should follow that they will produce more of the time than aquatics. Of course, during a hatch, a peak of activity will be reached that is never approached with terrestrials. Match the hatch when there's one on, but if there is not, look to terrestrials.

One cannot use just any terrestrial at any time and expect to have consistently good fishing. You must present a fly that will be on the water at that time of year and that time of day, for the most part. For instance, at our altitude of 7,000–8,000 feet, grasshoppers do not usually show up much before 10 July, so generally it is useless to fish a hopper pattern much before that date.

Also, since our nights are always cold, it is a waste of time, anytime, to fish a hopper pattern much before ten thirty or eleven in the morning, or much after four thirty in the afternoon.

So, you must use as much judgment in fishing terrestrials as you do in matching the hatch. At least, that has been my experience.

In order to know what terrestrials are worthwhile imitating in your area, you must do some study. It is futile to make and use a Japanese beetle imitation in this area; they are not found here, nor is anything much like them. There will be similar instances in every different area of the country.

Here, nearly everyone uses a hopper imitation in season, and it is one of the few terrestrial imitations found in most shops. Some few use cricket imitations, although I've never seen a commercial version. Beetles are not much used, if at all, but ant imitations are beginning to show up, both in the shops and on the stream.

I use hoppers, crickets, ants, mice, caterpillars, moths—and a Floating Streamer to imitate minnows struggling on top. The largest trout I ever caught by any method, eleven pounds, was hooked on my Floating Streamer, and it is a consistent taker of good fish. But so are the others, or I would not use them.

It can be said that a hopper does not require much skill to use. In fact, the chief complaint that some dry-fly fishers have about terrestrials is that one need not be a skillful caster to use them. Just the opposite is true, of course, with aquatic imitations.

Because hoppers do not require a great deal of casting ability to get them on the water in fishable form, I frequently recommend them to friends of mine who are beginners. Because this sometimes gets them into larger fish than they are prepared to handle, it can be amusing.

I took a beginner to a small creek one time, during hopper season, and set him fishing along the grassy banks and log jams. This man was positively the worst caster I have ever seen, and during the course of an otherwise delightful day, he found new ways to spook every fish we saw. Once he started to cast for a fish that we had just observed taking a real hopper. On the backcast, the angler snatched out a clump of grass as big as my fist, then, making the only perfect cast of the day, he dropped it right on the head of the trout that had just risen.

But fate finally smiled on him. Actually, it laughed out loud. It happened when he was attempting to fish the lower side of a log jam, from above. He bungled his forward cast *again* and the hopper fell about ten feet in front of him, upstream of the jam, with a juicy splash, as hoppers are wont to do.

A trout of about five pounds roared out from under the log jam, its mouth gaping like a clamshell shovel. It looked at least a yard long, and it took the hopper pattern with a splash that sent spray flying into the trees lining the bank.

The angler responded with a strike that would have derricked a yearling beef into a barn loft. I had provided him with a 1X leader, but it parted like grocery twine under that mighty heave. That finished our fishing, and all the way back to West Yellowstone, the angler sat beside me on the car seat, his head hanging between his knees, muttering, "That trout would have weighed *five pounds!* He would have weighed *five pounds!*"

Most terrestrial imitations seem to work better in meadow streams and in smaller streams. One of my favorite streams is a tiny creek that flows for most of its length through a meadow as flat as a table.

This little stream is unique, in my experience. It is never over ten feet wide, and in its most fishworthy reaches it isn't over four feet wide. It is also four feet deep. It cascades over a series of limestone ledges, which make both underfalls and potholes, choice hiding places for trout. The grass has been untouched by man or nature, perhaps for centuries. The roots form a solid mat that will support a bull buffalo, which is good because the banks are undercut as much as two feet in some places.

There are brook, brown, and rainbow trout in the little stream and they range from five inches to five pounds. There is absolutely no way of judging the size of the fish that takes your fly, so one has to promote a slow, lifting strike to avoid breaking off the larger fish. It takes me some time each year to get geared up to the striking technique, and I lose many fish on the strike in the spring before my touch is developed.

I took a friend here once, the only person other than Grace I have ever taken there. Jim is a good fisherman, but on this day he was superb. He hooked every fish that rose, and lost none on the strike, yet a few of the trout were under eight inches, and one was over twenty. Jim said at the end of the day that this was the most outstanding experience of his entire angling life.

Because of the factors above, angling with terrestrials is just about the most exciting form of fly-fishing. When fishing to a rise with a standard dry, you may occasionally misjudge the size of a fish, but with terrestrials you seldom know how large he is until you lift on him. Then the fun starts.

Grassy undercut banks and log jams are prime places to fish terrestrials, especially hoppers. During hopper season, trout will often lie under such banks or jams, alert for hoppers to misjudge a leap.

I had always thought that trout were passive in these circumstances, just waiting for the hopper to fall in. It never crossed my mind that trout might actually go hunting for hoppers to knock into the water.

One day, I had a student, Pat Gartland, up in Biscuit Basin Meadows on the Firehole. I had just pointed out several trout of eighteen to twenty inches lying over the weed beds, and along the bank, when one of those along the bank catapulted into the air and slammed into the grass a foot or so above the water.

"What the devil was he doing?" asked Pat, startled by the abrupt, ungraceful splash of the fish.

"I hate to say what I'm thinking," I temporized.

"It looked like he was trying to knock something off the grass into the water," said Pat.

Even as he spoke, the fish vaulted into the air again, turning over in midair and slamming his tail forcefully into the grass. This time there was no doubt about it; we were watching the exact spot where the fish appeared and we both saw clearly what happened. Then just to make it certain, the fish did it again, and this time he knocked a hopper loose and pounced on it the instant it hit the water.

The incident unnerved Pat and he botched up the job of trying to take the fish. But a week later, I got a letter from him. He had gone back the next day and taken the fish or one like it, from the identical spot, by dropping a hopper pattern in the grass and shaking it off into the water.

Terrestrials are most effective in the fall, when aquatics are much diminished due to the hatching cycle. This latter circumstance causes many anglers to put away their rods, and they miss some of the finest fishing of the entire year.

If no fly hatches have occurred in the preceding several days, it then takes a hatch of considerable duration with a number of adult insects floating down the same groove to start trout feeding. This is not the case with terrestrials; under the same circumstances the trout need only to see one on the surface to come and take it.

When the trout have entered small tributary streams in the fall, prior to spawning, the ordinary hatches will be sparse or nonexistent. The fish will often be along the bank looking for anything that might

Grasshopper.

fall into the water. There are no aquatics to imitate, but a terrestrial suitable to the time and place will often take the fish.

If it is hopper season, a hopper pattern will always be my first choice. I have found that the fly must be given some action in these situations. Trying to impart the proper action with the rod tip is an exercise in frustration. So I point the rod straight down the line at the fly, slowly take in the slack, then give a little pull with the line hand. Don't overdo it.

When the trout are in such waters they are very wary and fishing for them is a stalking proposition. I am amazed at the numbers of anglers I see each year who apparently never thought of stalking a trout. They wear light-colored clothing, walk right up to, or along the bank, or blunder into the water like stampeding buffalo, then complain they haven't seen a trout all day. No wonder.

While still in the main streams in the fall, after hatches have diminished, trout will often signal a wish or intent to feed by moving out of their holds, or resting places, to a specific area which past experience has told them will provide a chance of something to feed on. This may be where the current has established a "line of drift," it may be a location of high opportunity, or just a place where the trout can see in all directions. Since such places usually have no cover, the trout will generally be visible if you do not spook him in your approach.

During summer, a cricket imitation will often work, especially along toward sundown or later. These should be dropped along the bank; they seldom are found out in the main current as hoppers sometimes are. If dead-drifting them along the bank produces no rises, try imparting a little action to them such as mentioned earlier with the hopper imitations.

Late in the afternoon or in the evening, moth types are fine. These must be given considerable action because the natural is always buzzing and skittering around when on the water. These are best tied in subdued body colors. Plain deer-body hair tied on in bunches right up to the eye and clipped to shape is my favorite. I add a couple of pheasant breast feathers on top, flat, as wings and let it go at that. I've never seen a commercial version.

I've had indifferent success with small beetle and jassid imitations. In other parts of the country they do great execution, so the angler should always have some in his vest.

I have seldom found a time when an ant imitation would not work. It's an established fact that trout have great fondness for them; they exist in many parts of the country where aquatic hatches are sparse, and they are not a particularly difficult insect to imitate.

In this area, the trout, with that perverseness that seems to characterize their behavior, seem to prefer small to tiny ants. Sizes sixteen through twenty work best, and since these imitations float awash in the surface film, seeing them is a great problem. Unless the light is right I often cannot see them at all more than fifteen feet away. But I use them.

As with the cricket, they usually are found drifting along the bank. Even so, trout will accept them unhesitatingly in midstream, so they can be treated more in the manner of an aquatic than can other terrestrials. They apparently are so common that the trout expect them almost anywhere.

I like them made of two little bumps of fur separated in the middle, with one turn of hackle at the waist. I trim the top hackle off. The three best colors are black, amber or reddish tan, and a dark red. Oddly, trout sometimes seem selective to them and one color will work at times while the others will not. Also, at times the trout will take a size twenty but refuse the size sixteen. Why is a progressive puzzlement.

Caterpillars that will float are not as easy to make as it would appear. Chenille for body material is worse than useless, as are yarn and floss. Some glossy furs do a fine job of floating the imitation, but I've had little success with them; the trout refuse them. A dull fur-bodied caterpillar catches fish but floats poorly. What to do?

The new polypropylene yarn helps some, but after you've caught a fish, and also after prolonged use, it's necessary to change the fly.

I've taken to making the body of Styrofoam, shaped, split, and glued on the hook. I seal the pores with two coats of fingernail polish. Over this I wind fuzzy polypropylene of the proper color, a good palmer hackle, and have a fairly serviceable fly that catches fish. However, this is the one terrestrial I could do without and not feel too much loss.

Deer hair mice are different. Here is one of my summer standbys for larger trout. It will not take so many fish in a season as hoppers may, but they will be larger. I've taken most of my very large trout on this lure.

The method I have found best is to cast it into the grass along a bank, or into a log jam or drift, then slowly work it until it falls into the water. If you have chosen your spot well, you can expect an explosion when the mouse hits the water.

If I don't get a hit immediately, I try "swimming" the mouse downstream. I point the rod down the line at the lure, take in the slack, then hand-twist retrieve until the mouse is taken or the leader comes to the rod tip. You must use a strong leader with this lure, both to cast it and to withstand a strike that comes against a tight line with no rod tip to absorb the shock.

Some anglers doubt the value of the mouse lure. One such was my friend Bob Holmes, who always sort of chuckled when I mentioned them. Then one day Bob and I were fishing a meadow stream where the grass was unbelievably dense, and overhung into the water along the bank.

During the day we both saw several voles (meadow mice) working through the dense grass near the edge of the water. Several times the little creatures nearly fell into the water. This episode convinced Bob and he urged me to make up a mouse that looked more like the voles. They are a distinct brown, while our deer mice or whitefooted mice of the woods are gray. My deer hair mouse does fine for them, and I've worked up a vole with a cork body covered with brown mohlon. I'll be using it this summer along meadow streams and I fully expect a five-pounder or two.

I developed my Floating Streamer for summer pickerel fishing but it has proved most successful for large trout. This lure utilizes a large goose quill for a body, and this not only floats the lure, but gives a natural translucent look.

This is a large lure, 2/0 or 3/0 on 3XL light wire hooks, but because the quill, which is a major portion of the lure, is hollow, it is light and casts easily.

For surface fishing, a floating line and 7 ½ foot, 1X leader is used. I generally cast short and try to work the lure on the water surface in imitation of a small fish in trouble. When done properly, it gets a savage reaction from the fish, some of which engulf it so voraciously that it comes out the gills and hooks them in the side. This, with a three-pounder or larger, I guarantee, will give you your jollies.

The second method is about as successful, but not nearly so much fun. I use a sinking line, 6-foot, 2X leader for this method, cast out and let sink, then retrieve in pulls of varying length. At each pull, the lure will tip down and glide forward, and will rise sharply when tension is released. This is a good imitation of the actions of an injured minnow, and if the area contains a trout of good size, he will usually pounce upon it. Do not let the lure dawdle—it must be pulled and slacked, then pulled again rather rapidly, so as to preserve the illusion. I think that the large, staring eye is a definite help.

I've had a good deal of backchat from anglers who feel that my Floating Streamer isn't a fly, isn't effective, and isn't sporting. As I said earlier, to each his own. It's light, not difficult to cast, it catches big fish, and it is used with a fly rod. That's reason enough for me.

In the field of aquatic flies, the adult caddis has received about as much attention as an orphan girl at the Queen's Ball—this, despite the fact that more of our trout streams hold caddises than any other aquatic insect.

Though Halford and the "exact imitation" group gave it lip service, there is little evidence they considered it an important fly. Some writers give space to the underwater form but pass lightly over the adult. Marinaro gives it little space. Swisher and Richards give it slightly fuller treatment.

The fact is, the life history and emergence style of most caddis flies is not too similar to that of mayflies, and this, more than anything else, has led to their neglect.

The two forms most prevalent and widespread are *Rhyacophila* and *Brachycentrus*. They are found practically everywhere in the Temperate Zone. In a great many of our best trout streams they are the most abundant of all aquatic insects.

Like nearly all caddises, they undergo complete metamorphosis, going from larva to pupa to adult. During the pupal stage, they are inactive in rock cases on the bottom. It is when they break out of the pupal cocoon that they become of interest—and a problem—to the fly-fisher.

When the caddis chews through the silklike cocoon and emerges underwater, it is a full-grown insect. It is encased in a membraneous sac filled with air, with a pair of legs protruding. The air sac causes it to rise rapidly in the water, and it aids this movement with the protruding legs. A few inches from the surface, the air sac splits, and the caddis comes out flying, bursts through the surface, and zap! it's gone.

Caddises do not return until egg-laying time, and when you see clouds of them fluttering over the surface of the water, they are laying eggs or preparing to do so. At this time a dry imitation works very well. Sometimes, however, there are so many naturals that the chance of your artificial being taken is remote.

I've seen *Brachycentrus* adults so thick over the Yellowstone River in Hayden Valley that it looked like a snowstorm. At this time, it appeared as if every square yard of river surface held a rising fish.

Trout taking caddis pupae
in the surface film.

Adult caddis flying.

Fishing was poor, simply because the terrific number of naturals made it unlikely that the artificial would be selected more than once out of twenty or thirty floats. Moving the fly did not improve the taking percentage.

If the egg-laying caddises are not so plentiful, the fishing can be excellent. The standard no-drag drift has always been perfectly satisfactory at such times.

Commercial versions of *Rhyacophila* and *Brachycentrus* are hard to find. I'm told that in the East a fly called Grannom is sold to imitate *Brachycentrus*. The two flies are not difficult to imitate and instructions will be found for making the artificial in Chapter 9. An excellent commercial pattern is the Colorado King made by George Bodmer of Colorado Springs; George did not originate the pattern and doesn't know who did. It works extremely well.

Except for the salmon fly hatch in this area, it is not too profitable to use floating stone-fly imitations. These flies hatch by crawling out of the water and splitting the nymphal shuck. If they hatch in sufficient numbers, as they do during the salmon-fly hatch (really *Pteronarcys californica,* the giant stone fly), many of these clumsy fliers fall into the water and are gobbled up by the trout.

Here again, one can get into an area where there are so many naturals on the water that having a trout take your artificial is pure luck. However, salmon-fly time brings up some really huge trout, and if you work hard and get a break, you can tie into a fish over five pounds on almost any day.

Brown trout rising
to mayfly nymphs.

I've had some luck staying well at the front of the hatch (these

flies start hatching at lower elevations and the hatch progresses upstream from two to four miles a day, depending on weather) and trying to select the largest of the occasional risers. This is complicated by the fact that the hatching flies fly upstream, and locating the front of the actual hatch is a time-consuming process. The size of the fish makes it well worthwhile.

About the only skill required is to be able to cast the huge (number 4, 4XL) dry fly some fifty or sixty feet. If it comes down with a plop, hooray. So does the natural.

During the hatch, which will probably be on for six weeks on one stream or another in the area, a carnivallike atmosphere is evident. Things are a little wild, anglers galloping up and down the banks in waders, like ponderous pachyderms, waving and shouting to each other. "Where is it?" is the universal greeting at this time.

"It," of course, is the front of the hatch. After things have been under way for several days, it becomes almost impossible to locate the front, since flies line the bank for miles. One angler I met during this time said it was like grasshopper season but with ten million hoppers.

The figure is not an exaggeration. I have walked the banks of the Madison in the Varney area during salmon-fly hatch and found every tree, bush, and shrub covered with flies for five miles along both banks. Trying to find where the flies are actually hatching is a real chore.

It does no good to fish an area where the hatch has just passed, for the fish will be glutted. Above (upstream of) the line of hatch, the trout will be deep, gathering in the nymphs that are crawling over the rubble bottom to get to shore to hatch. Therefore, to enjoy the fabulous dry-fly fishing that *can* be had at this time, you have to find the exact stretch of stream, perhaps a quarter-mile long or less, in a five-mile or greater area.

The Madison River, from Meadow Lake near Ennis, to the foot of the cascades below Quake Lake slide, is about seventy miles long, around the bends. Since it is difficult or impossible to approach in many areas—it may be ten miles between approaches—this causes the local phenomenon known as "bank running."

I've got over charging up and down looking for the front of the hatch. When it has been on for a few days, the tackle shops will all know where the front of the hatch is, within a few miles. So I pick out an approachable spot that is pleasant to fish and where the hatch has not arrived, and go there, early each morning. I fish with my big Montana Stone Nymph until the first fish commence to rise, which might take two or three days, or even a week, if cool weather and rain slow up the progress of the hatch.

This is the most reliable method of locating the hatch, and is the best bet to avoid becoming a distance runner in waders, a sport that becomes less appealing the older I get. However, if you are a dry-fly purist, it can waste several days, though some men enjoy the rodeolike activity. They have a ball, and lose weight in the process, they say. They say it with broad smiles and every appearance of enjoyment, even while panting like puppies. One has to believe them.

The hatch on the Madison will run from early June to mid-July or later. While it is going on, there will be lesser hatches on other streams. The Box Canyon section of Henry's Fork has as reliable a hatch, and as many big fish as any comparable section of the Madison, but it is unapproachable except at either end. Floating in double-ended boats is used here, and, since this is a wild stretch of water, if one hits the hatch, the action can become so frantic as to be dangerous. It can also become addictive.

The mayfly hatches in this area can be exasperating. Due to our altitude and location, we have what is called a microclimate, in an area about one hundred miles across. Because of our climate, major hatches can vary as much as three weeks. Thus a visiting angler coming out to fish the western Green Drake hatch can spend his whole vacation and never see the fly once.

This goes on all season and, because of it, one must be prepared to fish caddis imitations, or even some tiny aquatics such as midges and blackflies if he is to fish on the surface. Fortunately, our caddises hatch with fair regularity throughout the season.

I often see anglers fishing to rising fish feeding on hatching caddises, but using a mayfly pattern in the standard no-drag drift. They catch few fish.

When caddises are hatching, the fly, because of its rapid rise from the bottom and because it does not rest on the surface, but bursts through the surface flying, is mostly caught by the trout *below* the surface. The trout pursue them up from the bottom and some-

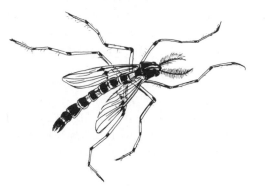

Midge adult *(Chironomus)*.

Tricorythodes, flying spinner.

times the speed of the pursuit causes the trout to break through and create a disturbance, which looks like a surface rise but isn't. Also, turning sharply just below the surface will cause a boil or bulge that looks very much like a normal rise.

At such times, the angler is better off fishing a pupal imitation of the caddis, my experience being that he will take ten times the fish that he would with even a very good imitation fished dry.

In fishing standard mayfly imitations, I prefer to fish when only a few flies are hatching and to fish the rise selectively. However, I am more inclined to use dry flies that are not standard—not yet, anyway.

Marinaro advocated a new type of dry fly, the Thorax Dun, with criss-crossed hackle, and some body in front of the wing. Swisher and Richards did away completely with the hackle. I fish a combination fly, tied as Marinaro does, but with the top hackle clipped off.

If, as Marinaro says, the height and color of the wing are the most important things in the dun, as is implied also in the no-hackle fly, then wing size, not hook size, is the governing factor. This allows

Baetis no-hackle dun.

the tying of a size twenty fly on a size sixteen hook, by limiting the size of the wing—and, of course, the body. This is my approach, and I like the results. The finished fly reminds one somewhat of low-water salmon flies.

In dealing with the vision of a trout, one thing to remember is that the trout's eyes are placed on the *sides* of his head. He does not have binocular vision; he sees independently with each eye, which suggests a lack of depth perception. It also tells us the trout can see everything except in a small area directly behind him. As R. D. Blackmore says in "Crocker's Hole," they have no eyes in their tails, the implication being they can see everywhere else.

Fishing for trout with standard dry-fly methods has been covered by scores of writers, in books that are thorough and explicit. Therefore, I'll not waste your time with any further directions, since most of these books are written by anglers who are better writers and better dry-fly fishermen than I.

Nonstandard dry-fly fishing—that is, fishing the water rather than the rise—has not been so well covered. Most writers on dry-fly fishing seem to regard it as a haphazard method, and give it little space.

This is surprising in view of the fact that aquatic biologists say that hatches on most streams cover less than 10 percent of the fishing day, and that stomach studies indicate that winged aquatics never furnish more than 20 percent of the food taken by the trout on such streams. This indicates that a dry-fly fisherman will spend 80 to 90 percent of his days either not fishing or fishing the water.

One reason that this phase of dry-fly fishing has received so little space in books devoted to dry-fly fishing is that it is very difficult to get a trout to rise to a standard dry fly when there is no hatch on. During such periods, trout will usually be lying deep and inactive, near or on the bottom.

Whether a trout can be induced to rise from the bottom to take surface food depends on a combination of depth and current speed and, of course, on the trout's hunger. The slower the current, the farther the trout will come up to feed. In faster waters, trout wishing to surface-feed will seek shallower water. In slow water, I have had trout come up as much as three feet for a floating fly, but this is not usual.

For a dry-fly fisherman to fish the water successfully, he must first know the water. He also must know something of the stream's insect structure, what flies are where. He should know the holds and lies of good fish, else his catch will be mostly yearlings and infants. It requires more study, thinking, and know-how to fish the water, and this, I believe, is why so little is written about it.

George LaBranche is credited with the so-called artificial hatch method of fishing the water. It works in some cases, especially if the angler knows the exact lie of the fish. Otherwise one can wear out his casting arm over blank water.

When fishing water one knows, the coverage should be thorough and careful. The water should be thought of as a checkerboard, and one starts by placing his fly on the nearest squares first, then gradually reaches other squares farther up and farther out, moving along as needed to keep the casts short.

The above kind of fishing with standard dry flies can be fun but is seldom very productive. If I'm going to fish the water with a floating fly, I either go to a "shocker"-type dry fly or to a terrestrial.

The shocker-type fly is a big spider or variant, or a big Palmer-tied dry. As the fellow said when he smote the mule between the eyes with a two-by-four, "First you have to get their attention."

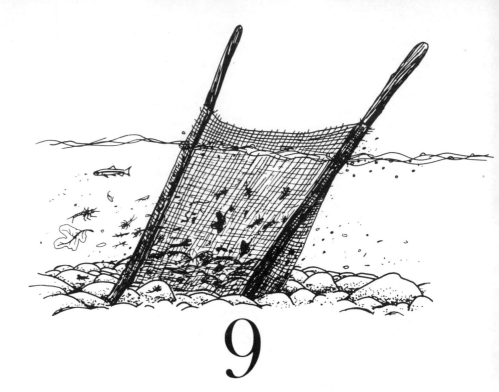

9

Fly Patterns and Their Dressings

I was walking down the street of the Ozark county town this day, completely unaware that I was about to encounter a man who would change my whole life. My whole life up to that time consisted of nine good years.

The fellow who stopped me on the street reminded me of Shadow Smart in the comic strip, "Harold Teen."

"Say, there, Little John Ernie," he addressed me, signaling at once that he knew my father. All my father's friends called me by his name.

"Yeah," I replied noncommittally.

"I hear you have a lot of deerskins over at your place," he allowed.

"They were all killed legal," I quickly assured him.

He laughed. "I'm not the game warden," he said, "I'm Howard Steen."

I recognized the name. He was a fishing guide, manager of the Hawes Clubhouse not far from my home, and the most famous fly-tyer in that part of the country.

140

"You cut the tails off those skins and bring 'em over to my place," he said, "and I'll give you fifty cents apiece for the good ones."

This was November, 1930. Fifty cents was big money in those days.

I was so excited I cannot recall even now how I got over the fourteen miles from the county seat to our log cabin in the hills. But I distinctly remember asking Pa if I could have the tails off those skins.

"Just don't spoil 'em for buckskin," he replied.

So, I whacked 'em off, put them in a shopping bag, and trudged the three miles over the hills to the Hawes Clubhouse on Current River. There were fifteen fine large whitetail tails in my bag and I spent the seven-fifty they would bring at least a dozen times on the way over.

I knocked on the door of the little cabin next to the beautiful stone clubhouse. It was about nine o'clock on a gray November day.

The pretty, plump woman who answered the door was Howard's wife, and the best mince pie maker in the world. She told me that Howard was in his shop, a little shed behind the house.

I walked back, entered the rickety door, and stood spellbound.

Howard had been turning out some twenty thousand flies a year in this shop for three or four years. The floor had not been swept in all this time and was covered several inches deep with brightly colored feathers and hair. Some five thousand bright bass flies hung on cards on the walls; scores of others hung on drying racks in front of the lone window. Howard was busy at his vise, turning out more.

He was quick to note the glazed look in my eyes, and offered me a large box of materials, a hundred hooks, one lesson, and a dollar and a half for my deer tails. When I took him up, he smiled secretively. Little did he know that I would have given him the deer tails and worked for him daily for six weeks just to learn the wonderful art of fly-tying.

I had already become hooked on fly-fishing through reading Ray Bergman. But I'd resigned myself to waiting thirty or forty years before I would accumulate the necessary tackle and flies. Now, at least, I'd have flies galore.

To help you understand some of the wonder and awe I felt on that November morning, let me quote from the writings of an English writer, H. C. Cutcliffe, over a hundred years ago, upon opening a chest of fly-tying materials for a young friend:

"Open the lid, oh! what an enthusiasm arises in the breast of the young piscator, emulated by the enchanting odour of the preservative spices which have now quite scented the box, there placed to prevent attack of intrusive insects. To turn out our old materials in the commencement, or even in anticipation of a future fishing season, affords a gratification to the sportsman, only equalled by meeting an old friend after a long and complete separation, with an interval of wintry times. It is the stirring up of old memories. Oh what pleasures rush upon the mind!"

So, I became a fly-tyer before I became a fly-fisherman. And I have not lost that sense of wonder at the beauty of flies and materials. I have, along with many others, become a collector of materials, my chests and drawers of fur, feathers, wools, and tinsels quite fill the little room where I work. Some of the material is at least twenty-five years old, and many and pleasant are the memories bound up in them and their association with the past.

Collecting fly-tying material can almost be described as a separate sport; I know anglers who spend more time at it than they do on the stream. I feel a strong empathy for these fellows for during the long Montana winters I wile away the happy hours adding to my collection, adding to a supply that is already sufficient for a hundred thousand flies, and most of which will never be used by me in my lifetime.

Over the ensuing forty-odd years, I have largely got over tying the experimental fly. And during the past twenty or so years I have narrowed my selection of patterns down to those that work in this area and in other streams of the Rocky Mountain West and Northwest. It is this list you will find at the end of this chapter.

Following, in alphabetical order, are the twenty patterns I use most, all of which were developed by me since about 1950.

Assam Dragon (nymph): size four, 2XL.

Represents *Libellula pulchella,* dragonfly nymph. Fished in any water with sand or sand-silt bottom. Let sink to the bottom, retrieve with short, sharp pulls. A fly for larger fish, and for times when no activity is evident.

To tie, you need the following materials: brown or tan seal fur *on the skin;* large grouse hackle or brown dyed grizzly. I once used cock capercailzie back and rump feathers but they have become unavailable.

Cut a strip of sealskin with fur on, an eighth of an inch wide and three to four inches long. Weight the hook with fifteen turns of .025-inch lead wire, centered on the shank. Taper one end of the sealskin strip to a point. Tie this point on at the hook bend, tightly.

Assam Dragon.

Coat the hook with cement, wind the sealskin strip on like chenille, keeping the fur outward. Do not overlap turns. Stroke fur toward the rear between turns. Tie off so as to leave one-eighth inch of clear shank back of the eye. Tie in the hackle, which must be very long-fibered. Wind one and one-half turns, tie off, finish head. I use 3/0 brown Nymo thread for this fly. It comes out rough and ugly, but then, so is the natural.

CREAM WIGGLER (larva): size fourteen, regular.

Using brown tying thread, tie a half-inch piece of cream-colored elastic about .030 inch in diameter to the hook about one-quarter inch back of eye. Rib this piece of elastic by half-hitching the brown thread back to the end and sealing it at that point with a drop of cement. The elastic should be attached to the hook at only one point. Put a wisp of short partridge hackle at the front and finish the head medium size. This fly represents midge larva, and should be fished in and around weed beds.

Cream wiggler.

DEER-HAIR MOUSE (mouse): size four, 3XL.

For a tail for this lure, I cut strips of car-washing chamois one-eighth by two inches. I bind this on by one end at the bend. Then bunches of deer-body hair are bound on tightly, pushed back with the thumb and fingers after each tie, to compress. Continue right up to the eye and finish off. Trim to a general teardrop shape, small at the eye. Flatten by trimming under the hook shank. Good anywhere there are trout. Fish along the banks and drifts. "Swim" by pointing the rod down the line and hand retrieving.

Deer Hair Mouse.

FAIR DAMSEL (nymph): sizes six or eight, 3XL.

Tail, two brown-dyed grizzly hackle tips three-quarters of an inch long, tied spread, on edge. Body, brown mottled fuzzy yarn or fur, tapered, full in the thorax. Body goes right to the hook eye. Rib with gold oval tinsel along abdomen, tie off at rear of thorax. Tie in one brown-dyed grizzly hackle, with fibers stripped off lower side when butt of hackle is to the right. Wind two separated turns of hackle, tie off about one-quarter inch back of eye. Half-hitch thread to eye, finish head rather large. Use brown tying thread. Represents *Argia* genus of damselflies.

Fair Damsel.

Foam Cricket.

FOAM CRICKET (cricket): size six, 2XL.

Shape styrofoam body in long oval or egg shape, flattened on bottom. Split underneath full length, halfway through body. Slip onto hook and glue slit closed. Bind tightly to hook just forward of center to make cricket's waist. Tie in some legs of peacock herl criss-cross under the bottom at this time, and finish the tying at the waist. Dose with black shoe polish; when dry, coat with lacquer or cement. Fish anywhere along banks and drifts.

Foam Hopper.

FOAM HOPPER (grasshopper): size six, 3XL.

Shape a piece of styrofoam about one-quarter inch square and as long as the hook shank. Slit one side halfway through, full length. Slip over hook shank and glue on.

Tie on a piece of dull yellow polypropylene yarn at bend, wind thread spirally forward, make a half hitch three-eighths of an inch back of eye. Cover abdomen and thorax with poly yarn. Tie off, then tie in a small bunch of brown deer tail on top. Over this, fold a piece of cinnamon turkey-wing quill fibers about a half-inch wide. Treat this fiber wing with sealer or fixer. Paint head of hopper dull yellow.

Fish as hopper during hopper season, dropping it down with a juicy splash. Twitch by pointing rod down the line and jerking lightly with the line hand.

GRAY OR BROWN CADDIS (dry): size ten or twelve, 2XL.

This is the only dry caddis imitation I've found necessary in this country, and as one can see by the description, it is a quite general pattern.

The body is gray, tan, or brown polypropylene wound about as thick as a kitchen match, to just back of the eye. Rib with a fine gold wire. On top tie a small pinch of gray and red squirrel tail, mixed, tying the butts about an eighth inch back of the eye. Make one turn of gray, ginger, or brown hackle, and finish the head. Trim the hackle off on top and bottom.

This is effective when adult caddises assemble in numbers to flutter over the water. It is not usually effective when caddises are hatching, nor is any other floater.

Gray caddis, dry.

IDA MAY (nymph): sizes eight and ten, 3XL.

Tail: grizzly hackle fibers dyed dark green.

Body: Black fuzzy wool to just back of eye, tapered to be full at the thorax.

Rib: Peacock herl and gold wire. Wind the herl first, then reverse wind the gold wire for strength.

Hackle: One and one-half turns of grizzly dyed dark green, tied to slant to the rear. Hackle should be very soft quality.

This represents the larger *Ephemerella* nymphs that swim with their legs folded back along the body.

Ida May nymph.

INVISIBLE (emergent): sizes eighteen to twenty-two.

Body: black wool or fur, thin, to eye.

Wing: wisp of wood duck fibers tied down wing.

When fish are taking something on or just under the surface, give this a try. It works very well during midge or blackfly hatches until the hatch is well under way.

Invisible.

LITTLE GRAY CADDIS (larva): sizes eight to ten, 2XL.

Make the body of gray wool somewhat thinner than a kitchen match. Over this wind peacock quill, spacing it so that the bands of quill and wool are about the same width. Wind both to just back of the eye. Overwind with gold wire in reverse direction. Wind one turn of very soft, very short black hackle, finish the head rather large, of black tying thread. The hackle should be about the length suitable for a size sixteen.

Fish this with a slow crawl along the bottom at the edge of the current. It is not too effective free drifting. Represents cased form of *Brachycentrus*.

Little gray caddis, larva.

LITTLE GRAY CADDIS (pupa): sizes eight to ten, 2XL.

Tie on at the bend a little bright green fuzz as an egg sack. Make the body regular length, about the size of a wooden match, of gray wool. Rib with fine gold wire. My gold wire is .005 inches, which is strong but not overly prominent. For a thorax, tie in three or four pieces of gray or tan ostrich herl; wind to make a definite bump. Clip the ends, after tying off, so that they are a little over a quarter inch long. Wind one turn of soft gray or brown partridge hackle. Finish head with brown tying thread, which can be used throughout.

Fish with a rising-to-the-surface motion, or the Leisenring lift.

Little gray caddis, pupa.

Little green caddis, larva.

LITTLE GREEN CADDIS (larva): sizes eight to ten, 2XL.

Make the body of dark *bright* green wool or fur, about as thick as a wooden match. Rib with fine gold wire. Make a bump of brown thread for a thorax. Tie in and wind one turn of soft black hackle, very short. Finish head of brown tying thread.

This is *Rhyacophila,* the naked caddis, which makes no case in the larval stage. How it survives, a soft, succulent, bright green worm, is a puzzle; but it does. And it furnishes food for all sizes of trout. Fish along the current edge, along the bottom.

Sparse Grey Hackle writes of making an imitation of this with a short length of fine bead chain, tied to the hook, and painted bright green. I wouldn't have thought it of Sparse.

Green caddis, pupa.

LITTLE GREEN CADDIS (pupa): sizes eight to ten, 2XL.

Make the body of dark green wool, about hunter's green—not as bright as in the larval form. Rib with gold wire. Make the thorax of several turns of gray or tan ostrich herl, tying off and leaving the ends a quarter of an inch long. Wind one turn of soft brown partridge hackle, finish the head in brown thread.

Handle this, in fishing, exactly like the Little Gray Caddis pupa.

MONTANA STONE (dry): size four, 4XL.

Wind black tying thread from eye to bend to form a bed for the other materials. Cut a hollow quill from some primary feather, as long as the hook shank. Stopper with a piece of cork and lash tightly on top of the hook. Tie a piece of dusky orange polypropylene yarn on at the bend, and wind forward, covering the quill. Tie a wisp of brown bucktail on top, one-quarter inch back of eye. Over this tie two broad grizzly hackles dyed dark orange, tied flat, and long enough to reach just past the bend of the hook. In front of the wing, wind one orange and one black hackle. Finish the head in black thread. Clip all hackle off top and bottom.

This is effective only during the salmon fly hatch and really is no more effective than Bird's Stone Fly, or Dave's Stone Fly.

Montana Stone (dry).

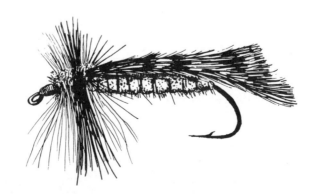

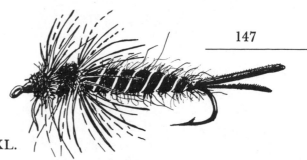

MONTANA STONE (nymph): size four, 4XL.

Montana Stone nymph.

Tail, six fibers from a raven or crow primary, tied forked. The body is black fuzzy yarn or fur. I use yarn, tying on at the bend. Rib is oval copper tinsel. Weight the hook with twenty-five turns of .025 lead wire. Wind the yarn forward to the eye, back to just short of the bend, forward to the eye, then back one third of the length of the body, and tie off. Wind the ribbing and tie off. Take one grizzly and one brown-dyed grizzly hackle, and two strands of gray ostrich herl. Strip the lower edge of the hackle so that the fibers are all on one side. Wind both hackles one turn at the base of the thorax, spiral forward on the bottom, one quarter inch, wind one more turn, tie off. Wind the ostrich herl at the base of the hackle windings and tie off. Half-hitch the black tying thread forward and finish the head.

When finished, this fly has one turn of hackle at the rear of the thorax and one a quarter inch forward of that.

I like my fast-water flies tied with separated hackle turns, and I like them tied "in the round"—unflattened, and with no top, bottom, or side effect. As the current works on this deeply sunken fly and the line and leader, the fly will be rolled over and over. If back and belly were not exactly alike, the fish would notice this, and refuse the fly because live nymphs do not roll over in the current. However, as this fly, and all my other nymphs, are tied in the round, it is difficult to tell which side is up.

This nymph represents *Pteronarcys californica,* the salmon fly of the West.

NATANT NYLON NYMPH (emergent): sizes twelve to sixteen.

Body is tan or gray fur, nymph-shaped, to the eye. Take two tiny hollow quill tips about one-quarter inch long, place in a pouch made of a small square of nylon stocking mesh. Tie this on in the wing position and lash upright. Tie a few wisps of partridge fibers at the front. Make the head small. Use dark stocking material with the gray bodies, light material with tan bodies.

Grease with line dressing and fish in the surface film. This is the deadliest emergent I know of, but it is delicate. The wing pouch will only hold for two or three fish.

Natant nylon nymph.

RIFFLE DEVIL (larva): size four, 4XL.

Riffle Devil nymph.

Weight with twenty-five turns of .025-inch lead wire. Tie on one long ginger or light brown saddle hackle, by the tip, and large olive green chenille at the bend. Wind the chenille to the eye, tie off. Wind the hackle forward, tie off, finish the head. That's it.

This represents the larva of the riffle beetle, *Dytiscus*, and is fished crawling quartering down, or downstream, on the bottom of riffles. Deadly at times.

SKUNK HAIR CADDIS (cased larva): sizes six to eight, 2XL.

Skunk Hair Caddis.

This is the most difficult fly to tie that I know of, and I wish I knew a better way to do it.

Weight the body with fifteen turns of .020 inch lead wire centered on the shank.

At the bend, tie on one brown hackle by the tip. Take a bunch of black skunk tail hair as long as can be obtained, and about as big around as a kitchen match. Tie on by the tips at the bend, very tightly. Use strong tying thread, black or dark brown. Twist the hair, and wind on, twisting between turns. Tie off one-quarter inch back of the eye. You will find it very difficult to lash the twisted hair down tightly enough to keep it from unwinding.

Wind the hackle forward in the segments formed by the hair, tie off. Clip off all the hackle as short as possible. Tie in medium oval copper tinsel, spiral to the bend and back to the front. Tie off, tie in one short, soft black hackle. Wind one turn, tie off, finish head large, varnish or cement well.

This fly represents *Hesperophyax* and other caddises that make their cases out of sand and small stones of generally dark color. Fish it on the bottom, slowly moving it near the edge of faster water, where the bottom is small stones and gravel.

WHITE-WING MIDGE (adult): size eighteen.

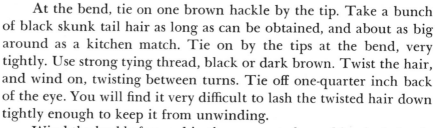

White-wing midge.

Tie on the wing, of white deer hair or polypropylene yarn, upright, in the normal position. Tie on black polypropylene yarn at the bend, wind the body to the eye. The thorax, around the wing butts, should be a little fuller than normal and this method of tying does this without any special attention.

The wing should be upright and trimmed, square at the top, the fibers flaring naturally. This fly rides along on the surface with its wings held up and buzzing rapidly to dry them. The fish are very partial to this fly when the natural is on the water.

YELLOW STONE NYMPH (nymph): size four, 3XL.

Weight the hook with twenty turns of .025-inch lead wire. The tail is six fibers of cinnamon turkey primary, tied forked. Tie on gold wire, then fuzzy brown yarn at the bend.

Yellow Stone nymph.

Wind the yarn to just back of the eye, back to just short of the bend, forward almost to the eye, then back one-third of the body. Tie off, tie in some thin dirty yellow yarn, rib to bend and back to base of thorax, X fashion. Tie in one brown dyed grizzly and one regular grizzly, both with the lower fibers stripped off. Tie in two pieces of gray ostrich herl, all this feather material at the back of the thorax.

Wind the two hackles one turn, spiral forward one-quarter inch underneath, wind another turn, tie off. Wind the herl at the base of the hackles. Wind the gold wire forward to the eye, tie off, finish head. Pull the gold wire quite tight.

This represents the *Acroneuria* genus of stone flies. It is found in the same waters as *Pteronarcys* but in lesser numbers. Very good in the Yellowstone River from Yankee Jim Canyon to Livingston.

The above flies comprise my regular list. None of them is tied in the conventional manner, and several have hackles tied *on* the body. If these hackles are not firmly tied on to start, they will slip from beneath the tying thread and unwind.

I have a few special flies that I do not use under normal conditions, or in the regular waters that I fish.

Floating Streamer.

FLOATING STREAMER (minnow): size 3/0, 4XL.

I use fine wire, gold-plated hooks for this fly.

The body is a goose primary feather quill, two inches long, as big in diameter as possible.

Using white size A tying thread, cover the hook from eye to bend to make a bed for the quill. Coat with cement. Stopper the cleaned-out quill tip with a small, bullet-shaped piece of cork. Place on top of the hook, with the tip of the cork just even with the eye. Take a couple of tight turns at this point with the tying thread. Place on top some long, green marabou plumes. Tie these with a couple of turns, then spiral the thread over them back to the bend and then forward to the cork, making sure that the marabou lies neatly on top, and that a good bunch extends past the quill tip an inch or so, for a tail. Whip finish at the head. Paint on a yellow eye with a black pupil. Give the belly a few small red spots. Varnish or lacquer, keeping this off the plume material.

This is the best injured minnow imitation I know.

STRIDER (impressionistic): sizes six to eight, 3XL.

Tie the body as thin as possible, with floss, to just back of the eye. Rib with fine gold wire, closely. Hackle, one or two turns of long-fibered, soft wood duck, grouse, or guinea. Body color should be bright red or orange.

This is used only for skipping and skimming on the broken waters of riffles. It works only at certain times, but I have no way of knowing just when those times are. It's a fly to experiment with.

SPRITE (impressionistic): size fourteen, 2X short.

This fly consists of two turns of long, soft hackle in the middle of the shank. The hackle should be about right for a size eight hook. I use only grizzly, badger, and furnace. I fish this fly only in eddies, at bends, or behind rocks. Use sinking line and try to get the fly to go 'round and 'round. It is the most effective fly, used in this manner, of any I know for this water type. Used here, your fish are apt to run large. This fly used in other water types produces only small fish.

All my wet flies and nymphs are tied with regular weight, English hooks. I specify English hooks because their regular weight wire is some thousandths of an inch smaller than Mustad hooks, but is stronger.

I _do not_ use coarse hooks for weight to get the fly down. Use lead wire for weight, because coarse hooks will cause a bunch of trouble in lost fish.

I got a letter a couple years ago from a reader of my first angling book who was losing many fish off the hook on nymphs. This was Harry Murray, of Edinburg, Virginia, who has since become an angling pal.

Harry sent me some samples of the nymphs he was using. The

wire was at least twice the diameter of the same size English hooks. I wrote him that I thought the coarse wire was the problem, that he simply wasn't sinking the hook over the barb, which was huge for the hook size. It turned out to be the right answer.

I am surprised at the number of fishermen I meet each year who do not know why our sport is called angling. Because this is apparently widespread, let me explain.

When metal fishhooks first started to be used in England, about 1300, they were made from iron needles. Steel was not yet known. To make needles, a bar of best quality iron was heated and hammered, reheated and hammered some more, into a sheet about one-eighth inch thick. This was cut into strips an eighth-inch square.

At this point the strips were cut into pieces two needle lengths long. This was ground to a point on each end, punched flat in the center, the eyes bored out, then the two needles were separated.

When a man filched one of these from his wife's sewing basket to make a fishhook, he heated it red, let it cool slowly, then chiseled and raised the barb on the pointed end. Then he bent the softened needle into a lopsided V shape, the shank end somewhat longer than the point end. This he called an "angle," for obvious reasons.

Even after this was retempered, it was pretty soft, and the angle bend was such that the fish wouldn't straighten it out, as they would a curved hook.

Our word, hook, comes from the Dutch *hoek,* meaning a corner or an angle. Make sense?

During the fourteenth and fifteenth centuries, the best iron for needles was imported from the Baltic states and Germany. About 1340, in Nuremburg, the wire-drawers guild was formed, to draw a better grade of wire for monochords, harpsichords, clavichords, et al. So, these wire-drawing guildsmen, by experiment, developed a better grade of wire.

England imported this wire for making needles, then made hooks from the needles. It was almost two centuries before hooks were being made directly from the wire.

The best fly-tying hooks are still English, or sometimes Scottish. No other country uses as good a grade of wire nor as many hand operations in hook making.

I would be perfectly willing to pay five cents a hook in order to get better hooks. Since a finished fly costs sixty cents to a dollar each, and the materials never more than a dime, it should be obvious that the major cost of a fly is in labor. In order not to waste my labor, I use the best hooks I can find. For the last twenty-five years I have got most of my hooks from Edgar Sealey in England, through an American distributor. Unfortunately, I was sometimes unable to obtain the exact size and style that I wanted. So I shopped around. But I always come back to using Sealey hooks.

Although I do not use as much dubbing as I once did, my interest in this material has not declined. It is, without question, one of the most useful and versatile materials the fly-tyer has.

Notice the contents of the dubbing bag of Charles Cotton, writing in 1675: "Dubbing of the tail of a black, long-coated cur, such as they commonly make muffs of; for the hair of such a dog dies and turns red brown, but the hair of a smooth-coated dog of the same color will not do, because it will not die, but retains its natural color."

Marten's fur, white fur from a hare's scut, hog's hair, dun bear's hair, hair from the flank of a brindle cow, squirrel's tail, brown spaniel hair, mohair, fur of black water-dog, hair of an abortive calf, down of a fox cub, black spaniel's hair, camel, and sable hair, fur from a black cat's tail, fur from black rabbits, hare's neck and badger were some of the dubbings Cotton used, and he was meticulous in blending them for color.

Looking in my own dubbing box I find the following: dark and light seal's fur, seal hair, polar, grizzly, cinnamon, and black bear hair, squirrel and rabbit, mole, muskrat, mink, sable, vole, weasel, goat wool, sheep's wool, fox, fitch, and wild pig's wool, and deer, elk, and antelope hair, plus the cheek of a peccary, for dry-fly tails.

Several authorities vouch for the excellence of dubbing as body material. W. H. Lawrie in *All Fur Flies and How to Dress Them,* and E. H. "Polly" Rosborough in *Tying and Fishing the Fuzzy Nymph* are two of the best. Both of these writers are excellent fly-tyers and make a splendid case for the dubbing body.

Why, if dubbing is as good and useful as it appears, do I use less of it than I once did?

There are several reasons. Yarn, which in spite of its detractors, is nothing but sheep's wool, is now available in fuzzy and very fuzzy types, blended with acrylics and mohairs, and dyed many different colors, so that it is really a very first-class, already made up, dubbing material.

Second, my huge nymphs require so much dubbing that making it myself would keep me tied down more hours than I can afford. So I use the beautiful imported fuzzy yarns one can find in better knit shops. I have not purchased yarn from a fly-materials house in over twenty years.

I've not had much luck dubbing on waxed threads; even the stickiest wax will not hold the quantities of dubbing needed to make my big nymphs. However, there is something that will.

This is a mixture of stick shellac and alcohol, made to the consistency of very thick syrup. Paint your taut tying thread with this, using a toothpick, then just touch the dubbing to the treated thread. It will cling at the slightest touch. When the mixture gets too thick, a little alcohol fixes it up.

One last fly is the Green Marabou Muddler.

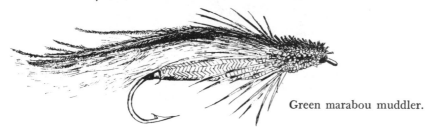

Green marabou muddler.

GREEN MARABOU MUDDLER (streamer): sizes 2 to 2/0, 3XL.

Body, silver Mylar tubing, large. Wing, a good clump of medium green marabou plumes. Make a collar of brown deer tail at the point where the wing is tied on. Make the head of deer body hair, clipped to a bullet shape, quite large.

The Brown Marabou Muddler is made exactly the same, except that brown marabou plumes are used in place of green.

Following is a list of commercial flies found useful in the Rocky Mountain West and Northwest:

Bi Fly	Mites
Big Hole Demon *	Montana Nymph
Bird's Stone Fly *	Muddler *
Bitch Creek	Picket Pin *
Black Nymph, Martinez *	Renegade *
Dunham	Trueblood's Otter Shrimp *
Fledermouse *	Trude
Goofus Bug	Whitcraft
Henry's Lake Nymph *	Woolly Worm
Missoulian Spook	Yellow-Bodied Grayback *

Flies marked with an asterisk can be found in *Flies of the Northwest,* a fly-pattern catalog issued by the Inland Empire Fly Fishing Club, Box 2926 Terminal Annex, Spokane, Washington, 99220. It can be obtained for two dollars plus postage, and is worth every penny. It contains the best selection of patterns for the West and Northwest available anywhere.

Most of the flies listed are available at well-stocked shops in the West.

10

Tackle Talk

IT has been customary in the past in books like this to begin a chapter on tackle with a discussion of rods. This would imply that the rod is the most important thing in fly-fishing. In my book it isn't; the most important piece of tackle, as far as I'm concerned, is the line. I can get by with a very poor rod; in fact just after World War II, I fished an entire season with a cane pole fitted with guides because I had no rod, and none were available in the shops. That is, none that I could afford.

In 1947 I was fortunate to fall in with a bunch of nuts in the San Francisco area who were miles ahead of anyone in the country in the matter of fly lines. J. P. Cuenin was the voice of this splinter group through his outdoor column, and Marvin Hedge would come down from Portland every six months or so to see that we were headed in the right direction. We had only silk lines to work with at this time, but we did great things with them. We also developed the needle knot, which someone renamed the nail knot and which is now becoming known as the needle knot again.

We spliced our own lines, making them up to suit the exact purpose they were intended for. Steelheaders spliced shooting heads of B through AA onto half a mile of monofilament, greased the works with graphite, then cast the whole thing across the river and into the trees. Small-stream fishermen spliced up exquisite lines of IHI for floating tiny flies down shining riffles. Striped bass fishermen made up "bull.ropes" of AAA shooting heads spliced to H shooting lines, and some even used lead-core shooting heads.

Those lines were so successful that I still splice my own lines. I have a far larger selection of materials and types, i.e., floating, slow sinking, fast sinking, and Hi-D. With these to choose from, I can splice up a line that casts like a dream and performs exactly as I want it to.

Four years ago while conducting a seminar on fly-fishing along with a representative of Scientific Anglers, under the auspices of Bud Lilly's Trout Shop in West Yellowstone, the tackle rep took me to one side.

"Charlie," he said, "if it isn't too personal, why don't you use our lines?"

"I'll tell you, Duane," I replied. "I don't use any commercial lines as made up by those companies. I splice my own to get lines that will do exactly what I want them to."

"I noticed your lines were spliced," he persisted, "but tell me what yours will do that ours won't. Your fast-sinking line that you demonstrated deep nymph fishing with, how is it different from our weight forward fast-sinking line?"

"In several ways. Your WF8S has a forward taper—a short forward taper, to be sure, but one isn't needed on a fast-sinking line. The purpose of a front taper is to promote turnover and delicacy of presentation. But a front taper *will not* turn over a leader with a weighted fly as well as no-taper. And delicacy of presentation of a deeply sunken nymph is a laugh, who needs it?

"Also," I went on, "you yourself suggested a four-foot leader for the fishing we were doing, so that the fly doesn't float up. But you defeat that purpose with a front taper, which does float up. Then, there's the shooting and running portion of the line. Your company's sinking lines all have sinking running, and shooting portions. You don't want that portion of the line to sink, in streams, because it is difficult to haul to the surface to recast. My line has thirty-five feet of level 8 fast-sinking line for a head, spliced directly to sixty feet of level 4 floating line. Thus only the shooting head sinks, and pickup and recasting is far easier."

I don't know what Duane reported back to his company, but two years later they came out with a fast-sinking head with floating shooting and running line. It still has the front taper but is the best commercial fast-sinking line presently available. If I were going to use it, or any fast-sinking or Hi-D commercial line, I'd lop off the front taper.

While spliced lines can be made for any specific purpose, they can sometimes cause a problem if one doesn't take care to keep the splices up. It happened to me a fall or so ago. I got a call from Bruce Peeples to come over to Lewiston, Idaho, to fish for steel-head in the Clearwater River. It was "greased line" fishing, using floating lines and no-drag drifts.

I took a couple of steelhead of five or six pounds the first day, then cast a thousand or more times the rest of the day without results. That night I failed to check the splice, and the next morning ran into trouble.

The fish had all been hitting on the swing, at the point where the downstream drift started to drag across. On this cast, however, a heavy fish hit as I was retrieving upstream to pick up and recast.

The splice was about halfway through the guides when the fish hit, and it immediately parted and the silk thread binding started to unravel. It was a weird sensation; it felt exactly as though a coil spring was running out through the guides. It was the first splice I've ever had let go and it will be the last.

Actually, commercial lines are so much improved in the last few years that one has to be a real fussbudget to splice his own. When my present lines are worn out, I'll probably start using commercial lines.

There are still some areas where one cannot find a commercial line to suit his purpose, at least in this country. Some ultralight tackle enthusiasts complain they cannot find weight-forward lines of size 2 or 3 for their willowy wands, and one famous light-tackle angler bemoaned the fact he could not find a size 1 for his four-foot-four-inch, one-ounce bamboo stick.

I am not a light tackle user, but if I were, I wouldn't go the short, wispy rod route. I wouldn't, because if fishing very fine and far off is your bag, there's a better way, at least as far as I'm concerned.

Some time ago, I helped a British consular official off a plane from Hong Kong. This fellow needed help, because his cabin luggage consisted of one large leather case containing about twenty fly reels with lines, and fourteen loose rod cases. How he convinced the crew to let him bring them aboard I'll never know.

When I asked about the fly-fishing in Hong Kong, he explained that he *hadn't* fished there, but he had taken advantage of the situation to have the fourteen rods made up from a supply of Tonkin cane that he'd managed to locate. He'd been able to get the rods manufactured to his exact specifications at a cost of less than fifteen dollars each. He'd had his reels and lines sent from England to balance up with the various rods.

Well, a bargain is a bargain and I was happy for him, and when I said so, he insisted on showing off his collection on the airport grass.

He was a beautiful and impressive caster, as a great many Britishers are, but I was bored with the whole thing until he began showing off his "light" rod.

This was a startling piece of equipment. It was *twelve feet* long, in three sections, the bamboo at the grip about the size of a lead pencil. It weighed four ounces and was equipped with a Hardy Flyweight reel and an IGI or number 1 silk line. What this gentleman could do with that outfit was an eye-opener.

With a single, easy, drifting backcast, he would shoot the line smoothly through the guides and put the fly down like a thistle forty feet away. No double-haul, no frantic sawing back and forth of line through the guides, no thrashing to get up line speed, just one gentle back-and-forth wave and the size 16 fly came down ahead of a nice straight line far enough away to be almost invisible. As I said, I do not use light tackle, but if I were enamored of midge flies, hair-fine leaders, and sewing-silk-size lines, this would be the one I'd choose.

Such tackle is not really necessary out here, although on the thin, clear, smooth, pondlike stretches of some Eastern streams, it probably is. The splash of an ordinary line coming down on such waters might spook every fish in the place. So, if you fish such waters, by all means have the line that will do the job. I would, even if I had to make it up myself.

Rods are personal; what suits one man will not suit another. Also, some anglers regard their rods as status symbols.

I was out with four very wealthy men one time, dry-fly fishing the Firehole. When we got out of the car to rig up, it was like a status seekers' picnic:

"My rod is a one-hundred-and-fifty-dollar Orvis."

"I have a two-hundred-and-fifty-dollar Payne."

"Mine is a three-hundred-and-fifty-dollar Leonard."

"My glass rod cost about fifty bucks."

The man with the fifty-buck glass rod was a better fisherman than all the others together.

I regard a rod as a tool; if it will not do what I want it to, it is of no use to me. I do not baby a rod, and I don't spend a great deal of time drying, waxing, polishing, or cleaning a rod. I take minimum care of it and I want it serviceable. That's about it with me. For that reason, I want a good quality glass rod. I put on, or have put on, nonfouling spinning guides for ease in handling and shooting the line. Snake guides are an abomination.

A longer rod, say eight to nine feet, will do more things more easily than a six- or seven-foot rod. Even when fishing a creek only four feet wide, I can place my fly more easily and more accurately with an eight-foot rod than I can with one of six feet.

You can keep more line off the water with the longer rod, and you can handle sinking lines and weighted flies much better with one.

Each year I take fifty or more experienced anglers for stream teaching and demonstration tours. Most of them have adequate rods, but several have been fanciers of very light, short rods. Almost to a man (or woman) when we return, they ask me to come into the shop and help them select a longer rod.

The first of such were Gordon and Corky Sherman, who favored six- and seven-foot rods. At one deep, fast run below a cascade, I noticed that Corky was having trouble lifting the sunken line and weighted nymph, and was in danger of hooking herself with the fly on the forward cast.

I gave her my eight-foot rod with its fast-sinking line and big spinning guides. In minutes she was shooting the line out over the water like a pro. She lost no time telling Gordy that she wanted an outfit just like mine, and when we came in, he ordered her one. Last time they were to come, Corky had domestic affairs to attend to and couldn't make the trip. But her rod made it. Gordy too had become a convert.

My teaching tours always include fishing at least four kinds of water. Seldom were my clients equipped with proper lines for such varied fishing, and nearly all of them purchased other lines when we returned. I've had letters from many of them telling how this opened up new angling vistas for them.

There is much confusion about the proper line for a rod. Some rod companies print the proper line size on the butt near the grip; most recommend only one line size. The fact is, any rod can handle three different line sizes, according to the use it is put to, and the average casting distance for which it is used.

Lines are numbered according to the weight of the first thirty feet exclusive of any front taper. Thus, if your rod is made for a size 8 line, it will handle perfectly with that thirty feet just past the rod tip. This is *not* a thirty-foot cast.

If the rod is eight feet, and the leader nine, then this is a cast of over fifty feet, because there are from five to seven feet of front taper on most double-tapered or weight-forward lines. Very few anglers

cast fifty feet on the average. Thirty-five would be a better guess. I
am speaking of the distance from angler to fly.

If you do not cast over fifty feet, you will get better handling
with the next number larger line, a 9 in this case. Fifteen feet of this
line through the tip, with rod length, leader, and front taper, will
give you a cast of thirty-five feet, angler to fly.

On the other hand, if you cast sixty to seventy feet on the average, you'll do better with a line a size light for your rod. Casting this
distance, you'll most always have the back taper through the tip;
this will give you forty feet or so of line in the air. An eight-foot rod
and a nine-foot leader will give you a fifty-five-foot or slightly longer
cast without line shoot. You can easily shoot ten to twenty feet of
line on the cast to get your distance.

My lines are all a number larger than the maker of my rod
recommends. This is because I prefer to cast short in order to exercise better line control on the drift or float.

So the line number printed on your rod should be thought of
only as a starting point. From your own experience, you should be
able to determine whether it is the proper size, or whether you need
a size larger or smaller. No one can really decide this for you; it's a
personal decision.

Lines are for fishing, more so than for casting, and one needs
the proper kinds of lines for the water he fishes, as well as for fitting
the rods he uses.

Different anglers handle the situation differently. Some, like
me, carry three or four kinds of lines on extra reel spools and change
as needed. Quite a few carry entire extra reels, and I met one man, a
real specialist, who had a different reel *and* rod for each type of line.
When I asked him how he carried them along the stream, he informed me that his rod caddy did this. I thought he was joking. Not
until some time later did I find out he was not.

For dry-fly fishing, one needs the best floating line he can find.
Even then, after prolonged use, the tip will sink. I know of no way
of preventing this; some profess not to be bothered by it, but it
bothers me. If I had wanted a sink-tip line, that's what I would have
bought.

When I dry-fly fished days at a time, some years ago, the sinking
tip problem was worse than it is now. In those days I bought the best
double-tapered floating line available, cut it in half, and spliced each
of the two sections to a floating shooting and running line. I carried
a fresh line with me on an extra reel spool, and when the tip of the
one I was using started to sink, I removed that reel spool, dried the
line, and put it in my vest. Then I would snap in the fresh line on

its spool, and continue on. I see some few fellows still doing this.

Some lines come with a cleaner that is supposed to stop the tip from sinking. It delays it, but it doesn't stop it, nor will any kind of dressing I've ever seen. If the tip sinking doesn't bother you, fine; if it does, I recommend an extra reel spool with a fresh line, and changing as needed.

Slow-sinking lines for streams should have a shooting and running portion that floats, although this is not as critical as it is in faster-sinking lines. Color in such lines is important; they should be highly visible so that the angler can have a better idea where his leader and fly are. Fish are not spooked by sunken lines. When I was doing underwater research on sunken flies some years ago, there were times when the brown sunken line would actually touch the back of some fish. They would simply move a foot or so forward, or to one side, with no sign of fright.

In all sunken lines I like a highly visible color—flame orange is the best. Yellow is better than white, and green is the worst for visibility.

Slow-sinking lines in stream fishing are useful in pools, in flats and some riffles, around weed beds, and for drifting a nymph along an undercut bank. Basically, in choosing a sinking line one needs to determine what kinds of waters he is going to be fishing with it, and what he wants it to do. Only then can he make an informed choice.

One way of relating line to fishing condition is to use the current as a guide—slow current, slow-sinking line; fast current, fast-sinking line. High-speed current calls for a Hi-D line.

So far, I've been speaking only of fishing in streams. All sunken lines used in streams should have floating shooting-and-running portions. In lakes, however, the entire line should sink, as it does in most such lines presently available. If you do mostly lake fishing, any of the current crop of sinking lines will do a good job.

Beware of the bargain line. The amount of whipping back and forth that a fly line does will wear out the best line in time; it will ruin a poor line in only a few days. I always recommend that the angler buy the top brand of line made by a well-known, reputable company. I have used lines by Cortland, Gladding, Scientific Anglers, and Orvis, and found the lasting qualities of all of them comparable and entirely satisfactory. The level lines I've used in the past to splice my own lines have always been one or the other of the above brands, except when only silk was available, some twenty-five years ago.

Leaders are not as important as lines, yet more anglers agonize over leader selection than do over line selection. Dry-fly fishermen especially are prone to spend more time on leaders than on all other parts of their tackle.

Considerable attention has been given in the past to the relationship of the line tip to the leader butt. One rule of thumb most often used is that the leader butt should be two-thirds the diameter of the line tip. This ignores completely the most important factor—not the comparative size of line and leader, but the comparative *flexibility*. That's the key to good line—leader compatibility.

For instance, I have two coils of .021-inch nylon monofilament. One is as stiff as piano wire, almost; the other is much limper. Attached to the same line tip they give completely different performances. Size is meaningless.

Most experienced fly-fishermen in this area deal with leaders somewhat differently than is done in other parts of the country. They needle knot about eighteen inches of proper nylon mono to the line tip. They tie their choice of leader for the day's fishing to this with a barrel or needle knot. In the course of a season, as leaders are tied on and clipped off, it is this permanently attached piece of nylon that grows shorter, not the line tip. If your line has a front taper, as most do, and you knot each leader directly to this tip, it isn't going to be long before your line has no front taper.

No experienced angler I know uses leader loops. Such are convenient for changing leaders, but they do not give good performance and a line loop wears out rather quickly.

I do things a little differently than do my friends. I permanently needle knot a tapered leader to my lines. Each will vary with the purpose of the line. On my floating dry-fly line, I knot a knotless leader six feet long tapered to 1X (.010 inch). I use it as is for some fishing—Floating Streamer, Deer Hair Mice, and so forth. As I use smaller flies, I step the leader down by adding tippets of twelve inches. Thus, if I change to 3X, my leader is eight feet; if I go down to 5X, it becomes ten feet long—a good length for such a fine tippet. This leader turns over well, and it isn't much trouble to change tippet size because I carry tippet sections of 3X, 4X, and 5X already knotted together. No matter which I use, I have to tie only one knot on the stream.

I use the same method on my sinking lines, but since these have no front taper, I first knot on a piece of heavy monofilament of about .023 inch and about a foot long. The butt of the six-foot leaders I use will run anywhere from .018 to .021 inches, but the needle knot can fasten the .018 to the .023 without too much of a hinging effect. This arrangement works just fine, since neither delicacy of presentation nor perfect turnover is required.

For a tip size on these leaders I use the "rule of four" method. That is, I divide the hook size by four to get the proper leader-tip size for that fly. Size-four fly calls for 1X, size eight for 2X, and so on.

A size-six fly can go on either a 1X or 2X tip, whichever I need. This method works just as well for dry flies. A size twenty fly needs a 5X leader.

As far as the exact steps one needs to tie the perfect leader for dry-fly fishing, it varies with the angler, and most long-time dry-fly fishermen have evolved their own pet leaders. Therefore I offer no advice in this area. Should one wish to explore further in this direction, any good recent book on dry-fly fishing will probably have much information on leader selection of more value than anything I could offer.

Reels are probably the least important part of the fly-fisherman's tackle. It used to be that all one needed was a good, sound, simple, single-action reel suitable for the rod it was used on. The development of many types of lines has led to the need for either additional reels or extra spools.

Most anglers like the extra-spool arrangement. This calls for a reel that allows quick changing of the spool, and there are many good ones available. In my reels I want simplicity of mechanism, quick spool changing, a reliable drag, and perforated side plates. I also like a click. There are many reels that provide these features, at prices ranging from fifteen to one hundred fifty dollars. My fifteen-dollar reel offers more for the money than any other, and extra spools are not expensive. It's a Pflueger Medalist, and at least 80 percent of the good anglers I know use it for the same reasons I do.

Some anglers are status conscious about reels as well as rods. I know fellows who wouldn't be caught dead on the stream without a Hardy reel on their rod, and I see anglers now and then fishing for trout with complicated reels more suitable for Atlantic salmon or tarpon. There is absolutely nothing wrong with this; some anglers get as much pleasure out of fine tackle as they do from fishing. I'm all for it—for them. Me, I'm a practical fly-fisher and like the simplest tackle that will do the job.

The above is somewhat of a justification for what follows. In the field of gear, I'm a collector of gadgets, so I understand the tackle collector and sympathize with him.

A reader of an outdoor column I conducted for four years wrote in to ask what the difference was between tackle and gear. My feeling is that tackle includes everything from the angler's hand down to and including the fly. Rod, reel, line, leader, and flies are tackle; anything else is gear.

Leader clippers, nets, creels, thermometers, fly boxes—these and many more are gear. I include as gear my storehouse vest, which carries all the rest.

It is only recently that fly-fishing vests have been designed by fly-fishermen. In the past, famous anglers have endorsed vests, but they didn't design them. There are several on the market today that are fisherman-designed, and these are by far the best available. They don't have to be designed by a famous angler; mine is designed by a nameless one, and there is none available anywhere that I would trade it for.

My vest was given me by my oldest and best buddy, Art Bock of Portland, Oregon. Art happened to be friends with Tim Boyle, the president of Columbia Sportswear of that city. Tim believed his North Umpqua design to be the best in its field, and Art sent me the vest to try out. I know of no better for my purposes, at any price.

First, I want big, roomy pockets on a vest, plus a full-length pocket across the back. My present vest has six very large pockets, two smaller ones, and the big pocket in the back. It is the only vest I've ever owned except ones my wife and I made ourselves that carries all my stuff with ease.

If all this seems commercial, let me state my position. For forty years angling writers have been writing about products in such vague irreproachable terms that they might as well have not mentioned them at all. I have never understood this reluctance to mention brand names. Gun writers name everything they use—make, model, caliber, who made the ammo, who made the scope sight, sometimes even who made the vehicle they haul the game home in. So why do angling writers steer clear of telling you what rods they use? (I use a Fenwick and a Heddon.)

Everyone won't need a vest with as large pockets as I do. My wet fly book is $7 \times 5 \times 2$ inches thick; my large dry-fly box is $7 \times 4 \times 2$ inches. These require large pockets, and very few commercial vests had such pockets until just recently.

The North Umpqua model vest has one drawback; the back pocket is closed at either end by snaps—the most stubborn, defiant snaps I have ever seen. You have to take the vest off to get anything out of the back pocket. I have suggested to Columbia Sportswear that they replace these snaps with Velcro material. Maybe they will.

A vest is the most personal piece of angling equipment one owns, and one should use great care in picking it out. If I were in the market for a new vest, I would put everything I normally carry on the stream in a box, take it down to the shop, and start trying on vests and filling the pockets. When I came to one that would hold everything I carry, and still have an extra pocket or two, I might consider buying it—if it were the right color.

Any *dark* color is suitable; brown or green, or a camouflage pattern would be fine. Light gray, tan, or, perish forbid, even white are what one mostly finds and they are worse than useless.

This past summer one of my clients showed up in a white vest. This was an expensive and well-made garment of a really good design. I suggested to him that it might, because of its color, cause problems. He said he didn't see that it mattered.

That afternoon we worked our way upstream to a deep curving glide that held several trout of eighteen to twenty inches. The water was silky smooth, and there were several good fish well up over the weed beds in feeding position, easily seen.

I took a position directly behind them, about twenty-five feet below the nearest fish. I told my client to take a position directly behind me, using my bulk as cover. (My bulk will furnish cover for about anybody.)

The client stood just at my back, peering over my right shoulder.

"Now," I said, "let's take a smooth, slow step sideways to the right, together."

We slid sideways a single step, in unison like a pair of robots. The fish maintained their positions.

"Now you take a single slow step to the right from behind me," I told him.

He did, and all the fish shot into hiding. In an instant not a trout was left in view.

When we returned that afternoon, the client got himself a new, dark green vest, relegating the white one to Atlantic salmon fishing.

Other than color, there are two mistakes anglers can make in selecting a vest. The common one is in not checking to see that one's gear will actually fit into the various pockets. Pockets are designed differently; a flat pocket on one vest may look as large as the bellows pocket on another, until you try to put something into it.

The other mistake, almost as common, is to buy the vest to fit. I've seen anglers, younger ones especially, buying vests and insisting on a nice snug fit. Then when they transferred their gear to it, they found that it lacked several inches of meeting in front. Buy your vest at least one size larger than you need. If you wear medium, buy a large, if you need a large, buy extralarge. Some friends have suggested to me that I buy a tent.

There are some vests on the market that contain flotation chambers and an inflating cartridge. For elderly persons, those who are unsteady in fast water, or who are merely uneasy in such water, these vests are literally lifesavers. They are great for fast-water float trips also. I recommend them highly for anyone who is not firm in the water for any reason. In the last two years, we have lost at least two anglers in this area, while they were wading. Safety first is more than a slogan; it should be a way of life.

The sixties were a bad decade for anglers trying to find new waders. Some companies that had made good waders went out of business. Other old and formerly good firms were trying to make cheaper waders with disastrous results. Assembly-line methods and poor quality control allowed many unserviceable waders on the market.

I was caught in the middle of this. My Hodgman Model 304 boot foot waders, purchased in 1948, gave up the ghost after seventeen years. The company had changed hands, and the new owners were not producing waders I considered usable. Many of them had the fabric separate from the rubber core after less than a season of use. I tried other brands, but none was satisfactory.

From about 1968 to 1972, nearly every experienced angler I met, several hundred of them, was bemoaning the wader situation. Poor quality control, regardless of brand, was the biggest complaint.

A good example of this occurred while I was instructing a fly-fishing school. I had taken the students to a deep, gliding run to teach them various nymph methods. It was spring, our snow-melt was at its peak, waters were icy.

One student, Larry Winn, standing waist-deep in the icy water, started complaining that the water was cold. He muttered and fussed until some of the other students started razzing him about being too tender to be a fly-fisherman.

Finally Larry announced he couldn't stand it and started wading out. As he reached shallow water he exclaimed, "My waders are full of water!"

I helped him to the bank. He was sloshing and floundering, almost helpless from the weight of water in his waders.

"My waders are full," he said, "listen to that," once on the bank. He extended his leg and kicked to make the imprisoned water slosh.

The entire boot foot on that leg came off and fell to the ground. It had never been vulcanized to the leg. The waders were brand new; this was the first time Larry had had them on. They were a very expensive wader by one of the major companies in the business.

I was fortunate enough, in 1972, to find a pair of older model Hodgman waders that had been in a warehouse for several years. They were new and my size, and I'm very happy to have found them. But as of late 1972, I have seen little if any improvement in the quality of waders. A pair of expensive hippers I purchased in early 1972 did not last two months before the feet split in several places.

What to do?

Frankly, I don't know. I've talked to several anglers who have purchased Canadian or English waders in the last few years. Quality control, even on famous brands, is poor, they say. Some have taken to having waders made up by a company that makes only waders, and to order. I've seen these. The quality is excellent, but the material used is a glossy light-gray synthetic. They reflect far too much light to suit me.

The only suggestion I can make at this time is to buy your waders from a dealer whom you know and trust, and to get from him an assurance of replacement or refund if they fail because of poor quality control. Last fall, one dealer I know showed me over a dozen pairs of waders he had sold, and which had been returned because seams had split, fabric separated, feet had split; all sorts of things were wrong with them. They were all expensive brands by well-known firms. This same dealer lists not a single wader in his latest catalog. The situation appears serious.

If waders have become shoddy, the same is not true in other items. Right now the angler has a far better selection of tackle and gear, and of better quality, than at any time in history. In the gadget field, this is especially true.

There is a thermometer, which, though not designed for anglers, is the neatest and best for angler purposes that I've ever seen. Last fall, Gene De Fouw, an automotive air-conditioning engineer, was fishing with me, and showed me this gadget. It consists of a stem five inches long topped with an easy-reading dial. It is unbreakable in normal use; the stem is stainless steel, the whole thing shock resistant. One can obtain them with dials of any one of six ranges. The one of most use to anglers reads from −40 to +120 degrees F. If you like Celsius, there's one with a range of −40 to +50 degrees, which is almost exactly the same range as the Fahrenheit one above. The instrument is the Taylor Hi-Visibility Bi-Therm Dial Pocket Thermometer. It comes in a little tube carrying case that can be clipped to the vest pocket, and costs about ten dollars.

I like several things about this little gadget; it is virtually unbreakable, and that I need. In the last three years I've broken four glass-tube angler's thermometers. It is instant reading—just stick the stem about four inches into the water, and zing! the little needle whips over to the temperature. It takes two seconds and the dial is very easy to read.

If you're concerned that the temperature just under the surface might not be the same as at the bottom, don't be. I've taken thousands of such readings and I've never found a trout stream where the bottom temperature was more than two degrees F. different from that a couple of inches under the surface. (I except the Firehole, which has hot springs in its bottom, and other streams which have cold springs in the bottom.)

One of the most important gadgets a fly-fisherman has is some sort of leader clip. I have used the standard Angler's Pal clip for over twenty-five years. Some anglers prefer scissors. They're fine until they get dull, which they will in a few years. Also, they get sprung and don't work.

I keep my scissors for trimming flies for all kinds of use and I want them sharp. They are in combination with a small knife, all stainless steel including the handles. Mine is two and one-quarter inches long, about as thick as a silver dollar. It is made in Switzerland by Hoffritz, and was given me by Dick Vance of Monsanto. A great many of my favorite gadgets have been given me by fellows I've fished with.

There are several of these little knife-scissors combinations; most shops carry one or another. I recommend them. They are handy and versatile little tools. In the interest of keeping my vest weight within limits, I like things small. My loaded vest weights seven pounds, and since there's nothing in it I can bear to be without, I try to keep down weight where I can.

A bodkin for cleaning out eyes of flies and picking out wind knots in leaders is invaluable. I make my own from old ball-point pens. Just nick around back of the ball point with a fine file and break off the point. Insert an ordinary sewing needle into the ink tube, eye first, until about a half inch of the point still protrudes, then crimp the tube onto the needle just firmly. Put a drop of epoxy cement on where the needle enters the tube, let dry, and that's it. I also make these using worn-out nylon point pens. Just cut the pen point off flush and force the needle back through the nylon material until only a half inch of needle protrudes. This gives one a protected

Steps in making a bodkin from a ball-point pen.

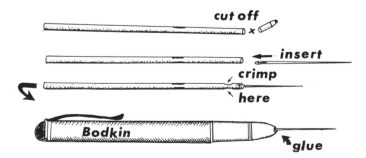

point when the cap is on. If your needle is reluctant to go through the nylon, heat it with a match. I like this bodkin better than the ball point because the cap protects the point while carrying it.

I make up about twenty of these each winter because I know my angling companions are going to relieve me of them during the season. I've never been able to get through a season with one left.

What other gadgets?

Well, even a casual leader maker needs a micrometer, and your dyed-in-the-wool dry-fly man needs a very good one. The best one I know of, and which I like better than any other, is the Starrett 1010, made by the Starrett Instrument Co., Norwich, Connecticut. It costs about forty dollars and is worth every penny of it.

Retrievers are very handy at keeping other gadgets out of the way. These are small, one-inch-across, one-quarter-inch-thick button-like devices that contain a coiled spring and a string or chain with a clip. They pin onto your vest and you hang things like leader clips, knife, scissors, and so forth on the clip. You can reach out about eighteen inches with your gadget and when you let go, the retainer will coil back out of sight in the button, taking the gadget with it.

I use a couple of them, some anglers use several, and Carl Richards and Doug Swisher keep the firms that make them in business. They must carry eight or ten each.

Another gadget that I make from ball-point pens finds great favor with fellows I fish with. This is a fly magnet. I remove the entire works from a ball-point pen, and insert a small rod magnet about one inch long and one-eighth inch in diameter. I leave about one-quarter inch of magnet protruding. I used to get the magnets at hobby shops, but so many of my pals wanted these gadgets that I ran out of rod magnets.

Now I use magnet-impregnated rubber, which I also get at hobby shops. It comes in strips, one-eighth inch thick. I cut a piece about an eighth-inch square and an inch long and insert it in the pen barrel leaving a quarter inch exposed. I shape the rubber so that it wedges.

It takes about two minutes to make one of these gadgets and they have no equal for plucking a single size twenty-two fly from a boxful. No muss, no fuss, no mashing of hackles, just touch the magnet to the fly you want and you've got it. Dry-fly fishermen dote on them, as do some steelheaders who find them far more dextrous than cold fingers.

A hook-sharpening file or stone is a must. If it is a stone, it must be knife-blade-shaped with a very thin edge to do a proper job.

A priest is necessary. I seldom kill a fish, except for research purposes, but when I do, I want it killed quickly and cleanly. I am

Converting a ball-point into a rod magnet.

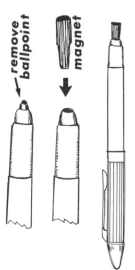

remove ballpoint

magnet

appalled at the number of intelligent anglers I see casually tossing live trout into their creels to suffocate. I'll bet they wouldn't do it if a fish could scream.

For releasing fish, one needs something to get the hook out with, without injuring the fish. I have used surgeon's needle forceps for this for years. Just as my old forceps gave up the ghost, Dr. Phillip Lightfoot of Healdsburg, California, gave me another pair. They're gorgeous, eight inches long, stainless steel with gold-plated grips. Long-nose pliers work nearly as well, but are much heavier and a bit harder to use.

For releasing fish with the least amount of trouble and with the most assurance that the released fish will live, you *must* have a net. I have always subscribed to the idea of getting a fish out of the water and into the net quickly, while he was still lively. I felt he had a better chance of surviving when released if handled this way.

Now I have found proof for my belief. Ruttner, in *Fundamentals of Limnology,* says that fish under exertion or stress accumulate lactic acid at up to nine times the rate that humans do under like conditions. When the acid in the system reaches certain levels, it becomes toxic and the fish is doomed. Thus, a fish played until "belly up" may appear to recover and swim off when released. But the acid accumulation is there, and about seven times out of ten your fish will die sometime later, within a day or so. Ted Trueblood may have had this in mind when he condemned use of ultralight tackle as being poor sportsmanship because, he said, a fish had to be played until "belly up" on such tackle, and usually such fish died soon after.

Your net should be large enough to handle a three-pound fish; smaller fish won't give you too much trouble, but I've seen several anglers lose large fish because their net was too small.

Notice the material the mesh is made of. There are some very well made but inexpensive nets on the market that have bags made of woven nylon monofilament. Avoid them. This material is so harsh and rough it literally scales any fish landed in it.

A landing net should float if dropped into the water. It should be durable, light, and easily carried. Other than that, the field is wide open.

After I have a fish in my net, I fold or wrap the mesh around it firmly. This quiets and immobilizes it so that you don't have to squeeze it until its eyes pop out in order to keep it still. I get the hook out as swiftly as I can, doing the least damage to the fish. For this reason the barbs on my hooks are always mashed down. They hold almost as well as a barbed hook and allow easy release of an unwanted fish.

A gadget I find very useful is a collapsible drinking cup. For some reason, I develop a raging thirst around running water, and I'm getting too old to be lying on my belly and draping my snout into the stream. There are several kinds of collapsible cups available. One is trade-marked Trik Kup and it folds flat, taking up no more room than a playing card. Others feature a telescoping action; I remember back in grade school we all had to have one of these to drink from.

I read a recent article by a fly-fishing optometrist in which he strongly advised anglers to wear sunglasses, even on cloudy days, because glare off the water can be injurious even on such days. The article offered several choices, each for a type or combination of conditions. Basically, the information was concerned with making sure the glasses were dark enough. Polaroid lenses were recommended *only* if the wearer understood that they were effective only as long as there was a right-angle relationship between the water surface and the lenses. Also, the user was to be made aware that people's eyes differed and that one type of lens would not be suitable for all people.

The above hit home with me. I wear prescription glasses and have had made, and been forced to reject, several pairs of prescription sunglasses. I now wear Polaroid clip-ons over my regular glasses. They are fine for me, but one should experiment until he finds sunglasses that do the job for him. If your eyes feel strained, or if they burn or smart at the end of a day's fishing, have your sunglasses checked.

Glasses of any kind offer an advantage one doesn't hear much about. They protect the eyes from flying hooks. I've known two persons who lost an eye because of a misdirected cast.

Eyes aren't the only part of the anatomy one may hook. In this country, where many large and weighted flies are used, doctors are kept busy extracting hooks from necks, cheeks, ears, arms, and you name it.

A hat of stiff material with a good-sized brim will help prevent one from being hooked in the face or neck. The only time I've ever hooked myself was one day when I forgot my hat.

Small head-hugging hats won't do the job. I was fishing the Widow's Pool one time with Grace, Bob Holmes, and Cliff Barnes. We started off using weighted nymphs. Bob, Grace, and I were wearing good, brimmed hats. Cliff had on the billed cap favored by deep-sea anglers.

After we had been there about an hour, I encountered Cliff

coming along the bank, wearing a sheepish grin and a number four
nymph in the lobe of his ear.

If you cast only small dry flies, you may go for years without
being hooked. But if you go in for sinking lines, weighted nymphs,
or big streamers, watch out. Your time will come. Wear a hat and
glasses is my advice. We're allotted only one pair of eyes per lifetime.

If you keep a fish now and then, some sort of creel is necessary.
Do *not* try to keep fish in the back pocket of your vest, even if it's
lined with plastic. Your body heat and lack of evaporation make a
pressure cooker out of that back pocket; your fish will spoil more
quickly than if left out in the hot sun.

I don't like wicker creels because of their weight and bulk.
Plastic creels do not allow evaporation. I use desert water bags for
creels and have since the late forties. Some of these have a long
metal clip on the top that can be slipped off easily, leaving the top
open full length. Others must be opened by slitting the threads that
hold them together. You may also have to modify the attachments
on your harness.

These bags are well worth the trouble. If dampened well before
the fish is put in, and dampened occasionally through the day, they
will keep fish as well as ice. Also, one can keep cold drinks in them
in cans or bottles. If I'm going for a day's riffle fishing or just moping
along the stream, I put a quart of beer in my creel.

The problem of putting a 5X tippet through the eye of a size
twenty-two hook is one that gets worse as one gets older. A magnifier
is needed by some even at a fairly early age. One generally has to
go outside angling shops to get a suitable one. Most available require
they be hand held, and along with the hook and tippet, one feels
as though he needs three hands.

I have a catalog which lists an incredible number of types of
magnifying lenses. Several come in a range of power from 2X to 5X,
there are others which have powers of 3X, 6X, and 9X, others are
stronger. Some of these lenses have headbands, some fasten to regular glasses, some screw into the eye (jeweler's loupes), some are
hand held, others are on stands. There is one for just about every
purpose and they are quite reasonably priced.

You can obtain one of these catalogs free just by writing to
Edmund Scientific Company, Barrington, N.J., 08007, and asking
for their catalog number 731 for 1973. This catalog contains a lot
of other goodies, including the magnetized rubber strips I use to
make fly magnets.

Jim Wilkie put me onto this when he gave me a little folding 9X Linen Tester this company sells. It's a great little mini-microscope for studying insects, leader knots, hook points, and the like.

I think it should be obvious that I cop many of my good ideas from brother anglers. I'm always alert for a better way or a gadget that makes things easier, as well as a better fishing method. One of the major joys of angling is that most of us are delighted to share ideas, gimmicks, gadgets, even flies. It is one of the things that makes angling so great.

I'd like to return for a minute to leaders, because there is something I passed over all too lightly—leader stiffness. Over the years I've become convinced that leader visibility has little to do with whether a fish will take or refuse a fly. I believe that when a fish refuses a fly on 3X but takes the same fly on 5X, it is the greater flexibility of the finer tippet that made the difference.

I've experimented along this line and am convinced that stiffer leaders impart an unnatural motion to the fly that causes a fish to refuse it.

I cannot remember an unattached dry fly being refused by a fish, and I've sacrificed several dozen to this experiment. Also, I've had cases of fish refusing my fly on 5X tippets only to take the same fly confidently when I replaced the monofilament with eighteen inches of size A white nylon thread.

If you doubt this, try it yourself. The A thread is about as strong as 5X monofilament, but is completely limp. Try it on rising fish that have refused your fly on monofilament. You can't cast many times with the thread tippet or it will untwist but if you put it over a rising fish in the first half dozen casts, I think you'll get him, because your fly will come over him with no false motion and I believe that this is far more important than what fly one uses.

PART THREE

AESTHETICS AND CONSERVATION

"Fly fishing is not all of a piece; it is an extremely diverse affair, with as many aspects as there are French political parties. Its major appeal lies in the fact that one can never learn all there is to know about it..."

11

Developing a Philosophy

NO one is born with a philosophy about anything, and you certainly don't pull one out of the air full blown. I've read some of the great philosophers and the evident thing is that even when their philosophy itself appears to be simple, the reasoning behind it never is, and there is always evidence of growing and changing. A friend has suggested that philosophy is merely a viewpoint and that a man's viewpoint keeps changing as his position in life keeps changing.

This I think, is oversimplification, for it suggests, among other things, that as a thinking man grows older, he also grows wiser, and we all know that this is not always the case.

Arnold Gingrich, in *The Well-Tempered Angler,* says that fly-fishing has always lacked a rationale. If one regards fly-fishing as all of a piece, I suppose that it has. But fly-fishing is not all of a piece; it is an extremely diverse affair, with as many aspects as there are French political parties. Its major appeal lies in the fact that one can never learn all there is to know about it, and even in the mere act of fishing each cast of the fly is subtly different from the one just before or after.

I like to compare the lure of fly-fishing with that of golf. In this game there are never two successive shots alike, no matter how many rounds one plays. Teeing off on hole number one today may appear to present the same shot as teeing off on the same hole yesterday, but the next shot will be somehow different from any you've ever hit before.

There is a story that Byron Nelson retired from golf because he grew tired of hitting his shots out of his own divots of the round before. When Byron was told this, he snorted. On the best round he ever played, he said, he had never hit two successive great shots. He had given up competitive golf because it was becoming increasingly difficult to command the concentration needed to play championship golf. But, he emphasized, he still enjoyed the game and he never stopped thinking about how to improve it.

This, on the surface, appears to be the philosophy of "enjoyment through excellence," and there are many who seem to have this as their philosophy.

Some, in fact, appear to make excelling at a certain phase of fly-fishing their whole reason for fly-fishing. There is nothing wrong with this as long as it does not become the ruling passion of life and lead one to shun or look down on others who do not share this passion. It can, however, have a terribly limiting effect on the person who holds such a philosophy.

I must tell you about a bear-hunting trip I took once, because it sheds some light on the above philosophy. It may also tell you something about my own philosophy.

It was the spring of 1951. I was living in Fairbanks, Alaska, and two of my buddies, Gene Gowing and Ray Stephens, talked me into a hunt. There were probably, at that time, more bears around Fairbanks than there were people. Did we just go to the outskirts of town, then?

The place we selected for our hunt was near Tok Junction, two hundred miles down the Alcan Highway, not far from the Canadian border. This was done on the advice of George Tweedy, another pal, who had hunted there and had great success.

"When you get to Tok," George said as we were departing in Steve's jeep, "go in to see Walt Sens, the highway patrolman there. He knows every animal in the area by its first name."

So, when we got to Tok, we turned down the Slana cutoff a few miles to Walt's house.

"I know just the place," said Walt when we told him what we were after. "There's an old sawmill site down the road a piece that will be great for camping. Flat ground, tons of slabs for firewood, and a little spring-fed creek for water."

He led us down to this place in his patrol cruiser. It was the best camping spot I've ever seen, green, flat grassy banks along a clear icy stream five feet wide, and a pile of dried slabs as big as the Pentagon. Someone had even hung a pole between two trees for hanging game.

As we were unloading our gear Walt spied my fly rod and vest, which I took everywhere, even on my honeymoon.

"Are you a fly-fisherman?" he asked, and upon being assured I was, he told me his wife had given him an outfit for his birthday and he didn't know how to use it. "Will you show me how to fly-fish?" he asked.

"Here?" I said in unbelief, indicating the tiny stream.

"Not here!" said Walt scornfully. "I know a great place just a little ways off."

The "little ways off" turned out to be ninety miles over a gravel road and we made it in a little over an hour in Walt's patrol cruiser.

The stream was very winding and it wound back and forth over the Alaskan-Canadian border. Because the border was ill defined here, Walt said, both governments honored each other's fishing licenses.

I took Walt upstream of the little wooden bridge where the road crossed, and got him started. In a half hour he was doing fine, so I went down about a half mile below the bridge and started fishing back.

Fishermen began to show up as if by magic. Where they came from was a puzzle, for the nearest village was fifty miles away. But you know fishermen. By six in the evening, when we'd been there about two hours, at least a dozen other fly fishermen had arrived.

I hadn't been able to raise a fish—on dries, wets, nymphs, or anything—very unusual for Alaskan waters. Neither had anyone else.

I'd worked my way back to a long riffle leading from the deep pool under the little bridge. I was fishing a number fourteen Brown Spider, the last untried fly I had left. But it wasn't producing.

"Guess I'll go see if Walt's done anything," I thought, and started walking upstream, reeling in. The Spider was skipping merrily on the broken surface of the riffle, when, bang! a two-pounder smashed it and was duly landed.

"Aha! They've just started hitting," I thought. Two dozen casts later I was sure I had caught a lone maverick and once more started off upstream to see Walt, reeling as I went. Bang! Another two-pounder.

This time I got the message. The fish wanted the fly skipping on the water, and no other way. After five fish, I went to give Walt the good news and had the pleasure of watching him raise and land his first fish ever on the fly.

When I got back, there was an Englishman standing on the bridge, drifting a dry fly over the head of the pool.

This man was the most beautiful caster I have ever seen, then or since. The rod appeared to glide rather than whip through the air. The line unrolled smooth and straight as a cable. At the last split second, a barely perceptible checking of the tip caused the fly to curve around, right or left, and alight on the water with just the right amount of slack for an instant, drag-free float.

I watched this fellow, fascinated, for a half hour, but he never raised a fish.

Finally, I said to him, "You have to cast downstream and bring the fly back skipping on the water to have any success."

He looked at me aghast.

"Cast downstream!" he said in something like horror.

"What's wrong with that?" I said in surprise.

He lifted his chin. "It isn't sporting."

"It's the only way they'll take the fly," I persisted.

He lifted his chin even higher. "You might as well *spear* them," he said haughtily.

Walt and I left about nine in the evening. Walt had taken sixteen fish, all two pounds and over, on our despised method. Our English fine-casting friend had never a rise.

Walt dropped me off where the dirt road to the sawmill site turned off and I ambled the fifty yards to our camp, carrying four fish for our supper. It was about 10:30 P.M. and was dusky, as dark as it would get until September.

As I approached the campsite, I could see the glow from the coals of the campfire, and off to the right, where the pole was, two long, dark shapes hung.

"Ha!" I thought, "those two yo-yos have hung up a couple of sleeping bags to make me think they've killed something while I've been off fishing."

But I was wrong. My two friends had each killed a bear while I was gone. The bears had walked right into the camp while Gene and Steve were drinking coffee and telling lies. Two shots, bang-bang, and it was all over. We went back to Fairbanks early next day.

Since then I've met many fishermen whose whole philosophy seemed to be included in excelling at one phase of fishing. But I've only met one other who took as narrow a view as that Englishman did. This fellow, too, was a Britisher and he took me to task for calling a streamer a fly. "If you're going to use those to fly-fish," he said disapprovingly, "you might as well stoop to snagging them."

Arnold Gingrich says that a fisherman's philosophy changes in proportion to his success, a rather cynical view, but there is some evidence that there are many who agree. It was Edward Hewitt, I think, who said we all start out as fish hogs at heart. Later on, he said, we change from wanting to catch any fish, to wanting to catch all fish, and finally, to wanting to catch the biggest fish.

There are a great many anglers who seem to play the numbers game. At the end of the day, these men's remarks all have a monotonous sameness: "I took forty trout today on small dry flies." "Me and Bill landed over sixty today." "We killed 'em on the Big Hole today; must have taken seventy between us."

The thought of fishing for mere numbers depresses me, and did long before I ever got to where I could fish every day if I wanted to. I find that, in anglers I have known, this pursuit of numbers has a terribly limiting effect on the angler's growth. In the past few years I have seen this disease overtake one of the most promising young anglers and reduce him to a working fisherman who goes out early and stays late merely to cram more fish-catching into his day.

There is much more to fly-fishing than the ability to cast well, or to catch large numbers of trout. While there is far more to be learned than can ever be learned in one lifetime, one can definitely increase his pleasure by increasing his knowledge. I like to know *why* I've caught a fish, and I like to know *why not* when I don't catch one.

When I go fishing and fail to catch fish, I feel I've failed in a task I've set for myself. If I know why I failed (and I usually do) then I am not depressed by my failure. My failures are nearly always attributable to human weakness—I didn't concentrate, I was lazy (most common), I failed to take note of some significant condition, and so forth. The trout are always there. I know where they are, and what they feed on. With that much knowledge, I should be able to catch fish anytime. But I don't. I think if I did I'd give up fishing.

A friend of mine says that what I call fishermen's philosophies are merely their attitudes. Attitude is merely the outward manifestation of one's philosophy: you are what you think. Thus everyone has a philosophy, whether he realizes it or not.

Oddly enough, America is where the philosophy of returning fish so that someone else may catch them got its start. Considering that other peoples often regard us as greedy and opportunistic, it is strange that this is the only country where this practice is widespread, and it is reflected in our fishing language. We speak of "taking" a trout; in all other trout-fishing nations the term "kill" is used.

As for me, I am devoted to fly-fishing for trout as more than a recreation. When I am down or depressed, or become cynical, a few hours on the stream gives me back my belief in things. It picks me up and clears my thinking. It restores my soul. For these reasons, when I depart the stream forever, I'd like to leave behind a little more knowledge and more and larger trout for others to fish for. That's why this book is more about the trout and the stream than it is about fishing.

12

Conservation and Fly-Fishing

THERE has been a concerted effort in the past decade to promote fly-fishing as a conservation measure, both by individual angling writers and by fly-fishing groups. I applaud the thought but deplore the lack of research behind the movement. The fact is, it ain't necessarily so.

This past year, at a meeting of the Montana Fish and Game Commission, a group asked that a certain stream be set aside for fly-fishing only, since there was strong evidence that heavy angling pressure was destroying the quality of the stream.

I was there representing my fly-fishing club on another matter. From past appearances, the chairman knew me and that I represented a fly-fishing group, and he apparently respected the approach we had used, for he asked my opinion of the proposal *as a conservation measure*.

"It has always been our belief," I said, "that conservation lies in the heart of the fisherman and not in the method he uses. Restricting this stream to fly-fishing *would* restore the fishing, by limiting the number of fishermen but not necessarily because fly-fishermen are more conservation-minded."

Some members of my club took issue with me privately on this   179 matter but none had done any research on it and I was able to convince them that fly-fishing as a method was not necessarily the conservation tool they thought it. Let me quote from a Bureau of Sport Fisheries and Wildlife study.

"In 1970 . . . in an effort to reduce the harvest, improve the catch rate and encourage catch and release fishing . . . all bait fishing was banned . . . a comparison of catch rates of anglers using flies and lures is shown. The catch rate on flies was over *six times greater* than that recorded for lures. . . . Since the mortality for released cutthroat trout was 4.0 percent on flies and 4.1 percent on lures . . . it can be shown that most of the fishing mortality . . . in 1970 was inflicted by fly-fishermen. . . . Why, then should lures be prohibited as a means of taking stream trout? It may be self-defeating to replace lures with *far more effective flies* as a means of reducing mortalities from 'catch and release' fishing." (The italics are mine.)

The report also stated that season-long observation indicated that hooking and handling mortalities of released trout could be minimized by use of a landing net and long-nosed pliers.

The 4.1 percent mortality rate for fish caught on lures and released is the lowest I have any record of. The next lowest was a 7.8 percent rate on single-hooked lures. In general, such mortality rates as I have knowledge of indicate that lures with one or more treble hooks produce a mortality rate of about 18 percent, and that the rate on fish taken on bait varied from a low of 48 percent where fish averaged better than twelve inches, to a high of 79 percent where the trout averaged under eight inches. However, if the catch rate on flies is six times greater, the number of released fish dying would definitely be far greater than the number caught on lures and released.

The study also showed that the fly-fishermen not only released more fish than lure fishermen, but kept more also, since more of them caught fish to keep, if for no other reason. In any event, the mortality rate from all causes, kept and released, was much greater for flies than it was for lures.

The entire study covered a period of nine years, on several lakes and rivers in Yellowstone Park. Its purpose was to find the causes of reduced angling quality and to institute measures to restore it. The one recurring fact throughout the report was that flies were more effective in taking fish *in all fishing waters surveyed* than any other method, and that probably the only method to restore angling quality was to limit severely the size and numbers of fish allowed to be kept. In effect, fly-fishermen would have to be restrained *as a conservation measure*.

If the above reflects somewhat badly on fly-fishermen, the report contained some encouraging news about them. When limits were sharply reduced, and fish had to be fourteen inches (or larger on some streams) to be keepers, the evidence was overwhelming that fly-fishermen not only accepted the restrictions but approved them. This is further evidence that conservation is not in the method but in the heart of the angler.

Fly-fishing *can* be a method of conserving and protecting our trout fishing but it must be pointed out in no uncertain terms that fly-fishermen are not automatically conservationists.

I have already mentioned that ultralight tackle causes excessive mortality in released fish because the prolonged playing of the fish induces acid toxicity that ultimately kills the released fish. But even strong tackle advocates kill a lot of fish that they intend to release unharmed simply because they give no thought to release procedures.

I've mentioned seeing well-informed, intelligent anglers tossing live trout into their creels to suffocate, instead of cleanly killing them. I've seen these same people kill trout they intended to release, by squeezing them until air bladders ruptured, snatching hooks out and bringing parts of tongue, throat, or gills with them, and by excessive and casually brutal handling of fish. As I said earlier, if fish could scream, I'll bet anglers wouldn't treat them like that.

There are several things a fly-fisherman can do to avoid wasting his fishing resources, and it all starts with not wasting trout.

Don't fish where greedy small trout come to your fly in numbers.

Mash down the barbs of your hooks; they'll hold almost as well and make releasing fish much easier.

If a fish takes the fly deep, snip off the leader tip and release him; the fly will soon dissolve in the fish's acid system.

Always use a net; you can handle the fish much better and with less chance of squeezing him to death while removing the hook.

Don't sacrifice trout on the altar of false sportsmanship; use leaders strong enough so that the trout can be brought to net while still lively. Handle the trout gently while he is in the net, but get him out of, and back into, the water as fast as possible. A dead trout is of absolutely no use to anyone unless it is meant to be eaten, and frankly, I find a trout on a plate very ordinary fare; in the stream, he is a joy forever. To paraphrase Gervase Markham: that which is worth millions to my contentment can be purchased by another for a few cents in a market.

Since I release over 99 percent of the trout I catch, and I fish the same streams over and over, I have refined my catch-and-release procedures to the point that I feel I am never wasting a fish. I want the fish I release to be there to catch another day since I think, with Lee Wulff, that a trout is far too valuable to be caught only once.

First, I do not fish for, nor seldom catch, fish under fourteen inches. If I lived where this was unreasonably large, I would still set a lower limit of not less than ten inches. I'd simply spend more of my time locating larger fish.

Second, I use good-size hooks and the strongest possible leaders. Yes, I horse them in, because I regard playing a fish as a cat-and-mouse game, and because I wish to release a live trout and one which will continue to live. Along this line, I note that Charles Ritz, who does not release many trout, really horses them in. He gives a two-pound trout, he says, no more than seven seconds from strike to net. That's *really* horsing them in.

Ritz gets them in fast because he wants not to lose the fish; I do so because I want to save them. It's not the same thing.

I use a net for *all* trout—a large, deep net that will easily hold a five-pounder. I get the fish in the net and quickly fold the net around him lengthways. This restricts his bending, and without bending he cannot flounce.

Once I've wound the fish firmly in the net, I snap my needle forceps into the bend of the hook and a little backward twitch removes the hook. I then put the net and fish into the water, unroll the net and allow the fish to swim out. A fish so handled will live. I'm convinced of it.

One thing that really burns me is to see a photograph of a famous angler holding up a large trout by the gills, then to read in the text that "all fish were released." If this is true, that angler has released a dead fish.

I was discussing this one time with Dr. Clint Pace, who demurred. "I don't see that it's all that deadly," he said.

"How would you feel about a man's chances of living if someone came along, thrust their hand into his lungs, took a good grip, held him up at arm's length and then tossed him back onto the floor?" I asked.

The trouble seems to be that most people don't think of it at all. Where one's happiness or pleasure are deeply interconnected with the existence of another creature, one's greatest concern in the relationship should be for the welfare of the other creature. Any other attitude seems either selfish or illogical.

So, if you are a fly-fisherman and you wish to conserve trout and trout fishing, it would be wise to start with the welfare of the trout, and this means giving considerable thought to how you handle him, in and out of the water.

13

Stocked and Wild Trout

FOR some years I have been doing research on trout hatchery management, or, as some might say, the lack of it. In 1938, in *Trout Streams,* Paul Needham said that trout-hatchery managers seemed to have for their slogan, "millions for hatching but not one cent for investigation." Other prominent biologists were equally disturbed by the liberating of millions of catchable (seven inches and up) trout in scores of streams, with no effort made to determine if the program was good, bad, or indifferent.

Fishermen seemed to accept the catchable program as the only one that would maintain a decent trout fishery, but some researchers felt that the fisherman was a victim of propaganda. One biologist, speaking of this, said that there were many ways of managing a trout stream but when hatchery catchables were stocked, you weren't managing the stream, you were managing the fisherman.

The figures I have been able to compile indicate that in the last thirty years, since 1940, eighteen states have spent 270 million dollars on all phases of trout-hatchery programs. Less than 2 percent of this was spent on direct research.

It is the considered opinion of every Fish and Wildlife department contacted that stocking of trout in streams has been a complete failure as far as improving fishing is concerned. Most departments would concede any form of success only to those streams which were managed almost as an extension of the hatchery pond, a strictly put-in, take-out program, with the only aim being to have as many of the stocked trout as possible caught out as soon as possible. And the only reason these were considered at all successful was the fact that it was discovered that—in streams—there is literally no survival of, and no reproduction by, stocked trout. The consensus is that—no matter how you slice it, no matter how good a natural stream may be involved—stocking trout in streams is now and always is going to be a put-and-take affair.

Late studies indicate also that stocking trout in large numbers in a good natural-producing trout stream is harmful to the wild trout therein, and if continued long enough will absolutely ruin the stream as far as natural production of trout is concerned.

Even short-term stocking can be harmful if not carefully done. There is abundant evidence that repeated dumping of 1,500 to 3,000 catchable trout in the same short stretch of stream will create a biological desert therein in as little as three years.

Stocking in lakes, in terms of survival past one winter, has been far more successful, and there is strong evidence that there is less harm to the wild populations than there is in streams. The carry-over of stocked trout in some lakes ranges as high as 30 percent past the first winter and, in rare cases, as high as 7 percent for three winters. This compares very favorably with wild trout carry-over, especially when five years is considered the normal life span for the average wild trout.

Best results in lake stocking are obtained by using brood trout not over three generations removed from the wild fish, and with each succeeding generation, the survival rate drops. There is also some evidence that there will be no significant spawning runs of stocked trout whose parents were more than two generations removed from the wild fish. Most hatchery brood stocks are seven to fifteen generations removed from wild stock.

Late research indicates that most streams will carry an excellent head of wild fish under conditions where no angling is permitted. This would seem to be a silly situation, like angling with no hook, but as a research measure it has contributed much knowledge to stream management. One result is that when stocks in such streams were surveyed by electric shocking, then opened to controlled and limited angling, then resurveyed, it was found that the fish remaining in the stream, plus the numbers caught by the anglers, never totaled more than 78 percent of the original stock.

At first researchers thought that other predators were accounting for the losses, but this was soon ruled out, such predators taking an average toll of 3 percent only. Were the trout cannibalizing the missing 19 percent? Well, they hadn't when the stream was closed to angling. So, what was happening to them?

The answers are not all in yet but there is good reason to believe that the missing trout are migrating, going downstream to deeper holes and better cover. In some cases marked fish have traveled as far as thirty miles downstream, and where angling pressure is very heavy, some biologists believe that trout, especially larger trout, will migrate downstream until they escape such pressure, or until they reach a lake.

This brings us to the inescapable conclusion that the number of anglers on a stream affects the habits of the trout to a marked degree. Thus, it should be evident that trout might not be found in the same type holds and lies on a lightly fished stream as they would on a heavily fished stream. On the latter stream there would have to be more cover and deeper water or the trout will migrate to where such conditions exist.

Thus, it seems apparent that on a heavily fished stream the number of fish present is governed by available cover and not by food supply, though food supply governs the size of the fish. Even so, the larger fish will be found in the better lies.

Birge and Juday, doing lake and stream research in Wisconsin many years ago, concluded that trout streams with the best possible food supplies could support 240 pounds of trout to the acre of stream bottom. They found no stream that approached this maximum. Their conclusion: not enough cover. These surveys were made over forty years ago, yet only now are biologists for state Fish and Wildlife departments beginning to note this important fact.

One of the reasons is that there has been, in the past, little coordination among the states in trout-hatchery operation and research. Each state does its own thing.

Research in New Hampshire done fairly recently—in fact, still being done—indicated that where adequate food supplies existed, a stream could support a one-pound trout for every 200 square feet of stream bottom where there was sufficient cover properly spaced. This translates to about 215 pounds of fish per acre of bottom, very close to the Birge and Juday maximum.

The research done here also showed that even very good trout streams could carry up to five times more fish per mile than they were carrying if they were improved by adding rocks, drifts, logwood, other forms of cover, and planting shrubs close to bank edges.

They found that the cost of such improvements ran from a low of $1,000 to a high of $5,000 per mile, depending on the original condition of the stream and the availability of materials. Based on an average of $2,700 per mile, as a guess, the 270 million dollars spent on hatchery programs in the last thirty years could have improved 100,000 miles of trout stream *permanently,* made them more attractive to man and fish, and not required constant redoing. I would hazard a guess that there are not 100,000 miles of trout streams in the continental forty-eight states.

Let me digress to talk about something I learned while collecting some of the above information.

I was attempting to find out the effect of float fishing on the possible downstream migration of trout or other stream fish. I wrote to the Missouri Conservation Department about the matter because I was raised on Current River in the Missouri Ozarks, and this is probably the oldest float-fishing stream in the nation.

The biologist who answered my letter was an ardent float fisherman, and he was not much impressed by what he called my attempt to rule float fishers off the water. But the statistics he furnished contained some surprising information, information even my biologist friend was apparently unaware of.

This thirty-year-study indicated a steadily rising angling pressure, something we are all familiar with. But the fish-per-hour catch rates indicated that a stream can produce steady and consistent per hour catch rates with rising angling pressure, until the saturation point is reached. Then there is a swift and dramatic decline.

This point was reached on Current River in 1959. In 1960 the catch rate was 59 percent of the twenty-year average. It further declined in 1961, '62, '63, and '64 in spite of massive restocking and sharply declining angling pressure. The situation stabilized in 1965 and remained so through 1969, even though restocking was sharply curtailed and there was a fairly stable angling pressure. The decline in angling pressure to about one-third the 1959 rate was not due to regulations but to the fact the stream was not as good fishing. The bulk of the fishermen came from the large cities—St. Louis, Kansas City, Columbia, and Jefferson City—and apparently would not make the trip for about one-quarter of the fish they had been catching ten years earlier.

The point here is that the amount of restocking had no effect on the per hour catch rates. Five times as many fish were stocked in the 1961–65 period as were stocked in the 1966–69 years. But the catch rate fell in the former years, rose slightly, and stabilized in the latter.

This is further evidence that stocking does not really improve fishing. Though the fish stocked here were smallmouth bass, not trout, I believe exactly the same thing would occur on a trout stream, given the same set of conditions.

Based on the information I have just presented, I firmly believe that improvement or maintenance of quality trout fishing will come through stream improvement to provide better cover, more holds and lies, and not through any restocking process, no matter how well financed and intelligently applied.

I do not believe restocking can be completely eliminated, however. There are millions of casual fishermen, who, when they visit the West, want to go trout fishing and want to catch trout. By and large, these fishermen will take neither the time nor make the effort to learn how to fish for wild trout. They already know, they will tell you. They've read a book.

For economic and political reasons, these people will be catered to. Since this is inevitable, I would suggest that we try to prevail upon the Fish and Wildlife people to cater to them in a manner that will make it easy for them to catch trout without too much effort.

Have the Fish and Wildlife stock lakes and only those streams that are deficient in food supplies and that lack qualities for supporting wild trout populations. Since stream-stocked trout are not going to survive the winter anyway, food supply is of no importance. Besides, being hungry should make them easy to catch.

Let us publicize to the maximum that certain streams are stocked, and make it easy for the casual fishing visitor to find these streams. Also, we should emphasize strongly that other streams contain only wild trout populations and therefore will be more difficult to take fish from. Eventually, I think, the casual fisherman will cease to fish wild trout streams in any numbers if he is provided with stocked streams that are easy to get to and easier to fish.

So, let us bend our efforts to get the Fish and Wildlife departments to refrain from stocking streams that are capable of supporting good wild trout populations, in the East and Midwest, as well as the West. Let them, rather, spend their time and money on improving the holding areas of these streams, providing more good holds and lies, giving the trout more protection, and halting his downstream migration.

Trout hatcheries will always be necessary as long as nonfishermen wish to catch trout; let us give them what they want and work like hell to try to get us what we want.

I was not the only person in this area, as I was soon to find out, who was wondering if the hatchery catchable program was causing harm to our wild trout populations.

In the 1960s Dick McGuire, a fishing guide and member of the

Southwestern Montana Fly Fishers, had begun to notice significant differences in the fishing in two identical appearing sections of the Madison River. Preliminary investigation could turn up only one thing that affected one section and did not affect the other. The section that had significantly poorer fishing had been stocked every season with large numbers of hatchery catchables; the other section had not been stocked for eight or ten years.

Dick made this information known to the Fish and Game fisheries biologist for the region, through our club. We were in luck. This biologist had just completed electrofishing studies on the river in that area for the purpose of determining mortality rates and age-group structures. The study showed that the two sections Dick had investigated had shown vast differences in mortality rates and in age-group structures, and that the section that had been stocked with catchables was poorer in both respects.

We took our information to the Fish and Game Commission and asked for a study to determine if stocking of hatchery catchables had a detrimental effect on a wild trout population. The study was granted for a two-year period, with another two-year study to follow if the first study produced significant results.

The first two-year study produced these results:

When catchables of seven to twelve inches were planted in wild trout streams, 70 percent died within four weeks, and 95 percent died within three months, in most streams. In the very best of circumstances only 15 to 40 percent of the planted fish were caught, making the cost of each fish taken by an angler about three dollars.

Study of several sections of the Madison River proved beyond any doubt that the best growth, highest population, and largest fish were in those sections of the river where no hatchery trout had been planted. As a comparison, the department planted one section of a stream, which had not been stocked since 1963, and checked it against a similar section of the stream in which planting was stopped. Population in the planted section decreased by almost half in two years; in the section in which planting was stopped, the population nearly tripled. In a control section, populations remained unchanged.

Further aspects of the study showed that almost twice as many fish over seventeen inches were found in *un*planted sections of the river compared to sections where planting had been done regularly.

The conclusion reached was that stocking of hatchery catchables in a stream containing a good wild trout population caused excessive mortality among the wild trout because more trout were in an area than there were shelters or barriers from the current. Wild trout, forced from their shelters by the sheer weight of numbers, were exposed constantly to the current force, and either migrated downstream, were taken by predators, or died from exhaustion. The latter two factors accounted for the largest percentage of lost wild trout.

The study is continuing in Montana, on other streams to make certain there wasn't some specific unknown condition in the first study area that might have caused the wild trout mortality. As the chairman of the Commission said, if we are going to scrap a program of nearly fifty years, we'd better be certain of what we are doing.

Montana is not the only state moving in the direction of not stocking hatchery catchables in streams containing a good wild trout population. In 1972, California began a program of not stocking on certain specified "wild trout" streams. It is too early to tell what the effects of the new program will be, but California is committed to a lengthy period of study of the matter.

The objection most often raised to stopping stocking is that there aren't enough wild trout to support a decent fishery for the number of anglers. If nothing else is done to alter the situation, then the objection might be valid. But where other things are done, there is proof that good streams *can* sustain a wild trout fishery to provide good to excellent fishing.

Stocking of hatchery trout in Yellowstone Park streams and lakes was stopped in 1958. Angling pressure steadily increased. In 1968, as a result of a study begun in 1962, it was noted that the quality of fishing had drastically declined. New regulations, based on the study, were instituted.

The new regulations banned bait fishing, to encourage anglers to release the major portion of their catch. Limits were reduced to "no kill" for grayling, "no kill" in the Yellowstone drainage, and to two fish, 16 inches or over in the Firehole and Madison rivers. Have the new regulations worked to restore a quality fishery?

Not yet, says a nine-year report on the matter, but there is evidence that the fishing *is* coming back, that more and larger fish are available to the fisherman.

The regulations did reduce the angling pressure by eliminating meat fishermen, on the one hand, and casual fishermen—those without the necessary skill to catch larger fish—on the other. However, the limits are still sufficiently large to allow anyone to catch a fish dinner any time he wants one. Actually, one of the reasons limits were reduced was because rangers were finding from 7,500 to 10,000 trout per month in garbage cans. Obviously, the larger limits were not needed.

I have fished Yellowstone Park waters since 1947, when the fishing was unbelievably good. I noted the decline in fishing and the increase in angling pressure, and made the obvious conclusion.

Since the new regulations went into effect, I have observed

conditions very closely. I have noted *no* decline in angling pressure on the Yellowstone River. Anglers number 4,500 per mile on open water from Fishing Bridge to Upper Falls during the season. The fishing was very much average before the new regulations went into effect in 1970, and the fish a good angler caught were mostly ten to thirteen inches.

Last year the Yellowstone was nearly as good fishing as it was in the late forties. Fish from twelve to fifteen inches ranged the stream in unbelievable numbers, and in a day's fishing, a few of sixteen and seventeen inches came to net. There has been no change in the river ecosystem, there have been no climate changes from normal. One therefore has to assume that the new size and numbers limits have done the job that they were intended to do.

What about the Firehole and Madison rivers? Here, though the increase in size and numbers has not been so dramatic, it has occurred. However, angling pressure has sharply declined, and thus one cannot say whether the new regulations or the decline in pressure is responsible for the increase in size and numbers of trout.

The angling pressure decline on these two streams commenced, not with the appearance of the new regulations, but with the arrival of Jack Anderson as Park Superintendent in 1968.

These two streams had been restricted to fly-fishing since about 1960, but the regulation had never been enforced. When I mentioned this to Jack at the Federation of Fly Fishermen Conclave in Jackson Hole in 1968, he had just been appointed to his new post in Yellowstone. He assured me that *he* would see that the regulations were enforced. He has done so, and this, more than any other reason, has caused angling pressure on the Firehole and Madison to decline.

The picture on the wild trout streams of Yellowstone, if not conclusive yet, is vastly encouraging. Coupled with the fact that stocking hatchery catchables has been uneconomical, has failed to improve fishing, and is now being shown to be detrimental to wild trout populations, I think we can look forward to the day when our good trout streams will contain only wild trout. And with logical limits and stream improvements, I think we shall have much better fishing, and that it will remain so in spite of increased angling pressure.

As for me, I feel certain that in five years the fishing in the Madison and Firehole in Yellowstone Park will be back where it was twenty-five years ago, and that these streams will be living proof that we *can* turn back the clock.

14

Stream Management and Improvement

THE future of trout fishing lies in managing and improving the streams we have, for the benefit of the trout, and in intelligent regulation pertaining to limits and seasons.

This is the consensus of most biologists who are active in the field of trout management. Most have long ago given up on planting and stocking as methods to improve fishing; these programs hang on because trout fishermen themselves have long pushed for them, and even today still urge their Fish and Game departments to "plant more trout," in the feeble hope that streams stuffed with trout will somehow make successful fishermen of them.

Some stream management in the past, though done on the best available advice and with the most sincere intentions, has proved harmful. I do not mean the misbegotten practice of dumping thousands of fry or hundreds of catchables in the same small area, year after year, but actual stream alterations that turned out to do more harm than good.

Ray J. White, in *Guidelines for Management of Trout Stream Habitat in Wisconsin,* says that much of the work done on Wisconsin streams in the 1930s was found to be ineffective—and some of it actually damaging. Since then, stream management has slowly taken the course of "doing what comes naturally"—that is, instead of building foreign devices in a stream, more of the natural features are enhanced, with the effort being aimed at helping the stream help itself.

Wisconsin has been in the stream-habitat-improvement business for forty years. As far as I know, it has done more of this kind of work than all other states together. I exclude work done by some states to make fishing easier, which is contrary to the real purpose of habitat management.

The entire stream must be studied before any logical approach to improvement can begin. Deepening and adding more rock shelters and barriers in a long riffle may look like a great way to improve a stream, until you discover that you've knocked out the only good spawning riffle for miles.

Trout-stream managers in the past have seemed to regard the "pool-riffle ratio" theory advanced by Paul Needham as being applicable to all trout streams; but in fact, there are scores of trout streams that do not have or need pools, and which have stretches of good trout-holding areas that are not riffles, either.

Very few stream managers have given any thought to current barriers or shelters in streams, yet all three studies on the matter that I have read rate this as the very best way to provide more and larger trout in any stream.

The reasons in all three studies are the same: such barriers or shelters provide relief from current force, shelter from predators, more usable room in the stream, less competition for such space, and therefore more trout and better growth and survival rates.

I have never read anything that indicated that such improvements were being carried out as a matter of policy; too often there wasn't any money for such projects because of the millions being gobbled up by the hatchery program.

Recently I read one of the latest fisheries-management reports which, though quite thorough in all other aspects, skipped over holding water with the briefest mention of the "pool-riffle ratio," the implication being that there were no other kinds of holding water.

Also, what little management that has been done in the past has too often treated trout streams as all alike or as all of a piece. That is patently absurd. Trout streams vary so much from one another that it is impossible to type them, and an individual stream will vary so much in fifty miles that the lower section will appear not to belong to the upper. This is especially true if the stream has been subject to dams, take-out and return of irrigation water, and other man-caused disruptive influences.

Rock, if it is available, is the best material to provide permanent shelters in a stream. Fallen trees provide more shelter for various sizes of fish; they protect better than anything else against aerial, terrestrial, or aquatic enemies, especially anglers, and they may prevent cannibalism. But they do not last as well as rock shelters and must be replaced every five years or so.

The advantages of rock are that it is usually available, it lasts forever, it is more stable in place, and it is natural-appearing. Therefore, even though the original cost will be higher for rock barriers and shelters than for other materials, once the job is done, it is done. Even if the stream rearranges the rock, it does so in a manner that results in an even more natural appearance, and benefits are generally retained.

One problem with fishery management people who are charged with maintaining and improving trout streams is that they are not fishermen. In the Wisconsin bulletin mentioned earlier, it is emphasized that only a man who was familiar with trout and their ways could hope to manage a trout stream in the best possible manner. Also, in improving a stream, a management official who was also an avid fisherman would be less likely to disturb the natural appearance of a stream.

Another problem is that lake and pond management has been done to a greater degree in the past, and that persons who have been in that line of work are now managing streams and are attempting to apply the same theories and practices that they have used on ponds and lakes.

This is borne out by the fact that in a great many streams that have been "improved," the improvement consists of a series of low dams and weirs, which have turned a natural, free-running stream into a succession of ponds and short runs, which these misguided managers regard as "pools and riffles." They have improved the holding areas by building more pools.

If a very shallow stream is involved, some method of deepening the water is helpful, but there are other ways to do this that will not turn a stream into a succession of small ponds joined by shallow runs. It takes more time and thought than the dam-building method, but what else are stream-management people for?

I once fished a trout stream in a bedrock-shale area. This was a small stream and, in its original state, was a succession of shallow-to-medium deep runs with no bottom cover and only a few very small trout.

In the 1930s, someone with imagination and foresight had improved about one and one-half miles of this stream with the materials at hand.

Broken shale had been dumped in many stretches to create a

rubble bottom. Some piles of broken shale here and there created areas of relief from current force and caused a broken surface. Many small, secure holds and lies had been made by placing a piece of flat shale across two piles of broken shale, with a small ridge of broken material just upstream that blocked most of the current from this tunnellike lie.

The result was fair fishing for fair-sized trout in this stretch. To be sure, these holds could all be seen and the angler could concentrate on them, but here was a case of definitely improved fishing without creating a series of ponds.

Based on actual catch records, this stretch was more than five times as productive in terms of poundage as the stream average. Yet though this was well known to the Fish and Game Department, there was no effort by them to improve other reaches of the stream, or other nearby streams in this or any other manner.

Streams must wind and the bottoms undulate to provide a diverse habitat for food production, shelter, and reproduction. In the past some streams were made to wind by installing deflectors of logs or even lumber in a stream. Even when well made and well placed these were not long lasting enough to create a natural sinuosity.

Riprapping with rock, thicker at the downstream end, has proved more successful, but even if those earlier deflectors were short term or wrongly placed, they served very well to advance the cause of stream management by demonstrating what not to do.

Creating bank cover gives a double benefit in many cases. If done at the outside, deeper portion of a bend, it not only provides some shelter for the fish, but halts or slows down erosion and stabilizes the area. Some species of small willows work best, larger trees are a no-no, and willows are helped in their effort by some kinds of tough grasses.

Stabilizing such a curve will, by the very nature of streams, create another curve downstream and on the opposite bank. This, too, should be stabilized, and over a period of years, a long, straight stream will gradually become meandered due to the cause and effect of one upper stabilized curve.

Straighter streams have more undulating bottoms in most cases. Where the stream is straight and the bottom even, food production and shelter are at a minimum. It is this type of water that has been much dammed in the past. Productivity has been increased, but at the cost of appearance.

Something that can be used to undulate the bottom without creating a pond is the Hewitt ramp. This device looks almost like a small ski jump built into the stream. It can be designed to deepen the water upstream, or it can be designed so that there is little deepening. The downstream face is designed undercut in all cases.

Water pouring over the top of the undercut face creates a pothole and plunge pool, where the water strikes the stream bed, and the nature of these causes underfalls in the undercut face of the device. All of these provide current relief and shelter, and are very natural-appearing.

Such devices are normally constructed of wood. Construction of rock is difficult and expensive, but in the long run, say forty years, would actually be cheaper.

In brief, more shelter in a stream for trout means more shelter for all creatures, and this means less predation, more food, a higher survival and growth rate, and more and larger trout. That's what stream improvement is all about.

The stage of the water must always be remembered in constructing barriers and shelters. It is sheer waste to construct a barrier or shelter that at low water will have only a few inches of depth. Thus, planning includes study of the stream in all stages and all seasons.

Sometimes a stream can be improved by stopping something that has been detrimental. This means bringing to a halt bad logging practices, overgrazing, badly managed irrigation projects, bad dam operation; it means preventing channelization, and stopping the building of highways along a stream, which are nearly always detrimental.

In Montana, the greatest villain right now is overgrazing of public lands, with the accompanying erosion and siltation due to loss of turf and ground cover. Badly managed irrigation projects are the next worst offender.

Less is known about shelter for the insects that trout feed on than is known about shelter for trout. Insects are the key to growth in trout, provided the trout have adequate barriers from current force. If there is plenty of *available* food, then trout will grow and do well. However, not all trout food in a stream is available to the trout and it is this area that requires more study.

To summarize, the size of trout is directly related to barriers and shelter and *available* food, and numbers are directly related to available shelter. Thus, it should be quite apparent that more and larger trout in a stream depends upon the increasing of available shelters; available food will usually follow.

Why does the fisherman need to know any of this information? It appears to have nothing to do with catching trout.

It *does* have to do with having trout to catch; then there's the point I made earlier, if you go before your Fish and Game people to importune them to improve some X miles of the Upper Neverkill, you'll do better if you have the facts.

The first thing that will happen after you've made your request is that the official will fix you with a fishy stare and inquire silkily how much it is going to cost.

If you say you don't know or have no idea, he's got you, and he'll take you and your request apart like a cheap watch.

On the other hand, if you have enough knowledge to know what needs to be done, how to do it, and with what, then you can estimate the cost. Then you've got him.

He asked for a figure, you gave him one, based on information that he almost surely does not have. In order to attack your project, a survey will have to be authorized and that is always the first step to commencing a project. If the figures turned up by the survey are reasonably close to those provided by you, the chances are excellent that you will get your improvements.

This chapter is not a how-to on getting such projects done; it only seeks to provide some information on what might be done to enable you to find the information you need.

I get much information from the conservation departments of all states that have trout streams, excluding Alaska. I find some information in books; the reference list at the end of this book will be of help.

However, one of the most helpful places to seek information is in the library of your state university, among the unpublished masters' and doctors' theses on the subject. Here you will find current and late information as well as invaluable bibliographies. Also, there's a fair chance the man you face at your Fish and Game Department may have written one of those you read. I don't need to tell you how much help this will be.

15

Reading for the Serious Angler

THE two lists of books at the end of this chapter comprise those forty or so out of nearly two thousand angling books I've read that I think have special merit. This is not to say they are the best forty books; if one hundred anglers chose what each thought were the best forty angling books, it is probable that the total number of titles would exceed two thousand. This is great; difference of opinion is what makes horse races, sells books, and develops fishermen.

So these lists can only be considered as suggestions, with the hope that readers will find them as delightful and informative as I have.

The separation of the books into two classes, pleasure reading and informative reading, is purely arbitrary; you will find passages of pure reading pleasure in some of the informative books, and thousands of bits and pieces of solid information in those in the "pleasure" list. You will, of course, sort and fit to suit yourself, even reject, as a friend of mine did, some of the reading outlined here.

That's good; don't ever let anyone tell you what to read. It is, I think, our greatest freedom. Hold onto it, at home, at work, wherever. Let no one judge your taste; if it pleases you, it is literature—if it also informs, it's worthwhile.

I've read some eight thousand books in my life; to save you figuring, that's about a book every one and one-half days for forty years, with time off to fish now and then. Some of what I've read could be considered trash. There's no such thing for a person with an open mind. You get something from any book-length work, or your mind is so ossified, so encrusted with prejudice and prejudgment, that it has stopped growing. That means no growth in any direction, and that includes fishing. However, if you were that type person, you would not have progressed this far in this book.

In *Larger Trout for the Western Fly Fisherman* I wrote that I considered *How to Fish from Top to Bottom,* by Sid Gordon, the most valuable purely fishing book I've ever read. In the four years since publication of that earlier work I've had no reason to change my mind. I met Gordon while he was researching the work; he talked my ear off, gave me a couple of really valuable tips, and left me with a great desire to see the finished book. I was not disappointed; Gordon's wit has all the heavy grace of a pregnant rhinoceros, but in factual matters, if he has an equal, I haven't met him, in print or otherwise. His book covers fresh-water fishing like the dew covers Dixie. If you have to go with only one book for freshwater fishing, including fly-fishing, this is it.

This brings me to a particular, violent hate of mine, the "Complete" book. Any author who titles any book "Complete" on anything, is, I feel, insulting my intelligence. Nobody knows, not in a dozen lifetimes—nor can gather—that kind of information. Then there's the undeniable fact that from the time the manuscript is finished until the book is published, things will be changing. Some "Complete" books are obsolete before they hit the bookstores. That doesn't mean that some such books aren't loaded with information; they *are*. But if you think such a book can be written, buy the one entitled *The Complete Book of Love Making*, take it home, read it to your wife, and listen to her snicker. Even if she's a brand-new wife.

Having got some sex into this work, however obliquely, let us get on to some more good reading.

The most nearly "Complete" work that I know of is Mr. George Leonard Herter's *Professional Fly Tying and Tackle Making Manual and Manufacturer's Guide*. George delivers more BS to the square inch than anyone I've ever read, including Casanova, but he also delivers more sound, easily followed, first-class, usable information than anyone, including Gordon. This paradox makes Herter the most controversial writer since Lord Timothy Dexter and his *A Pickle for the Knowing Ones.* Herter is unique; either you hate him, but use him, or you love him, but wish he were less omniscient. But you'd better read him; he knows and tells much you will never see elsewhere.

Taking Larger Trout by Larry Koller is an excellent book. But Koller borrows extensively from Herter on his insects, and is best read for technique. Even so, this is one of the better books on trout fishing. It has in it, also, some of the finest descriptive passages I've ever encountered in a fishing book. To my mind, nothing excels the beauty of "strange it is that this most abundant of Earth's inert compounds becomes a living, breathing thing when put into motion by forces of gravity." He has better described running water than anyone else I know.

There is another writer, not well known, who excels in description of trout waters and the joys of fishing them. Alexander Mac-Donald, a southern California attorney who wrote *On Becoming a Fly Fisherman,* is one of those, like Dana Lamb, John Taintor Foote, Haig-Brown, and others, who wrote of fishing not for money, and not from pure knowledge, but from love. No better reason exists. For anything.

There are more people who fish, in some form, than who do any other form of activity, work and other frivolous things excluded. The reasons are, at first glance, simple. A three-year-old can fish; so can a ninety-three-year-old. Paraplegics can—and have—fished. Peter fished—and so we may assume, did Jesus. So did Cro-Magnon man. Why?

Because fishing is the simplest of all food-procuring processes. The hunter *must* possess some skill; his quarry, in a sense, must be pursued. Not so with fishing; one can fling in a worm, sit forever, and eventually catch a fish. Or so reads history. What isn't said is that more hunters than fishers starve, not because theirs is the more difficult art, but because water supports many more and simpler creatures than does earth. Survival is and always has been more difficult on land. This is why man, the most successful of land creatures, turns to water for relaxation. He figures he can catch a fish while his mind is in idle cutoff; in effect no thinking or action is required to catch a fish. This, of course, is why brown trout survive nine to one over other kinds of trout when planted in equal numbers in streams. As Gervase Markham wrote in 1614: "The angler must entice, not command his reward, and that which is worth millions to his contentment, another may buy for a groate in the market."

Having come to, and glided over, the proposition that fishing is "a jerk on one end of a line waiting for a jerk on the other," let us proceed.

If you are an Easterner, you have a much richer pasture to graze than people from other parts of the country. Sadly, I must admit that Eastern writers, while no more informative than Western writers, have a literary style more graceful and readable. Backhandedly, however, their works have little practical value in the West, even those Eastern writers who have had extensive experience in the West.

The Fly and The Fish by John Atherton, is an excellent work for the Eastern fisherman, as is *The Lure and Lore of Trout Fishing,* by Alvin R. Grove. Both are well written, full of good information for trout fishers *east* of Michigan. Much of the same is true of Marinaro's *A Modern Dry-Fly Code,* a beautiful and thoughtful work. Marinaro, as more recently do Richards and Swisher in *Selective Trout,* comes a cropper on the multiplicity of stream types and the insect inventories therein. No one, absolutely no one, can write a book that can cover our great number of vastly different streams. This is *not* England; our streams offer greater differences and a greater variety of insects than any others in the world.

A recent example of this comes to mind. Doug Swisher, Carl Richards, and I were conducting a three-day school on fly-fishing on streams hereabouts. Carl and Doug based their demonstration on the appearance of a certain adult mayfly on a certain stream during that three-day period. It didn't happen. However, more experience on the same stream wouldn't have made it happen either. Nevertheless, *Selective Trout* is a must for the thoughtful angler. And, incidentally, these two young men are the most serious, intelligent, trained, and dedicated in the field of trout fishing of whom I have any knowledge. They definitely are our hope for the future.

Ray Bergman, God love him and care for him, must bear the burden of having aroused my interest in both fly-fishing and trout. I wrote Ray to this effect once; he indicated it was a burden he bore lightly. It is probable that Ray Bergman, by his writings, converted more people to fly-fishing than any other person. Considering that fly-fishermen, as I know them, are a shifty, devious, sneaky, underhanded lot, Ray has a lot to account for.

To be informed on trout fishing, you must read Bergman. If you stop at *Just Fishing* and *Trout,* you're cheating yourself. Some of the best trout fishing episodes of all are in *With Fly, Plug and Bait.*

I first heard of Helen Shaw in the late 1930s; she was, it was said, the best woman fly-tyer in the world. I met Helen and her husband, Hermann Kessler, in 1968, and I remember them as among the most dedicated and sincere people of my acquaintance. Helen is the author of *Fly Tying* and Hermann did the photos, which take this work completely out of the realm of the ordinary fly-tying book. Hermann was Art Director for *Field & Stream* magazine during the years that magazine acquired greatness.

For pure pleasure, I nominate *Fishless Days, Angling Nights* by Sparse Grey Hackle. It is my feeling that Deacon, as he is affectionately known, is the finest fishing writer in America at present, and perhaps for all time. His writings are all too few and are to be treasured.

Along with Sparse's works must be rated *The Spawning Run* by William Humphrey; *Any Luck?* by Eugene Connett; and the works of John Taintor Foote—the collection, *Anglers All* being superb.

A charming small book is *The Waters of Yellowstone with Rod and Fly* by Howard Back. It is something of a guidebook but one that is totally delightful. I recommend it highly—if you can find it. Like many of our finest books on the subject, it has been long out of print.

Three publishers, Winchester, Crown, and Freshet Press, are reissuing many of our fine out-of-print works and I, for one, have been taking advantage of this to obtain books I have long desired, such as John Waller Hills's *A History of Fly Fishing for Trout.* This is a fine book, but it is not quite a history; it is, instead, a development of a theory of important advances in fly-fishing, as the author sees them, through the writings of others. According to Hills, there are only four such: the origin of fly-fishing in the *Treatise of Fishing with an Angle,* which first brought it to notice, the advancement by Charles Cotton's "Instructions How to Angle for a Trout or a Grayling in a Clear Stream," Stewart's *The Practical Angler,* which made the case for upstream fishing of the fly, and Halford's works, which codified dry-fly practice.

These may have been the great happenings in fly-fishing but what has made it what it is today are the numberless smaller but still significant changes in flies, tackle, gear, and methods that have taken place since the writing of the *Treatise,* and which are still taking place. Hills's apparent conviction that all further advancement stopped with Halford, is, I think, an epic mistake.

It was only thirty-five years from Halford's first work on dry-fly fishing to Hills's history, and things move slowly in angling. However, Skues and Hewitt with their introduction of artificial nymphs, circa 1900, were passed over all too lightly; Hills apparently forgot that Pulman introduced the dry fly exactly thirty-five years before Halford first wrote of it. He notes the fumbling advancement of the dry fly up to Halford in some detail, but skips over the same type of movement in the use and development of artificial nymphs. The reason Hills slighted nymphs, I think, is the same reason their development has moved so slowly: all takes place underwater and unseen. This, plus the difficulty of properly imitating and fishing the artificial nymph, has caused most angling writers to ignore them or damn them with faint praise.

Thus, *Nymphs* by Ernest Schwiebert has been a long time in coming, and it only begins to fill a gap that has always existed in this most important form of fly-fishing. Hopefully, now that the dam has broken, there will be more books devoted to nymphs, their imitations, and methods of fishing them.

I've had a long and rewarding correspondence with Austin Hogan of Cambridge, Massachusetts, who probably knows, in theory, more of the world of fly-fishing than any man alive. He has also done much practical work, but his mind outstrips these limits and makes great leaps, founded only on intuition. He is an artist also, and has given considerable time, thought, and research to the color vision of trout. The fact that he recommends *Sunshine and the Dry Fly* by J. W. Dunne is strong medicine indeed. As in all such works of a half-century ago, credit must be given to the author who was working with techniques and instruments that are obsolete today. How much this author contributed may be shown by the fact that no *equal* work has been done by anyone since, in spite of better techniques and instruments.

The works of G. E. M. Skues are written in a more wordy style than I care for, this being one stamp of a Victorian writer, which Skues was. But from the standpoint of practicality and historical significance, they are well worth your time to plow through.

Also from the standpoint of history, you must read *The Origins of Angling* by John McDonald. This, in addition to being a thoughtful and perceptive analysis of the *Treatyse of Fyssinge Wyth an Angle,* is a masterful scholarly work that is wholly delightful. Further, it contains amplified descriptions and analyses of the first known trout flies, which are pictured in color, tied according to the best judgment of McDonald and Dwight Webster, who tied them, as they might have been tied by the fishers of that day (circa 1420).

Collections of pleasure reading about my favorite subject have always appealed to me, because most of them contain some of the greatest writings ever to appear on the subject, and the only way most of us get to see these gems is in such collections.

The Fireside Book of Fishing, edited by Raymond Camp, is one of the first such collections I ever read (*Anglers All* was the first). Among the truly wonderful stories in this anthology, Camp's own "Stouthearted Men" and Sparse Grey Hackle's "The Lotus Eaters" are by themselves worth the price of the book, which contains forty other fine pieces.

Other collections are *Fisherman's Bounty* edited by Nick Lyons; *American Trout Fishing* (originally *The Gordon Garland*) edited by Arnold Gingrich, whose *The Well-Tempered Angler,* is also fine reading; *The Seasonable Angler* by Nick Lyons; and *This Wonderful World of Trout* by Charles K. Fox. The fact that some collections are the work of a single author in no way affects the fact that most of them are fine reading.

Fly Patterns and Their Origins by Harold H. Smedley and *Favorite Flies and Their Histories* by Mary Orvis Marbury are two fascinating, completely different books on a similar subject. Both are classics, and my particular copy of Smedley's book is a collector's item, with more errata than I've ever seen in any other book, plus something else I've never seen, a loose insert page amplifying at length a comment in the bound section.

The works of Roderick Haig-Brown reflect the philosophy of a master angler, as well as being some of the finest descriptive writing about angling that any writer has ever put between covers. Haig-Brown has the enviable capacity for making his happenings real and his subject come alive for the reader.

Two unrelated books of considerable value are Francesca La Monte's *North American Game Fishes* and Joe Bates's *Trout Waters and How to Fish Them.* La Monte's work is the handiest complete work on the subject that I'm aware of, since it can be carried right along in the fishing vest or tackle box. I have used it to settle problems of identification in many states and waters in other parts of the world, including one amusing experience off the coast of North Africa.

A group of us had chartered a large commercial fishing boat to take us sports fishing out into the Atlantic. As is usual in such affairs, there was a pool, one dollar per person for the first, most, and biggest fish caught.

Along in the afternoon, I came down with a touch of mal de mer, to which I'm intensely subject. I went below and lay down in one of the bunks.

About an hour later, there came a tremendous commotion on deck—people running, shouting, such a stamping, pounding, and threshing on the steel deck that I was sure some of the many beer drinkers on board had overimbibed and got into a fight.

A few minutes after the to-do had died away, one of the younger members of our party came bolting down the ladder and into the room where I lay.

"Brooksie," he said urgently, "bring your book and come up. We're getting ready to go in and there's a terrific argument you'll have to settle."

The book of course, was *North American Game Fishes,* and the problem was that one member of the party had caught a tremendous conger eel, over four feet long, as thick as a man's thigh. The commotion I had heard had been the group trying to subdue this beast after it had been hoisted aboard. The question: Was the eel a fish and therefore, did it take the pool for the largest fish? It was and it did.

Bates's *Trout Waters and How to Fish Them* is probably his least-known work, yet I consider it to be of more value to the serious angler than all his other works together. A friend of mine who is also a good friend of Bates says the reason the work is so little known is due to the lack of color plates, and he cites Bates and Bergman as two authors who convinced him that any how-to fishing book would never become popular unless it had fly or lure plates in color. I'm inclined to agree with them.

Sir Edward Grey's *Fly Fishing* was published over seventy years ago, but it is the soundest of English books on all-around fly-fishing. Grey was the only author of note of that period who was not taken in by Halford's dry-fly-only campaign. Skues was a dry-fly man of strong convictions at first and admitted that Grey's was the work that brought him to his senses. This is fortunate, for Skues was the first writer of authority who started looking seriously at the underwater fly before it was hatched.

Possibly the most underrated book on fishing ever written is *Fly Fishing; Some New Arts and Mysteries* by James Cecil Mottram, recently brought back from oblivion by Arnold Gingrich. W. H. Lawrie, writer of several excellent books on English flies and fishing, attributes this to the fact that the book was published and literally vanished from view during World War I, when there were other serious things to think about.

Mottram's book contains an astonishing amount of up-to-date and pertinent information for a book written over fifty years ago. The fact that the book was years ahead of its time may have contributed to its demise; anglers are a hide-bound lot and do not wish their pleasant reflections upset by new and startling assertions.

Charles Ritz's *A Fly Fisher's Life* is flawed, in my opinion, by the inclusion of the chapters on the form of casting known as High Speed–High Line. Ritz admits he is a nut on tackle and a fanatic on casting technique, but this section, I think, mars an otherwise fine book. I have never known a serious angler who was at all interested in this form of casting *unless* he was also a tournament caster.

American dry-fly fishermen will be astounded that Ritz almost never goes below .010 inches for a leader tippet in dry-fly fishing chalk streams and other glassy waters for wary brown trout. Also, he cares little whether his fly resembles or imitates that on the water. He bases his use of thick leaders on presentation, and that, he feels, is 90 percent of the dry-fly game.

One book in the list is my own *Larger Trout for the Western Fly Fisherman*. I will close this chapter with the suggestion that he who reads it will be better able to appreciate this one.

PLEASURE READING

HOWARD BACK, *The Waters of Yellowstone with Rod and Fly*

RAYMOND R. CAMP (editor), *The Fireside Book of Angling*

EUGENE V. CONNETT, *Any Luck?*

JOHN TAINTOR FOOTE, *Anglers All*

CHARLES K. FOX, *This Wonderful World of Trout*

ARNOLD GINGRICH (editor), *American Trout Fishing*

ARNOLD GINGRICH, *The Well-Tempered Angler*

RODERICK HAIG-BROWN, *A River Never Sleeps*

JOHN WALLER HILLS, *A History of Fly Fishing for Trout*

WILLIAM HUMPHREY, *The Spawning Run*

DANA LAMB, *Bright Salmon and Brown Trout*

NICK LYONS (editor), *Fisherman's Bounty*

NICK LYONS, *The Seasonable Angler*

ALEXANDER MACDONALD, *On Becoming a Fly Fisherman*

JOHN McDONALD, *The Origins of Angling*

MARY ORVIS MARBURY, *Favorite Flies and Their Histories*

CHARLES RITZ, *A Fly Fisher's Life*

H. H. SMEDLEY, *Fly Patterns and Their Origins*

SPARSE GREY HACKLE, *Fishless Days, Angling Nights*

John Atherton, *The Fly and the Fish*

Joseph D. Bates, *Trout Waters and How to Fish Them*

Ray Bergman, *Trout*

Charles E. Brooks, *Larger Trout for the Western Fly Fisherman*

J. W. Dunne, *Sunshine and the Dry Fly*

Art Flick, *New Streamside Guide to Naturals and Their Imitations*

Sid W. Gordon, *How to Fish from Top to Bottom*

Edward Grey, *Fly Fishing*

Alvin R. Grove, *The Lure and Lore of Trout Fishing*

George L. Herter, *Professional Fly Tying and Tackle Making*

Preston Jennings, *A Book of Trout Flies*

Lawrence R. Koller, *Taking Larger Trout*

Francesca La Monte, *North American Game Fishes*

Vincent Marinaro, *A Modern Dry-Fly Code*

James C. Mottram, *Fly Fishing: Some New Arts and Mysteries*

Paul R. Needham, *Trout Streams*

Ernest Schwiebert, *Matching the Hatch*

Ernest Schwiebert, *Nymphs*

Helen Shaw, *Fly Tying*

G. E. M. Skues, *Minor Tactics of the Chalk Stream*

Doug Swisher and Carl Richards, *Selective Trout*

Some serious reference works on the trout and the stream:

"Trout Streams," Paul R. Needham, Holden-Day, 1969.

"How To Fish from Top to Bottom," Sid W. Gordon, The Stackpole Co., 1955.

"Fundamentals of Limnology," Franz Ruttner, University of Toronto Press, 1957.

"Guidelines for Management of Trout Stream Habitat in Wisconsin," Ray J. White and Oscar M. Brynildson, Department of Natural Resources, Division of Conservation Technical Bulletin No. 39, 1967.

"The Ecology of Running Water," H. B. N. Hynes, University of Toronto Press, 1970.

16

Of Streams and Trout, Laws and Anglers

STREAMS AND TROUT

A stream is a living thing, never static, always altering and changing in accordance with physical laws. Thus if one has been away from a stream for a number of years, he will find it has changed almost beyond belief.

Streams constantly carve and gnaw at their banks, and this same ceaseless activity works away unseen in their beds. A curve in a stream bank moves upstream, due to cutting at the upper end and depositing of material at the lower. A rock or boulder in a stream bed moves downstream, due to material being washed out on the lower side. This motion is so slow that it cannot normally be observed, but in times of high water, it can be seen. It can be heard anytime, streams underwater are so noisy that it's a wonder the fish can stand them.

Weed beds migrate downstream and so do islands, as the water erodes the soil or particulate matter from the upper end, dropping it in the slack water lower down. This kind of thing has been going on since the beginning of time, and it is what gives a stream its particular identity. It is also one thing that makes it so difficult for the angler; the stream that he fishes this spring is not quite the same one he left in the fall.

When weather and water have been cool, fish will generally start feeding on underwater forms in the tail of a run sooner than they will in the middle or upper end. Temperature probably has little to do with this; in general, the trout in the tail will be smaller than those farther up and smaller trout feed more often than larger ones. Ounce for ounce, an eight-inch, two-year-old trout burns three times the energy of a three-pound, six-year-old fish, and has a much smaller stomach, thus must feed more often. It is this, more than a lack of sophistication, that causes more smaller fish to be caught.

Ruttner says that young and yearling fish generally eat their own weight in food every ten days, four- or five-year-old fish, once in every forty-five days, large and old fish, once every sixty days.

Smaller fish feed more and more often, thus are most apt to be caught, especially by the unskilled angler.

Trout vary somewhat in their feeding selectivity according to species, and this affects the ease with which they may be caught. Rainbow trout tend to be more adventurous, and will try more kinds of food than will other species. This leads them to be less selective in taking artificial flies; quite often they will be taken on flies that resemble nothing at all. Cutthroat have this same affinity for sampling anything and everything.

Brook trout while young are often taken in by flash and color. But very large brook trout become more selective than any other trout, except large browns. Brown trout are more selective throughout their lives, and more wary of unnatural-looking flies or unnatural motion. Each species of trout differs in its susceptibility to being taken on artificial flies.

Laws relating to stream use and to water rights are in a thorough muddle in this country. Laws not only vary from state to state, they sometimes vary from county to county. The poor angler thus is left at a loss; he may find himself fenced off from waters to which he has every right, and find himself trespassing on other waters that appear no different.

In general, on navigable streams, all land below the high-water mark is public property. But laws vary on where or what is the high-water mark, and also on the definition of navigable.

"Capable of being used for commerce," is one definition. But what is commerce? In some states it is held that if a farmer can take a rowboat-load of produce, or a trapper a canoe-load of furs, down to market on a stream at low water level, the stream is navigable. Others specify larger boats, or a raft of logs. Wisconsin holds that a stream with the ability to float a twelve-foot saw log is navigable. Some states define all free-running streams of a certain width or flow as navigable. If such streams have a dam anywhere on them, they then are no longer navigable. Montana does not define navigable at all. We now have a petition in the state legislature asking for a law defining navigable streams.

The importance of all this lies in the fact that a state cannot legally manage or improve streams where the waters and bed do not belong to it. In order to know that, there has to be a clear-cut law defining such streams. But in most states, it would take a Philadelphia lawyer to decide what the state's or the angler's rights are.

AN ANGLER'S NEEDS

The attributes an angler needs above all others, if he is to be consistently successful, are skill and know-how, and it is these that every angler thinks that he possesses from the day he commences to fish. No amount of logic will ever convince him that he is not a master angler, even though he returns from the stream for days on end without having caught, or even seen, a decent fish.

He has all the excuses of a thousand generations of other non-anglers to fall back on. The weather was too hot, or too cold, the stream too high, or low. The wind was from the wrong direction. The barometric pressure was at fault, or the water wasn't warm enough or cold enough. He forgot his solunar tables. The flies he bought at Jake's were lousy; next time he'll get his flies from Sam.

A man may admit he is a poor talker, that his social graces are few or absent, that he cannot dance as well as an uncoordinated giraffe. He will cheerfully agree that, as an athlete, his best event is the standing broad grin. Most will admit to being poor poker players and that checkers and chess baffle them. But *no* man will admit to being a lousy lover or a poor fisherman. Why is this? Because man, in order to survive, has to be incurably optimistic in these two areas.

Every year some few friends show up at my house with no waders, no tackle or gear, no skill or know-how, and less patience.

They arise in the morning, eat a breakfast that would stun an ox, give me a toothy grin, and say, "Let's go catch some fish."

When we return, fishless (I do not fish on these occasions) I try to console them with the statistic that only X percent of anglers are ever successful on this or that stream. It is a futile effort. They consider themselves in that X percent.

It reminds me of a story told in the Army during World War II. If an officer lined up ten men, went the tale, and told them that he had to send them on a dangerous mission in which nine of the ten would be killed, each man would look at the others and say to himself, "Well, I'm sure gonna miss these guys."

The only anglers who will admit to not being all they should be as fishermen, oddly, are the ones who are actually very good, and who study and work continually to become better.

Yea, verily, the fisherman is a strange creature, and not like other men.

If skill and know-how are the major tools of the successful angler, there is one other almost as important. This is concentration. Some anglers have this talent to a degree that makes them completely oblivious to all else.

I fished two days in the fall of 1972 with Jim Glenn of New Kensington, Pennsylvania. On the first day, we encountered some of the most miserable weather I have ever fished in. It was cold, below freezing, a steady drizzle of rain came down, and a chill wind added to the discomfort. Ice formed in the guides all day.

I was dressed for the weather, with thermal underwear, woolen clothing, rain jacket, and brimmed hat. Jim had no warm clothing and no hat.

By the time we had fished three hours, it had become a torture for me. My hands had become so cold that the line running through my left hand felt like a hot wire. Twice I lost fish of over three pounds because I could not control the line. My face had no more feeling than sculptor's clay.

We had fished back to where the car was parked. I left Jim to fish the far side of the deep run there and waded across.

I started the car, got the heater going, and drank some hot chocolate. Meanwhile, I could see that Jim, who seemed unbothered by the cold or wet, even though icy water had been running off his unprotected head and down his back the whole time, was into a heavy fish.

I waded back across to witness the landing, a brown of twenty-one inches. After Jim released it, I talked him into joining me in the car for some hot chocolate.

It was only after we were in the car, with the heater going, and drinking our hot drinks that Jim began to shiver and shake.

"You know," he said to me through chattering teeth, "we've got to be crazy. They couldn't pay me enough to do this kind of work in this kind of weather, yet here I am paying for the privilege."

Yet, he admitted, until he had got into the warm car, he really hadn't noticed how cold he was.

Two days later I witnessed another example of the terrific concentration Jim brings to fly-fishing. We fished a tiny meadow stream which harbors very large trout. Jim did superbly, finishing with another twenty-plus-inch brown, and later said it was the most outstanding day of his life as an angler. Yet, he fished the entire day with such a horrible, ferocious scowl that it was almost frightening. This kind of concentration makes great fishermen.

Over the past four years, it has been constantly brought home to me how important *willingness to learn* is to an angler. During that time I have taught a great many anglers to fish nymphs and to read water.

It got so that I could predict how well a student would do by his attitude during the few minutes I talked with him before we left for the stream. These were all experienced fly-fishermen, and some of them had become pretty set in their ways. I was unable to help these men much, because they really weren't there to learn, but to see if I had anything earthshaking to show them. Unconsciously, they were ready to reject anything I had to offer. I have found that there are quite a few anglers in this category, and generally they are one-method fishermen who have no real desire to advance.

To advance as an angler, one must, in the fullness of time, develop to the point where he *welcomes* more knowledge—and goes forth to meet new experiences. Yet his mind must be able to go beyond experience, or sure knowledge, to imaginative and often highly successful experiments. Then, if he is to become ever more competent, he must know what the factors were that he possessed that made this possible and he must have the physical skills and the perseverance to test these against the will of the trout, over a period of time, to determine if the wish was supported by the deed, if in fact, he dreamed, or if practice supported belief.

As for the no-kill rule, it is my feeling that man is too intelligent and skilled and has too long a memory to be a mere predator, and my hope for the future of trout fishing is based on a belief that he is coming to know this.

Index

A

Acroneuria, 44, 100, 104
Alaska, 6, 31, 93
algae, 5, 6, 7, 8, 10, 13, 16, 25
Anderson, Jack, 190
Armitage, Kenneth B., 34
Assam Dragon, 72, 106, 142
Atherton, John, 200
Au Sable, 11

B

Back, Howard, 42
baetis, 35, 36, 51, 53, 100
Bailey, Dan, 105
Baker's Hole, 44, 67
Barnes, Cliff, 170
Barns, river section, 104
Bates, Joe, 203, 204
Bear Traps, 104
Beaverkill, 8
Beaver Meadows, 44
Begley, Jim, 56
Begley, Lew, 56
Bergman, Ray, 85, 94, 141, 200, 204

Big Bend, 42, 43, 57
Big Springs, 4, 52
Bird's Stone Fly, 53, 54, 105
Bird's Stone Fly Nymph, 105
Birge and Juday, 6, 185
Biscuit Basin Meadows, 25, 35, 36,
    37, 39, 42, 44, 57, 91, 129
Bitch Creek Special, 44, 105
Blackmore, R. D., 138
Blue Dun, 86
Bock, Art, 163
bottom types, six, 65
Box Canyon, 53, 104, 136
brachycentrus, 35, 36, 53, 102, 133,
    134
Brooks, Grace, 25, 26, 67, 106, 128,
    170
Brooks, Ken, 25, 118, 119
Brown Bivisible, 42
Brown Hackle, 86
Brown Marabou Muddler, 44, 90,
    91
Brown Spider, 42
Buffalo Ford, 102
Butler, Dr. Robert L., 21

C

Cable Car Run, 43, 57
Cahill, 86, 108
calcium bicarbonates, 10, 11, 33, 41
callibaetis, 53
Camp, Raymond, 203
Centennial Valley, 105
chironomus lobiferous, 36
chironomus modestus, 105
Cook, Doc, 118
Cook, Pete, 118, 119
Cotton, Charles, 152, 201
Cucnin, J. P., 154
Culver Springs, 105
Cutcliffe, H. C., 141

D

Dark Spruce, 44
Dave's Stonefly, 54
deer hair mouse, 131, 132
De Fouw, Gene, 166
Deschutes River, 4
Dunne, J. W., 202

E

Ecology magazine, 34
Ephemera, 11, 84, 85
Ephemera danica, 84
Ephemerella, 51, 53, 85
Ephemerella grandis, 35, 85, 100
Ephemerella infrequens, 52

F

Fair Damsel, 39, 106, 143
Feather River, 106
Firehole River, 20, 23, 25, 29, 31,
    32–41, 44, 57, 91, 92, 105, 107,
    129, 190
Fledermouse, 72
Floating Streamer, 92, 125, 126,
    132, 133, 161
Foote, John Taintor, 26
Fountain Freight Road, 39, 40
Fox, Charles K., 203
Fraser, Joe, 27

G

Gallatin River, 8, 32, 48, 49, 57, 104
Gartland, Pat, 129
Gibbon River, 41
Gingrich, Arnold, 174, 177, 204
Glenn, Jim, 128, 210, 211
Golden Olive Dun, 52
Goofus Bug, 54
Gordon, Sid, 198
Gray Hackle, 86
Green Marabou Muddler, 44, 90
Grey, Sir Edward, 204
Grove, Alvin R., 200

H

Haig-Brown, Roderick, 203
Hare's Ear, 72, 186
Hat Creek, 107
Hedge, Marvin, 154
Henry's Fork, 4, 20, 32, 52, 57, 104,
    105, 107, 136
Herlyn, Ted, 119
Herter, George Leonard, 198
Hesperophylax, 36
Hewitt, Edward, 84, 112, 177, 201
Hewitt ramp, 195
Hexagenia, 11
Hills, John Waller, 89, 201
Hogan, Austin, 202
Hole number one, 43, 44, 190
Hole number three, 44, 119
Hole number two, 43
Holmes, Bob, 23, 132, 170
Holtzman, Jed, 119
Hot Creek, 107
Hyalella, 53
Hynes, H. N. B., vii, 19, 99

I

Ida May, 100, 103, 145
Inland Empire Fly Fishing Club,
    153
Iron Creek, 35
Irresistible, 54
Isonychia, 85

J

James, Red, 87
James, Ron, 87
James, Vallie, 87

K

Karwell, Bob, 119
Kessler, Hermann, 201
Kiely, Jack, 119, 120
Klamath River, 6
Koller, Larry, 199

L

La Branche, George, 138
La Monte, Francesca, 203
Last Chance, 53
Lawrie, W. H., 152, 204
Leadwing Coachman, 84
Leisenring, Jim, 116
Letort, 4, 67, 107
Lilly, Bud, 91
Lilly, Greg, 91
Little Green Caddis, 103
Little Grey Caddis, 103
Lower Madison River, 32, 53, 54,
    57, 65, 104, 135, 136
Lyons, Nick, 203

M

McCammon, Dr. R. D., 21
McClane, Al, 52
MacDonald, Alexander, 199
McDonald, John, 202
McGuire, Dick, 90, 187
Madison Notch, 42
Marbury, Mary Orvis, 203
Marinaro, Vincent, 125, 137
Markham, Gervase, 181, 199
Martinez Black, 35
Matching the Hatch, 110
Meadow Lake, 135
Merced River, 106
Montana Stone Nymph, 44, 105,
    135
Morning Glory Pool, 35

Mosquito Gulch, 50
Mottram, James Cecil, 204
Muleshoe Bend, 40
Murray, Harry, 150, 151

N

Needham, Paul, 183
Neversink River, 8
Nez Perce Creek, 41
Nine Mile Hole, 42, 45
"Nymphs," 96, 202

O

Otter Shrimp, 72, 86

P

Pace, Dr. Clint, 20, 182
Peeples, Bruce, 54, 156
phytoplankton, 6, 16
Pteronarcys, 44, 49, 53, 104, 105
Pteronarcys californica, 100, 104,
    134

Q

Quake Lake, 53, 79, 135

R

Railroad Ranch, 31
Rhyacophila, 35, 36, 53, 102, 122,
    133, 134
Richards, Carl, 96, 137, 200
riffle beetle larva, 88
Ritz, Charles, vii, 6, 7, 110, 182, 205
Rosborough, Polly, 123, 152
rubble, as composite bottom, 12
Ruttner, Franz, vii, 19, 99, 169, 208

S

Sawyer, Frank, 112, 113
Schaplow, Barry, 91
Schwiebert, Ernest, 96, 110, 202

screen, insect, 24, 27, 28, 97, 98
sculpin, 15, 78
Sealey, Edgar, 151
security hold, 29
Selective Trout, 96, 200
Seven Mile Bridge, 43
Shaw, Helen, 200
Sherman, Gordon, Corky, 158
Silver Creek, 107
Skues, G. E. M., 84, 89, 94, 112, 113, 201, 202
Skunk Hair Caddis, 106
Smedley, Harold H., 203
snails, 25, 27
Sofa Pillow, 53, 54, 105
South Fork, 4, 32, 50, 52, 57
Southwestern Montana Fly Fishers, 16
Steen, Howard, 140, 141
sulfur, 10, 11
Swisher, Doug, 96, 137, 200

T

temperature, stability of, 9
Terrell, Sid, 48
Treatyse of Fysshynge Wyth an Angle, 82
tricorythodes, 53
Trout Magazine, 21
Truckee River, 106
Trueblood, Ted, 63, 169

U

Upper Madison, 20, 27, 28, 32, 41–

48, 57, 67, 90, 104, 105. 119. 190

V

Vance, Dick, 167
vision of trout, 21

W

watertypes, the six, 64
White, Ray J., 191
White Hair Winged Variant, 42
Whitlock, Dave, 105, 123
Whit's Stone Nymph, 35, 44, 105
Widow's Pool, 105, 170
Wilkie, Jim, 172
Winn, Larry, 165
Wulff, Lee, 181
Wulff fly, 54

Y

Yankee Jim Canyon, 104
Yellow Stone Nymph, 105
Yellowstone Park, 11, 27, 28, 32, 58, 59, 90, 107, 180, 189
Yellowstone River, 31, 32, 54, 57, 65, 102, 104, 133, 190
Yuba River, 106

Z

zooplankton, 6, 8, 11, 16
Zug Bug, 35, 72, 86